PENGUIN BOOKS

THE WORKING-CLASS MAJORITY

Andrew Levison is a graduate of the University of Wisconsin and a former blue-collar worker, having once been employed as a radio-television repairman and an air-conditioning installer. He is now Senior Research Fellow at the Martin Luther King, Jr., Center for Social Change, in Atlanta, Georgia. His duties for the center range from voter registration and campaigning to writing studies commissioned by the U.S. Department of Health, Education, and Welfare and the National Institute of Mental Health. *The Working-Class Majority* is his first book.

ANDREW LEVISON

THE WORKING-CLASS MAJORITY

Penguin Books

Penguin Books Ltd, Harmondsworth,
Middlesex, England
Penguin Books, 625 Madison Avenue,
New York, New York 10022, U.S.A.
Penguin Books Australia Ltd, Ringwood,
Victoria, Australia
Penguin Books Canada Limited, 2801 John Street,
Markham, Ontario, Canada L3R 1B4
Penguin Books (N.Z.) Ltd, 182–190 Wairau Road,
Auckland 10, New Zealand

First published in the United States of America by
Coward, McCann & Geoghegan, Inc., 1974
Published in Penguin Books 1975
Reprinted 1977, 1979

Printed in the United States of America by
Offset Paperback Mfrs., Inc., Dallas, Pennsylvania
Set in Janson

A substantial portion of this book appeared originally in
The New Yorker in slightly different form.

Although it was once considered obligatory to dedicate one's first book to one's parents, that convention, along with many others, has been swept aside by the honesty of this generation. Therefore, this book is sincerely dedicated to the man who was genuinely the most important source of inspiration and support, not only for this book, but throughout the years.

His involvement in politics and the struggle for progress stretches over forty years, from the '30s, when he had an almost chance involvement aiding several union locals, which became the basis for the CIO (Congress of Industrial Organizations), to long years of work with Dr. Martin Luther King, Jr., beginning soon after the Montgomery bus boycott and continuing on in the years after Dr. King's assassination. For dedication, political knowledge and competence, and in that far more rare combination of simple courage and utter selflessness, I have never known his equal.

His name is Stanley Levison, and he is, in fact, my father. But, that is, in a real sense secondary. Everyone has a father, but few have fathers like him.

Contents

Acknowledgments

THE FIRST AND MOST deeply felt acknowledgment I must make is to Mr. Stephan Klein. Although the statement that "this book could not have been written without him" is often used (and is frequently an exaggeration) in this case it is the simple truth. Although the words themselves and the ideas in this book are those of the author, terms like "researcher" and "assistant" do not describe the full role Mr. Klein played in the book's development. He was not only a researcher and aide, but a genuine co-worker, doing not only library and field research, but contributing ideas and analyses in countless discussions of the facts that lay before us. There is not a single chapter that does not bear some imprint of his work, and were this an academic article, his contribution would surely merit a credit as "junior author."

I must also express my gratitude to Congressman Andrew Young and Mrs. Martin Luther King, Jr., president of the Martin Luther King, Jr. Center for Non-Violent Social Change. When the opportunity to write this book arose, I had a range of commitments to both of them, many of which had to be put aside. Though they could have felt, with perfect justice, that the book should be postponed, they gave their full and wholehearted support, despite the difficulties my absence created for them.

I also owe a debt of gratitude to the many people I interviewed or who otherwise assisted with information and advice. In particular, Mayor Richard Hatcher of Gary,

Indiana, and Mr. Irving Bluestone, international vice-president of the United Auto Workers, took time out of their packed schedules to give long and informative interviews, such as few writers ever receive. Franklin Wallick of the UAW and Moe Foner of Local 1199 of the Drug and Hospital Union also gave interviews, filled with invaluable information, as did local union officials of the United Steel Workers and The American Federation of State, County, and Municipal Workers among others. In this case, however, the caveat that the opinions and conclusions in this book are solely those of the author applies with special force. Whenever as many controversial topics and issues are considered as are in this book, almost everyone will find something with which he disagrees. The author alone bears full responsibility for the ideas and conclusions presented.

Another person who deserves the deepest thanks is Carey McWilliams, editor of the *Nation*. Though he is deluged with articles every day of the year, no editor could have devoted more time or given more assistance to a fledgling writer. The basic information in the first chapter, as well as some material in others, originally appeared in the pages of the *Nation*, and it was as a result of those articles and Mr. McWilliams' early interest and able assistance that I received the opportunity to do this book. Morris Rubin, editor of the *Progressive*, must also be credited. His thoughtful comments and incisive revisions not only made the articles I have done for his magazine far better, but have been a kind of on-the-job training course in the skills of writing.

A last, but by no means least, acknowledgment I must make in regard to the writing of this book is to Mrs. Peggy Brooks, senior editor of Coward, McCann & Geoghegan. She quickly saw, in the very first article done for the *Nation*, the potential for a book. But in addition, she immediately grasped not only the central points, but the author's desire to make the book as clear and readable as possible. Her frank and helpful comments guided the book through its various revisions and in its final stages, and her thorough editing, rewriting, and deletions made the book far closer to what the author ultimately desired than he could ever have done himself. Mrs. Louise Lee must also be thanked for handling the thankless task of typing and transcription with consistent skill and good humor.

The work and research of Professor Richard Hamilton of McGill University must also be acknowledged. His original critiques and rigorous and systematic analysis of the popular myths about American class structure and political attitudes, developed during the '60s, affected the thinking of many, and his ideas were an early and important influence on this book. His 1972 book, *Class and Politics in the United States*, remains the best and most systematic study of social class and the political attitudes of American workers.

Finally, this book owes much to a man who probably is not even aware of its existence, Professor Maurice Zeitlin of the University of Wisconsin. Although it has been more than six years since I sat in his course on Contemporary American Society, and although I have not seen him since, the inspiration, and more than a few of the concepts, I first encountered in his lectures on working-class America. He was informing his students about the problems, discontents, and political role of American workers long before George Wallace even appeared on the national political scene and while most of his colleagues were still reciting the clichés of the '50s. But more than any specific point, I hope this book reflects his insistence on hard facts and independent, empirical observation as the only way to draw meaningful conclusions about American society and how it can be improved.

Preface:
Blue-Collar Workers and
the Future of American Politics

WATERGATE and the energy crisis have dominated the headlines for so long they have obscured the far more critical and basic political problem facing liberals, the Democratic party and all Americans who hope for progress today: the blue-collar vote. The exposure of the Nixon Administration's long tangle of deceit, corruption and illegal activity may have decisively crippled the "emerging Republican majority" touted by the conservatives. But the problem remains. In 1972 blue-collar voters defected to Nixon. What will they do in 1976? That is the central issue in American politics.

The reason for this is simple. If, as the centrists claim, the 1972 election indicates that American workers have lost their faith in liberal goals and chosen the right as their political home, then, for the foreseeable future, there is little hope of winning a majority of the American people to the side of progress. According to this thesis, the Watergate scandal in all its ramifications is only a temporary setback in a long-range conservative trend, and 1976 will see the election of a President who, if not Nixon's equal in arrogant lawlessness, will be his match in political conservatism.

Bleak and depressing as that prospect is, many Democrats,

liberals and progressives have come to accept it. They have decided they must either compromise their ideals or ignore the workingman and seek a coalition of women, youth, the alienated. They sidestep the blue-collar issues and look elsewhere for a constituency.

These opinions are widely held. The central thesis of this book is that all of them are basically and profoundly wrong. The hope for a progressive majority in America need not be forgotten, the basic progressive principles and ideals do not have to be jettisoned, and more widely disparate groups with few common interests need not be proposed as solutions to the current political dilemma.

All such approaches are tactics born of desperation rather than a serious understanding of the real problems, legitimate discontents, and, in significant measure, decent democratic instincts of American workers. They are conclusions reached on the basis of a common wisdom about workers and working-class life that is simply without foundation.

Consider the basic social and economic conditions of blue-collar workers. Although the euphoric image of the "affluent worker" of the '50s has been modified in recent years, to the less ecstatic "middle American," it is generally accepted that the classic discontents of blue-collar life have become a thing of the past and workers are now "lower middle class," unofficial junior partners in affluent America. No thousand-dollar stereos perhaps or Christmas trips to Aruba, but still, in the popular conception they are increasingly identical to their middle-class neighbors in suburban America.

As we shall see, for all the talk of overpaid craftsmen and narrowing income gaps, the truth is far different. The majority of America's blue-collar workers live not only far below affluence, but below the modest government standards for a fully comfortable "middle American" life. The gap between the working class and the middle class, between those who work basically with their hands and those who work with their minds, is enormous, and like the notion of similar life-styles, is belied by the reality of a deep economic, social, and geographical segregation between workers and the middle class that approaches the distinction between black and white. On the job and in the community workers often face not only the most harsh and pressing problems, but often clear injustice as well. While genuine improvements over the years are undeniable, so is the persistence of a real and basic inequality. Even the venerable cliché of America as a white-collar society turns out, on examination, to be a simply deceptive misstatement of the facts. For the rest of this century, the majority of Americans will be essentially manual, rather than professional or managerial, workers.

The popular notions about workers' political attitudes are equally flawed. Although often caricatured as far worse racists and militarists than the middle class, careful evidence fails to back up the claim. Strong currents of racism and militarism are certainly present in working-class America, but a vision of all workers as hate-filled "hard hats" assaulting students is no more valid today than the shamelessly romanticized image of Tom Joad was in the '30s, when Henry Fonda acted the part in *The Grapes of Wrath*. The results of elections and other real-life behavior in fact suggest that, in certain vital respects, blue-collar workers are still a largely liberal, not conservative, force in American politics.

For many readers, these assertions will sound so contrary to everything they have read and heard that they will be tempted to reject them out of hand. But though each one flies in the face of a common wisdom which has been accepted for more than twenty years, they are all supported by fact. And it is vital to note that, despite its wide acceptance, virtually every prediction about workers made on the basis of the conventional view has been wrong. It proclaimed that blue collar and white collar had become almost indistinguishable. But in 1968 workers identified themselves with a vengeance, in the Wallace campaign and later in the clashes between workers and students. On the basis of these events it was assumed that workers were suddenly captives of the "social issue" and were suckers for Agnew or any other reactionary politician who appealed to racism or knee-jerk patriotism.

Once again, Democratic victories in the 1970 elections proved the predictions of this common wisdom wrong. Yet, in July, 1972, while the Democratic party fought diligently to ensure that the convention represented women, youth, and blacks in the proper numbers, a similar concern with the number of workers represented was never seriously debated. Underground newspapers were allowed on the floor of the convention, but some union officials, all of them supporting McGovern, could not even get passes for the gallery. Nor was this lost on the blue-collar workers who watched that convention on TV. A mechanic who was steward of a Southern union local summed it up with the simple comment that "the only working people I saw there were wearing Wallace hats."

There are many other examples, but this is sufficient to show how destructive this liberal confusion about social class has been.

The myths about the shrinking numbers, increasing affluence, and political extremism of blue-collar workers has led again and again to defeat. It has antagonized workers and isolated liberals every time it has been accepted. The lack of concern and outright condescension it generates have created stumbling blocks for almost every social movement of the '60s, peace and ecology in particular. It played a role in electing Nixon twice to the Presidency, and it will elect a Wallace or worse in '76 if we cling to it. These concepts have led to defeat every time policy has been based on them. And if, as we will argue, they are basically false, it is time to get rid of them, once and for all.

That, in a nutshell, is the purpose of this book.*

---

* One final comment needs to be made. Because the subject of this book is of interest not only to specialists, but to every person with an interest in the future of America, every attempt has been made to keep the book straightforward and readable.

But on the other hand, since conclusion after conclusion challenges widely held beliefs, the slipshod and oversimplified style of avoiding charts and footnotes (which is characteristic of many "popular" treatments of technical subjects) was also judged inappropriate.

The result is, I hope, a happy compromise. All facts have been footnoted and where full data are appropriate, a chart has been used.

On the other hand, no statistical notation more complex than percentages have been used, and correlations, etc., have been translated, as best they can be, into common English. Equally, while several footnotes in a paragraph and page-by-page footnotes are a real convenience for the specialist, to many readers they are as foreign and intimidating as Latin services were to a churchgoing peasant in medieval Europe. In many cases, therefore, where a series of related anecdotes or facts are presented, a single footnote at the end of the paragraph or related series of paragraphs refers the interested reader to all the sources used.

CHAPTER ONE

The American Working Class

IT WAS ONE of the cold, chilly, gray days of fall, for which the Midwest is famous, when I sat in a university classroom and took notes in a bored and abstracted fashion from one of the faceless army of professors who drag one from freshman to senior year in the colleges of the "Big Ten."

I was sitting toward the back with a friend who was equally distracted and bored. He was a Vietnam vet who was born in a working-class suburb of Milwaukee. The topic of the lecture was "The Working Class," and had there been a spark of interest in the professor's presentation, my blue-collar friend, at any rate, would have been roused from his doldrums.

But instead of anything dramatically new, the professor was simply reciting the common wisdom of postwar American society. "The working class," he asserted, "is, for several reasons, no longer a central force in American society.

"First, they have become a minority. White-collar workers now outnumber blue-collar.

"Second, rising income levels have eliminated the rigid distinctions between blue-collar and white-collar—some blue-collar workers, like plumbers and mechanics, make more than white-collar workers like clerks and teachers.

"Third, the suburbs have created social and cultural integration, a common life-style that makes the distinctive working-class neighborhood or culture a thing of the past."

The professor went on to declare the political implications of this change, which, in his view, was the end of any distinctive "working-class" political attitudes.

This lecture was delivered in the fall of 1967—and within six months George Wallace would end the idea that the man who works in a factory was politically the same as his university professor cohort in suburban America.

The other points, about the percentages, life, and conditions of American workers, would not die so easily. In one form or another they have continued up to today and many still believe them.

I did not doubt my professor at the time. But if I had, I might have turned to my friend and learned from him a good deal more about working-class life in postwar America than I could have gained from listening to the lecturer. But most university students and liberals have lived without ever really coming in contact with workers and the three points that the professor listed seem perfectly logical and unquestionably sound. But, each of these conclusions is wrong and politically dangerous to any rational strategy for progress in America in the seventies. They are, in fact, simply myths that must be put aside.

II

The first conclusion, that a majority of Americans are white collar, seems hard to deny. If a student in that classroom, for example, had not been convinced by his professor's assertion, he would have found little to support his skepticism. His economics textbook had a full-page chart which made the white-collar occupations appear to be spreading throughout America like some advancing army charging across a map of Europe. The one relevant paragraph in the text began with the rhetorical question, "Why has this dramatic shift from blue collar to white collar, from brawn to brain occurred?" [1] The rest of the page was devoted to an answer.

Ordinarily, this would end any doubt. But, if the student was suspicious of his "establishment" textbook and professor, and turned to the most popular liberal and even radical social theorists, he would have found the same thing. John Kenneth Galbraith certainly did not challenge this myth. In *The New Industrial State* he said:

> By 1965 there were nearly eight million more white than blue collar workers, 44.5 as compared to 36.7 million. During those years the number of professional and technical workers, the category most characteristic of the technostructure, approximately doubled. [2]

Herbert Marcuse also endorsed this common conception in *One Dimensional Man*:

> An assimilating trend shows forth in the occupational stratification. In the key industrial establishments the "blue collar" work force declines in relation to the "white collar" element. The number of non-production workers increases. [3]

Finally, even in the "pop" best seller, *Future Shock*, Alvin Toffler presents a particularly lyrical version of this same idea:

> In about 1956 the U.S. became the first major power in which more than 50% of the non-farm labor force ceased to wear the blue collar of the factory or manual labor . . . within the same lifetime a society for the first time in human history not only

threw off the yoke of agriculture, but managed within a few brief decades to throw off the yoke of manual labor as well.[4]

Confronted with such an overwhelming unanimity of opinion, it is not surprising that the student in that class immediately dismissed blue-collar workers and turned instead to theories of youth and consciousness for the way forward.

But, while it is understandable that a note-taker in that class would give up in despair, it is a shame. If he had pressed on one more step, he would have found that the terms white collar and blue collar were used in a specific and technical way that was not the way we use them in ordinary conversation.

So, before taking the further steps that the student omitted, let us be clear about the "commonsense" definition of blue collar or white collar; working class or middle class.*

In terms of occupation, the division is basically between manual, essentially physical or menial, labor and managerial or intellectual work. Blue-collar workers mean people who work with their hands, not with their minds. The images are the factory worker or the garbage collector, the construction worker or the man who carries your bags in the airport. People instantly recognize that there is something fundamental that separates all the people who "punch a clock" or just "bust my ass all day" from the doctors, lawyers, and executives whose jobs are an important, creative part of their lives and mean something to them. Working-class jobs are almost

---

* Some will object to talking about occupations separately from income, life-style, and all the rest. However, for the last twenty years these three issues have been mixed together on the assumption that the "old" notion of American society as stratified by occupation simply couldn't be correct. In many discussions of social class, occupation is not even mentioned, instead income is used to describe social position. But it is worth separating out the various issues of occupation, income, and life-style, looking first at the occupational structure, blue collar vs. white collar, then at the income these occupations provide, and finally at the life-style one can purchase with that income. Before that, few sweeping conclusions can safely be drawn about the entire American working class.

inevitably relatively low paying and low in prestige. Day to day, they offer little independence or control, certainly in comparison with a doctor or lawyer.

On the other hand, "white-collar jobs" bring to mind the image of the man behind the desk: William L. White's *The Organization Man*, angling for the vice-president's job. Or else the doctor or lawyer, the "professional" man comes to mind.

These jobs are relatively high in status and pay, and offer more independence, control, and satisfaction than work which requires only rote, mechanical labor.

Some jobs fall in a gray area between these two poles. These are, in general, the lowest level clerical positions. But this basic brain vs. brawn dichotomy is how we really think about class in America. In 1970, when construction workers beat up students in downtown New York, the horrified reactions of many intellectuals clearly expressed the real way class is viewed. Liberals said, "Those thugs are beating up our kids. *They* don't understand. *They* must all be fascists. *We* have to do something!"

All of the clichés which said construction workers were really middle-class and shared the life-style of the intellectuals were forgotten. It was *us* and *them* and *they* meant working class. Thus, if we want to think in practical political terms about American workers, this simple commonsense division is what we must use as a guide.

In a way, it shouldn't even have been necessary to justify this point of view. Since most people use blue-collar and white-collar as synonyms for brawn and brain, for manual labor vs. professional and managerial work, one would reasonably expect that when statistics are quoted, they are based fairly concretely on this dichotomy.

But the problem is that they are not. If that suspicious college student had gone to the publications of the census bureau he would have found that the more than 20,000 specific jobs that people have in the United States are not directly classified into brawn vs. brain, but into ten different categories, some of which are then labeled white-collar or blue-collar. They are:

White-collar	Blue-collar	Other
Professional, Technical, and Kindred	Craftsmen and Foremen	Service
Managers, Officials, and Proprietors	Operatives	Farm Laborers
Clerical	Laborers (non-farm)	Farmers
Sales		

This sorting looks fine on the surface. The categories are not crystal clear, but they seem adequate. But, while for twenty years these categories seemed reasonable enough for commentators to proclaim the end of manual labor, had the commentators or a student in that classroom gone beyond these ten categories to the specific jobs they contain they would have found that the white-collar majority was very much like a desert mirage; the more carefully one looked, the farther away it became. The precise definition of the category "blue-collar" limits it to production and distributive workers, who are only a fragment of all the Americans who are still employed in essentially rote, manual labor.[5]

First of all, the "service" workers were excluded from the blue-collar classification. But within this group are such occupations as janitors, waiters, porters, ushers, elevator operators, doormen, and even shoeshine boys. These jobs just listed are a "who's who" of the most menial and low-paying occupations in America. Yet, when writers quoted the percentage of "blue-collar" workers at 37.5 percent they were automatically including everyone else, including the service workers, in the middle class. Other workers in the service category are equally manual: guards, watchmen, cooks, housekeepers, hospital and other attendants, barbers, police, and firemen. Only a tiny handful of people who hold jobs such as FBI agents and detectives could even be suggested as middle-class.

In addition, the male clerical and sales category, considered as part of the white-collar group, proves to have many working-class jobs concealed within it. The postman is a clerical worker. So is the young man in the supermarket who punches the prices on the cans. Baggagemen, messenger boys, bill collectors, newsboys, auctioneers, peddlers, office machine operators, bus and train dispatchers, telegraph operators, and so on, are all contained in the white-collar category and hence called middle class.

All of this becomes clear just by looking at the specific occupations for men. But on turning the page to the breakdown for women, suddenly we realize we have been thoroughly bamboozled.

When people read those quotes about the end of manual labor and the new white-collar majority they automatically thought of doctors and lawyers and "corporation" men as the "new class." But what they were reading were statistics not only about men, but about all women too, even those who only worked a few hours a week.

These women comprise 70 percent of clerical and sales workers, a key part of the "middle-class majority." They work as telephone operators, cashiers, salesgirls, typists, and in other low-paying, low-status jobs. The euphoric image of a society of professionals and executives is irrevocably lost Eighty percent of the labor force are either manual or clerical workers, with the majority in manual jobs.

Some sociologists have tried to salvage the "middle-class majority" by suggesting that these women clerical and sales workers are a "new" social group, a lower-middle-class "salariat." This is an appealing solution since one would hesitate about calling these women "working-class."

Many writers have been seduced by this concept since it seems to apply to the many "career girls" whom one meets and who seem more middle-class than working-class. The image of the women clerical and sales workers that these writers have is the New York single girl, perhaps a Vassar graduate, who is working as a secretary, but dreams of "getting into publishing." She lives with two other girls in an expensive East Side apartment, reads *Ms.*, takes courses at the New School on some strange subject like existential pottery, smokes pot on occasion, and goes skiing on the weekends. Such a person, however, is not at all typical of the clerical and sales category. Most women clerical and sales workers are married and about half are *married to working-class men.*[6]

Suddenly the career girl secretary is joined by a somewhat less romantic figure, a welder's wife who works part time as a cashier in the A&P. Instead of *Ms.*, imagine *Reader's Digest*, instead of the ski slopes, it's Wednesday night bowling. Lastly, not pot but one of her husband's beers. If a sociologist met her on the street, she would be one of "them," not one of "us."

The best way to clarify this confusion is to look at the occupational structure for men alone. Most women are married and therefore live in the class and culture of their husbands. They follow their husbands lead in politics and all their social life is with their husbands' class. Thus the occupations for men gives a much clearer indication of the relative size of the working class and middle class in America. The following chart shows the proportions quite clearly:

MAJOR OCCUPATION GROUPS FOR MALES, 1969* [7]

Professional and Technical	14.6%...29.2	
Managers, Officials and Proprietors	14.6	/...42.4 Middle Class
Clerical	7.4.....13.2	
Sales	5.8	
Craftsmen and Foremen	21.4	
Operatives	21.4............57.5 Working Class	
Laborers	7.6	
Service	7.1	

When we remember that there are many working-class jobs like mailmen hidden in the clerical and sales category, the true manual figure is probably 60–62 percent. Thus, three-fifths, 60 percent of America is working-class. The euphoric concept of a middle-class majority, the end of manual labor, and the new age in human history were all based on including the wives of steelworkers who went to work as cashiers and salesgirls as middle-class.

This chart, however, includes black and white Americans. Since blacks are disproportionately employed as manual workers, one might suspect most *white* people could be white-collar.

This, however, is not the case: 55.3 percent of white men are in the four manual categories, and with the misclassified clerical workers one can estimate about 58 percent, perhaps

* The reason for using 1969 figures is simply that the Nixon recession threw many blue-collar workers into the ranks of the unemployed, and made statistics on employed males in '70–'72 very deceptive. No one, to my knowledge has ever called men out of work part of the middle class, but so it would appear if '70 or '71 figures were used.

more, are what we would call working-class. Thus, the difference is about 2 percent—57.5 to 55.3.[8] *

The chart above also excludes students, and therefore seems to underestimate the size of the middle class. But even if one added in students and other groups outside the employed labor force, the conclusion would not change. If students tend to be middle-class, then several other excluded groups tend to be lower-class (or at any rate, not middle-class): unemployed blue-collar workers, for example, old people living on pensions, and the armed forces, which recruit a disproportionate number of working-class youth.[9]

All of these groups together far outnumber the students in America. America is not a white-collar or middle-class society. Sixty percent of American men still work in essentially rote, manual jobs.

For all practical purposes this is the key point. Next Monday 60 percent of American men will begin a new week at nine to five jobs which they do basically with their hands. To anyone who is involved in organizing communities, winning elections, or passing legislation this is the reality they must face.

But, it does leave open the possibility that blue-collar work may be rapidly disappearing and perhaps in a few years we will have our beloved middle-class majority after all. Social analysts most certainly jumped the gun in announcing the end of manual labor, but perhaps they were right in saying that fundamental changes occurred in the postwar period and that the long range trend is toward the end of manual labor.

If one presses the expert for the facts about the "great" changes in the work force, one usually gets a very complicated set of statistics about "relative rates" of increase and decline, all

* The complete figures for the white occupational structure are presented in Footnote 8.

of which seem very impressive and all of which point to a disappearing working class.

Unfortunately, while these statistics are very useful for publishing in the academic journals, they are not very good for getting a practical understanding of what is going on, because they conceal some of the most important information.

If we look at the actual number of people in different occupations, there is one absolutely stunning fact. The number of working-class Americans has not decreased at all—in fact, since 1950 it has increased by roughly four million! There are four million more workers in America today than in 1950. The declining trend the analysts notice is totally relative—as the population grew, the working class increased, but the minority of Americans who are middle-class increased at a faster rate.

Here are the figures for men in terms of our commonsense definitions and rounded off:

	1950	1969	Change, 1950–69[10]
Middle Class	13,000,000	19,000,000	+6,000,000
Working Class	22,000,000	26,000,000	+4,000,000

This white-collar increase is significant, but let us put it in perspective. The relative percentage of workers goes down, from 62.4 percent to 57.5 percent, a 5 percent drop in twenty years (not counting the misclassified clerical and sales workers).

But first of all, that still leaves us with 26 million working-class American men and 19 million middle-class. That is a raw social and political fact that cannot be denied.

Second, the middle class needed an increase of three million people just to stay even with the working class and hold the working-class majority at 62 percent. So there are only a bit less than three million middle-class people who indicate something new in the occupational structure since 1950.

Again, the raw number is striking. The whole "great change," the postwar "revolution," the end of manual labor comes down to less than three million men in a male labor force of 45 million. It may be significant, but it hardly constitutes a fundamental change in the very nature of society. At this rate there will be a working-class majority until the next century. At least another generation of Americans will be predominantly working-class. Seven presidents and thousands of congressmen will be elected by a working-class majority.

The Department of Labor estimates for 1980 confirm this. *No* manual category will decline in absolute numbers, and the relative decrease is small. In the seventies the figures for craftsmen and foremen will show no real change; operatives a decline of 2 percent; laborers, 1 percent; and service workers will in fact, grow.[11]

A closer look at changes in the particular occupational categories since 1950 shows some further points of interest:

EMPLOYED MEN BY OCCUPATION (*in thousands*),
1950 AND 1969[12]

Middle class	1950	1969
Professional and Technical	2,700	6,800
Managers, Officials, and Proprietors	5,400	6,700
Clerical	3,000	3,400
Sales	2,400	2,700
Working class		
Craftsmen and Foremen	7,500	9,900
Operatives	8,800	9,900
Laborers	3,400	3,500
Service	2,700	3,300

In the white-collar category the striking fact is that the three million "new" workers are clearly in the professional and technical category, whose growth can be largely traced to two concrete events of the postwar period. One is the sudden growth of the educational system in response to the postwar baby boom and Sputnik. A second is the massive allocation of resources to scientific research and development, much of it directly related to military projects.

Obviously, a large part of the "great change" was the result of some very concrete political decisions on how to spend the taxpayers' money and not an earth-shattering revolution in the nature of American capitalism. This is not as exciting as "postindustrial states" or "new eras in human history" but it is very likely closer to the truth.

The lower half of the chart also blows the whistle on some other cherished illusions. For one thing, skilled workers have clearly been growing rapidly, and the least skilled blue-collar category hardly at all. But in 1969, the majority of American workers, 61 percent in fact, were unskilled or semiskilled. We will see that skilled workers have been the victims of many myths, but at this point, we can at least dismiss the belief that they are typical blue-collar workers. A significant minority yes, but a majority no.

With these conclusions we are almost finished. We have had to follow a tortuous route in dissecting twenty years of mythology. But the facts are now fairly clear. The majority of Americans are working-class—60 percent of American men and their wives, sons, and daughters. They are not disappearing and not until the next century, perhaps, will middle-class men equal them in numbers.

III

If manual workers live exactly like white-collar workers, however, then the fact that they work in factories instead of offices is probably not of great political significance.

This is, of course, what most commentators have told us. The message that blue-collar workers are now "middle class" or "middle Americans" has been repeated so many times that no one ever thinks of questioning it. Although no longer called affluent, they are never called poor.

As a typical case in point, Herman P. Miller, in his article, "A Profile of the Blue Collar America—A View Through the Census Data," says, "By 1969 the median annual income of white families headed by blue collar workers was $10,700 . . ." [13] But, the mention of the census bureau should make us a bit wary. Who is he talking about? The answer— only craftsmen, foremen, and operatives—no one else. Service workers are excluded, laborers are excluded, people unemployed at the time of the survey are excluded. Not to mention the somewhat more defensible exclusion of blacks as a special case.

If we check back a few pages we find that Mr. Miller has excluded about 25 percent of the *white* employed working class and even more if we include the long-term unemployed and blacks. A far better approach is to include all four groups of manual workers (craftsmen and foremen, operatives, service and laborers; the manual clerical and sales workers unfortunately can't be separated from the rest of their category) to see, not just an average, but the distribution of income—how many workers are what we would consider poor, middle American, or affluent.

These figures would be difficult to arrive at or very

arbitrary if the divisions had to be made by just guesswork or instinct. Fortunately, the Bureau of Labor Statistics calculates "standard budgets" which tell us what we need to know. Each budget is geared for a family of four.

Although they use the neutral terms, upper, middle, and lower to describe three standards of living, these budgets automatically define the three distinct socioeconomic cultures in the United States, the culture of poverty, working-class culture and the life-style of middle-class affluence. Most affluent people, for example, buy a certain kind of clothing, rent or buy a distinct kind of house or apartment, buy a certain kind and amount of food, and so forth.

Every year the B.L.S. sends its employees out into the stores, car lots, and real estate agencies to find out how much these characteristic kinds of purchases cost.

The result is three budgets which reflect the average cost of obtaining the basic goods and services on each of the three levels. Thus, in 1970, for example, the lower standard of living budget was $6,960. This meant that a poor family needed $6,960 to obtain the typical shelter, clothing, etc. of most "lower-income" people in America.

The intermediate budget is immediately recognizable as the world of the blue-collar worker, the world of Sears, Roebuck furniture, four-dollar bourbon and two-year-old cars, traded in every six years. It is not a standard of affluence or anything remotely resembling the American dream. It constitutes the cost of living that some unions call a "shabby, but respectable, life."

In 1970, this intermediate budget required $10,670 and the affluent budget required $15,950.[14]

The chart on the following page shows the distribution of working-class income in 1970.

WORKING CLASS FAMILY INCOME, 1970[15]

Income in thousands	Percent	Percent of all working-class families below this level
1–7	29.5	29.5—30% Poor
7–8	8.1	37.6
8–9	8.6	46.2
9–10	8.2	54.5—60% "Below Intermediate"
10–12	14.8	69.4
12–15	15.2	84.4—85% "Below Affluence"
15+	15.5	100.0

The conclusion is striking. The majority of American working people do not even earn enough for the "middle American," "intermediate" budget.

The majority is not hovering midway between affluence and poverty. The majority lives below the "shabby but respectable" standard of comfort and security.

Thirty percent—almost a third of employed American workers, are living in what is really poverty. They made less than $7,000 in a year when the "lower" budget called for $6,960. This means a total family income of $135 per week *before taxes*. Another 30 percent were above the poverty budget, but below that "shabby" intermediate level. Thus, 60 percent of the working class is either poor or hovering between poverty and the very modest level contained in the intermediate budget. A United Auto Workers study shows just how "modest" that budget is.

    The BLS budget is much more "modest" than "adequate." It assumes, for example, that the family will own:
   . . . A toaster that will last for 33 years;
   . . . A refrigerator and a range that will each last 17 years;

. . . A vacuum cleaner that will last 14 years;
. . . A television set that will last ten years.

The budget assumes that a family will buy a two-year-old car, and keep it for four years. In that time they will pay for a tune-up once a year, a brake realignment every three years, and a front-end alignment every four years . . .

The budget assumes that the husband will buy one year-round suit every four years . . . and one topcoat every 8½ years.

It assumes that the husband will take his wife to the movies once every three months, and that one of them will go alone once a year. The two children are each allowed one movie every four weeks. A total of $2.54 per person per year is allowed for admission to all other events, from football and baseball games to theater or concerts.

Finally, the budget allows nothing whatever for savings.[16]

This or less is the condition of 60 percent of American workers. The affluent worker, who until recently was supposed to be typical, constitutes 12 to 15 percent of the working class, white and black. Eighty-five percent are not "typical." The average worker earned $9,500 in 1970, much closer to poverty than to affluence. It is an ironic fact that, while many commentators spoke of the affluent worker with two cars in the garage and a color TV, even today, the majority of blue-collar workers have neither.

These statistics do include black workers. But a simple calculation shows that excluding them would only increase the "well-being" of white workers by about 2.5 percent[17]—this is more than counterbalanced by the simple fact that these figures are the before-tax income. They are also the income of the entire family, working wives and children included. These statistics do not include the long-term unemployed, the ill, or old people on pensions. These figures describe the working poor, not poverty in general.

To some people this concept will seem incredible. For many years the economic condition of workers has been shrugged off with easy references to a handful of plumbers and electricians making eight to ten dollars an hour. But all that time other workers were getting $4.00 to $4.50 and some even less.

In fact, more than anything else, it is working wives who have made possible even the modest standard of living workers enjoy. The earnings of the husband, even if employed full time, shows very clearly what a worker's paycheck looks like:

MEDIAN WORKING-CLASS INCOME BY OCCUPATION, 1970[18]

Craftsmen and Foremen	$9,253
Operatives	7,644
Laborers	6,462
Service	6,964

In May 1970, the typical manufacturing production worker with three dependents had earnings of $132.93 weekly and spendable earnings (i.e., after taxes, etc.) of $115.27. For construction workers average earnings were $194.31, $165.13 spendable according to the Department of Labor.[19] It is worth keeping this in mind when one imagines a working-class family which has an income of $10,000 a year—he earned only seven or eight thousand and his wife the rest. Or the skilled worker's family who has $12,000. He often gets $9,000—she, the balance.

Suddenly, all the analyses which say workers don't really have any legitimate economic complaints look rather doubtful.

As we will see, a single illness, a period of unemployment or the loss of the wife's income when she becomes pregnant can wipe out a lifetime of savings and send many working-class families into a permanent cycle of debt and economic crises. The conclusion is inescapable: millions are still living far below the level needed for a full, decent life.

But, if the objective situation of most workers comes as a surprise, when we compare it to the middle class, the conclusion is so stunning and so disruptive of anything that we have heard that some people may find it difficult to accept despite the facts.

To make the comparison clear, let us first look at something we know, the economic inequality between black and white.

The average family income of blacks is 60 percent of whites, a difference of about $4,000.[20] What this means is that in order for black people to be on the same economic level as whites, once a year we would have to give every black family a check for an average of $4,000. This 60 percent or $4,000 is a shorthand way of understanding the degree of inequality between black and white in America. Obviously, some families will need more and some less to reach the average white income, but $4,000 is the average difference between a black family and a white one.

When we turn to working class vs. middle class, however, the clichés about the similar life-styles and a narrowing income gap lead us to expect something far different. The image of the typical worker as an overpaid craftsman, who has a life-style more affluent than many white-collar workers has become a national cliché.

However, the average white-collar income is about $12,500, while blue-collar, as we saw, is $9,500. This is a difference of about $3,000 or, to put it another way, blue-collar income is about 77 percent of white-collar.[21]

But, as we noted, the white-collar total includes many clerical and sales workers who are really manual workers. If we look at the two predominant categories, professional and technical, and managers and proprietors (75 percent of all white-collar men), we find their average income is about $14,500. Manual workers earn only 65 percent of the

upper-middle-class average, and the difference between them
is $5,000. We would have to give every worker in America
$5,000 to create real equity in income between the pro-
fessional and managerial middle class and the working class.
In percentage terms, the inequality between manual workers
and most white-collar workers is almost as great as the gap
between black and white, and in the absolute number of
dollars that separate them, the distance between manual and
professional and managerial workers is, in fact, greater.

This doesn't mean that workers are as poor or as exploited
as blacks. They are not. What it does mean is that the
inequality, the distance a factory worker sees between himself
and the middle class is almost as great as the distance the
average black person sees between himself and white America.
There is a profound economic inequality between black and
white America, but there is also a profound inequality between
social classes, as well. If a black skin means economic
inequality, so does a blue collar. Economic inequity and
injustice in America come in both colors.

A number of intellectuals, in particular, will find it hard to
accept this conclusion. They have a strange emotional commitment to the idea that, if anyone is underpaid, it is they, not
blue-collar workers. One professor criticized an earlier version
of this thesis by first making a few disparaging remarks about
statistics in general and then said, "There are workers in New
York City's Department of Sanitation who earn as much as
some City University of New York professors and more than
Columbia assistant professors."

This self-indulgent notion that professors and intellectuals
are suffering the same or even more severe economic deprivation than most workers is remarkably widespread. In fact, it is
probably the most popular myth about workers among
middle-class intellectuals.

But, for all its popularity, it is a myth, and a deeply destructive and pernicious one. Probably, more than any other, it is this notion that led liberal intellectuals to ignore the legitimate discontents of blue-collar workers and expresses the thinly veiled condescension that has been George Wallace's greatest political asset. So, it is necessary to get specific and show very clearly that this particular idea is nonsense.

The average professor's salary in 1970 was $11,745.[22] As we noted before, operatives get on the average $7,644 and craftsmen and foremen $9,253. Even the lowly assistant professors received more than skilled workers, $10,698 vs. $9,253. And even this does not show the magnitude of the error. This income of $11,745 in general, or $10,698 for assistant professors, includes a *three*-month vacation. This is a nine-month work year, one of the most popular features of the professor's job. If we compare weekly salaries to correct for this difference; we find that professors average $293 a week. Full professors make, on the average, a whopping $419 a week. The lowly assistant professors make $267.

The highest paid construction workers, the skilled journeymen, got an average of $6.54 an hour in 1970, or $262 a week.[23]

There it is. An assistant professor, who considers himself to be at the low end of the academic totem pole, and who has the chance of advancing to associate and finally full professor, averages more per hour than the worker who has reached the very top of the working-class hierarchy. It is a bitter pill to swallow, but the popular concept of workers as grossly overpaid craftsmen with their speedboats is about as valid as the image of all blacks as welfare cheaters with their Cadillacs. For all the clichés and myths, workers and the middle class are divided by a real and profound inequality.

If one doesn't personally know and talk with blue-collar

workers it is possible to think that this inequality has little practical impact on the average worker. Yet the fact is, blue-collar workers really are deeply aware of it. All through the fifties and sixties, while intellectuals were talking about the disappearance of class, workers saw the chasm between themselves and the theorists who wrote about them. The auto assembly line worker who owns a five-year-old Chevy he bought second hand, spends eight or nine or even ten hours a day building Cadillacs or Torinos he will never buy, and he knows it is the middle class that is buying them. As middle-class people go flying to Acapulco or San Juan for Christmas, they leave under the watchful eyes of mechanics, maintenance men and cabdrivers, who get two weeks vacation a year, and usually spend it at home, or perhaps take a drive with the family to Disney World or a national park for a few days. Social inequality is not abstract for these people. It is a visible daily reality.

IV

The one myth which remains is the "suburban worker." According to the authorities, it was here that the American dream of social and economic equality became a practical reality. The blue-collar worker no longer came home to his dreary tenement, still dressed in his work clothes, where he was packed together with his fellows. Now he changed clothes in the factory and drove to his suburban home, looking just like his middle-class neighbor who arrived alongside him. The common suburban life-style and daily personal contact, they said, was rapidly eliminating all of the distinctive "working-class" qualities of blue-collar America. America was a country of suburbs and the great social problem was crabgrass.

In the last few years this euphoric image has been tarnished by white resistance to residential integration, and suburbs are now counterposed to the image of the decaying inner cities. But, the vision of the suburbs as a single, undifferentiated mass of middle Americans still remains. Suburban whites and ghetto blacks define the way most people think of American society.

As usual, this concept was supported by a few statistics and affirmed by a host of writers and social theorists. A student in that college class, as he bicycled back to his apartment, probably did not even think too much about this idea. He was too young to remember the way it was years before when every town had. a "wrong side of the railroad tracks," where working-class people lived and worked. It probably did not occur to him even to look around him as he rode, and compare it to what his professor had said.

But, if our student did decide to make such a comparison, he would have suddenly realized a truth which had been staring him in the face all the time. If he were in one of the largest midwestern state universities, and began his tour from the precise center of town, he would have found that to the west he encountered one kind of "suburb," while turning east led him to a very different kind of "suburban" community.

To the west, beyond the university he would find the suburbia he was expecting. On the residential streets the houses were set far back from the tree-lined streets and there were, at most, three to a block. Many were recently built, with garages and dens and guest rooms and all the trappings of the American dream. If he were very acute, the student could even distinguish subtle differences between his professor's house, which was not new, but a carefully remodeled building in an older "good" community and the new houses of business executives. Finally, miles from the city, the student would encounter lavish houses that looked like something clipped from the pages of *Better Homes and Gardens*, set so far back from the street that they were invisible behind a screen of trees or hedges.

Everything else about that community conformed to the image of the suburbs. The cars were new and more than half the houses appeared to have two of them. The air was clear and fresh. It was a typical suburb.

But when our student returned to the center of town and began to ride in the other direction, the difference was striking. Down the main avenue, within a mile, he passed a massive industrial plant that covered four or five square blocks. Beyond was another, a meat-packing plant which let off an odor that could be smelled and almost digested, for half a mile. Low-flying planes announced that the airport was nearby. Turning off the avenue to the residential streets, the student found houses thirty or forty years old, eight or nine to a block. Had he tried, he would have found that they were sometimes so close together that he had to turn sideways to walk between them comfortably. Here there were no spacious front lawns, no garage, and rarely a newly constructed building. In backyards he could see wash hanging from clotheslines. There was one car in front of each house and it was old.

Along the streets our student could see other things that did not exist on the other side of town. Bars. Automobile part and body shops and small warehouses with signs saying "Parts and Supplies."

Our student would probably come away a bit depressed by the atmosphere of this community. There was something almost foreign about it; the people there did not share in the life-style nor live in the culture of his parents. It was not desperate poverty he saw, but in relation to the better side of town, it was clearly second class.

As he returned to the center of town, our student might have made one final and ironic observation: within a few blocks of the very center, he would cross a series of railroad tracks, which neatly bisected the city in half. If he had used these railroad tracks as a dividing line, he would have found that in census tracts to the east of them about two-thirds of the inhabitants were blue-collar. In census tracts to the west, about two-thirds were white-collar. In 1970, the railroad tracks still defined the social and cultural cleavage between working class and middle class in America.

Of course, no one city is "typical," and geographical and historical factors or the presence of a large black ghetto can make the picture more complex. Sometimes it is north and south and not east and west. Sometimes a river or other geographic factor complicates the situation, and frequently there are no actual railroad tracks. But, in every city in America, one can drive in one direction and find affluent suburbs and, in another the working-class community. In Milwaukee, for example, Richard Hamilton, a sociologist, says:

> There are not enough middle class suburbs to allow the assimilation of any significant proportion of the blue collar ranks . . . Most of the city's blue collar workers obviously live in neighborhoods with other blue collar workers. Typically, between three and four of every five neighbors would be blue collar families. Children who are born and raised in these areas will attend school with other working class children. Their friends and later co-workers will, overwhelmingly, be from other blue collar families. As far as personal contacts and influences are concerned, the structure of the city is such as to almost guarantee exclusive patterns of association.[24]

And again, about Buffalo:

> The city of Buffalo, admittedly an extreme case, contained seventy-five Census tracts in 1960. Only fourteen of these had

a non-manual majority. More than eighty percent of those in seventeen of the city's tracts were in manual occupations. Another ten tracts contained between 75 and 80 percent manual workers. One part of the city, the largest part, approximately 4 miles wide and 6 miles long, contains no tract with a middle class majority and only two (of 38) having less than 60 percent of the population in manual occupations.[25]

Nor do these working-class suburbs offer a life-style the same as the affluent ones. In a later chapter we will deal with the working-class life-style in greater detail, but just for the moment two points should suffice. First, the median value of a worker's home in 1964 was $13,237, while that of the upper middle class's was $20,375. In addition, fewer workers owned houses than did the upper middle class (61 percent vs. 83 percent).[26]

Also, as Hamilton notes about Milwaukee:

There are a number of other details that make it clear that the "look-alike" thesis is rather exaggerated. In the suburban working class tract, we find the following elements: Interstate highway 94 cuts through the district; the Chicago, Milwaukee, St. Paul and Pacific railroad also cuts it; the Howard Avenue water purification plant is located on one corner of the tract; touching another corner is Mitchell Field, the city's airport. A major runway points directly at this area of working class suburbia. Although the individual houses may look like houses elsewhere, the overall "tone" of the area is obviously very different from that of middle class suburbia.[27]

In general, working-class suburbs get the freeways, airports, or public housing which lower community values.

One could assemble a staff and spend a year confirming this reality with detailed studies of every city in America. But in fact we know that the middle class does not go to the bars and bowling alleys of working-class America, and that workers do not go to the same "art" films or expensive restaurants. If we think about it we realize that the suburbs we pass on the way to work are different from our own.

The truth is that working-class people are shadowy figures to most middle-class people. Contact is limited to a quick glance at a knot of construction workers sitting on the sidewalk eating lunch. Or else it is a few words exchanged with a postman, doorman, or telephone installer. Beyond this, few have gone.

This profound isolation of workers from middle-class liberals explains the reason why the latter could believe the myths for so long. If one lives in a middle-class suburb and works in an office, one never sees blue-collar workers and, naturally, one never talks to them. From this distorted frame of reference, it is easy to believe that workers are disappearing, or living like the middle class. If many of the income statistics seem startling to some readers, it is simply because they never saw a worker's paycheck or his bankbook in their entire lives. It is likely that more students have walked through the slums of Mexico with a copy of Oscar Lewis in their hands than have ever done so in the working-class neighborhoods of Hammond, Indiana, or Flint, Michigan. In fact, there is no comparable book for middle-class people to read.

But those three startling points, our point of departure, are now fairly clear, and the political implications are that every social program and blueprint for the future which accepted the "middle-class" majority has been fundamentally wrong.

The discontents of blue-collar workers have been dismissed as unimportant, their economic demands called greedy, and their particular interests almost systematically ignored. Condescending and elitist theories of working-class psychology have been developed to explain their behavior, inevitably assuming workers have no legitimate complaints.

The principal beneficiaries of this myth have been George Wallace and Richard Nixon and, since it is dangerously wrong, it is time to base our social and political strategies on facts. Self-interest and justice both demand it.*

V

Before turning to the real discontents of workers, on the job and in their communities, we must deal with two very special groups whose situation we have mentioned only in passing, black people and women.

The condition of blacks in America is, ironically, easier to deal with than that of white workers. While most liberals are ignorant of the most basic facts about blue-collar workers, many people have in their memories certain statistics like the fact that there are almost 25 million, perhaps more, black people in America, that the unemployment rate is usually double that of whites, and so forth.

However, the undeniable injustices of unemployment and welfare have often led to a visual image of the black community as entirely composed of unemployed ghetto youths and welfare mothers. This, along with the social crises of bad

* It must be noted that the isolation of middle-class intellectuals from workers is worst in the two places where, probably, a majority of the nationally prominent writers and commentators live—New York and Washington, D.C. There are simply no factories in these cities—Washington has 4 percent of its population engaged in manufacturing. New York, as a whole, has only 20 percent and Manhattan Island probably no more than Washington.[28] The commentators who live in the suburbs of Chevy Chase or the East Side of Manhattan never see a factory worker. Blue-collar workers, aside from construction craftsmen and personal service workers like cabdrivers and superintendents (who, in fact, aren't even workers) are no more a part of their experience than Chinese peasants. And, on the other hand, the number of national opinion makers who live in the cities like Flint and Saginaw, Michigan, could probably be counted on the fingers of one hand. Agnew's attacks on the media were filled with demagoguery but they contained a deep demographic truth—and a profoundly dangerous one.

housing and medical facilities, narcotics, and crime results in a liberal vision of the black community as some unique "underclass" or "culture of poverty."

The problem with this "underclass" view is that, while it highlights some of the most critical problems, it obscures certain key facts. Most black people are not welfare recipients or "street dudes." They are blue-collar workers who work in some of the dirtiest, lowest paying, and often most dangerous jobs in America. This means that, in economic terms, the problems of black people, although significantly worse than the problems of white workers, are part of the general pattern of social and economic inequality in America, and not some accidental, special case in an otherwise egalitarian society. Most black people, for example, are poor because of *low wages,* not inadequate welfare payments or unemployment. Although concern with the poverty of unemployed youths and welfare mothers is valid and important, it should not lead us to ignore the poverty of black janitors and dishwashers, maids and laundry workers. In an economic sense, the most important source of black poverty is the exploitation of black workers through low-paying jobs. Even among black youths, whose unemployment is at crisis level in some communities, nationally, the majority are still employed.

The focus on a romanticized vision of a culture of poverty, all too often, ends up agreeing, in substance, with the right-wing myths about all blacks living on welfare.

Meanwhile, however, most black people are working long hours in hard jobs, earning salaries that do not even provide a poverty budget standard of living.

One young, southern black, who joined a job training program which paid a certain salary to people as they learned, provided an ironic case in point. He described how, in addition to being given training in some rather dubious skill, the white instructor spent a good deal of time talking about the cultural factors and how he truly understood the desperation and despair that the trainees felt about finding work.

The irony was that this young black and several of his friends had been employed before they joined the program. They started the program because it literally paid more than the jobs they had held. Their previous work, with a temporary employment agency, gave them a take-home pay of about nine and a half dollars a day—$8.75 after busfare to the agency and back. To be sure of work they had to get up at 4:30 and be at the agency by 5:15–5:30 A.M., although their pay did not start until they actually began work at 8 or 9.

So, here were men who had been spending over twelve hours a day to earn $8.75 a day now in a training program whose central thesis was that psychological, social, and cultural factors were their real problem, not the $8.75.

In general, the scandalous conditions and real discontents of black workers have been the most ignored aspect of the conditions of blacks in America. Yet it is a central factor in the current crisis.

The census figures in this area are especially untrustworthy. There is ample evidence that blacks are often undercounted. So, although we will use census statistics, it is with the caution that they are not as trustworthy as they are for whites.

Of the 22–23 million blacks the census counts in America, about 6 million are adult men outside institutions such as school, jail, and the army. Of these:

Employed	4,770,000
Unemployed	410,000
Out of the labor force	889,000 [29]

The unemployed figure includes 266,000 who were actively

seeking work, and 144,000 which the AFL-CIO estimates were unemployed but not actively seeking work, which excludes them from the census calculations. Even this number is an underestimation because it includes as "employed" anyone who worked even one day in the two weeks before the survey as "employed." It also understates, due to the under-counting of blacks by the census. The unemployment noted above is about equal to 9 percent of the black labor force, and a complete figure would probably be 12–15 percent, if it included the people who only worked a few hours. This is confirmed by a study of black and white unemployed in central cities, which suggests that about 13 percent are unemployed or subemployed.[30] For black youth, the situation is far worse, and in some cities the unemployment figure is 25–40 percent or more.

1969 PERCENT DISTRIBUTION, BLACK AND OTHER MALE EMPLOYEES BY OCCUPATION GROUP AND MEDIAN INCOME[31]

Occupational group	Percent		'70 Median income, year-round, full-time workers
Professional and Technical	7.4		$8,675
Managers, Officials, and Proprietors	4.5	22% Middle Class	8,752
Clerks	8.1		7,668
Salesworkers	1.9		Not Available
Craftsmen and Foremen	15.1		7,353
Operatives	29.9	78% Working Class	6,273
Service	14.3		5,670
Laborers	18.9		5,410

When we compare these incomes, which are only for those lucky enough to find year-round employment, with the national averages the magnitude of black working-class poverty becomes clear, as does their concentration in the less skilled end of the working class occupational spectrum. The service and laborer categories, in particular, are huge compared with the occupational distribution of all Americans.

However, it is worth noting that operatives are the largest single category, constituting nearly 30 percent of the total. While this often hides the continuing pattern of occupational segregation of blacks into the worst "black" jobs, the sixties did see a dramatic increase in the number of black factory workers in industries like auto and steel. There has been a corresponding increase in black union membership. Today there are more blacks in unions (3,000,000) than in any other organization, aside from the black church. In a later chapter we will see that this has tremendous political implications, some of which are already becoming apparent on the national scene.

The basic point is clear. The majority of black Americans are working people, and for these close to five million black men, their discontents and poverty result from being the most oppressed sector of the working class. An increase in the minimum wage and serious enforcement of the minimum wage laws would do more to end black poverty than anything an army of social workers will ever accomplish. The problem is not values or culture. For the majority it is the typically working-class issue—the size of the paycheck.

VI

As we have seen, a great deal of the confusion about the class structure of America resulted from the role of women.

When we turn to an examination of women as a special group, the reason becomes clear.

Essentially, there are two parallel but different occupational hierarchies in America, one for men and one for women. When one looks at the two combined, one sees strange cases of white-collar workers earning less than blue-collars. But when they are separated, both the male and female hierarchies show very clearly the continuing superiority of white-collar over blue-collar and service jobs. The unskilled or low-skilled jobs in service and sales, like maids, salesgirls, and waitresses are the lowest paid. Semiskilled women factory workers do a bit better and the huge clerical category, which is split between skilled and semiskilled workers (for example, the secretaries, stenographers, and receptionists), are better still. At the top of the hierarchy are the small group of managers and proprietors and the far larger group of professional workers like grade school and high school teachers, medical technologists, nurses and so on.*

Thus, the brain vs. brawn distinction that we used for men is equally valid for the female hierarchy, even though the specific jobs they do are different. If we divided these jobs up into unskilled, semiskilled, skilled, and the college-trained professional and technical workers, we would find that the female labor force is, in its majority, unskilled or semiskilled

* EMPLOYED WOMEN BY OCCUPATION GROUP, 1969[32]

Occupation	Number of workers	Percent	1970 full-time median income	1970 % full-time
Professional and Technical	4,018,000	14.1%	$7,850	62.5%
Managers, Officials, and Proprietors	1,261,000	4.4	6,369	74.3
Clerical	9,975,000	35.0	5,539	60.3
Sales	2,017,000	7.1	4,174	32.8
Craftsmen and Foremen	339,000	1.2	4,955	58.7
Operatives	4,489,000	15.7	4,465	54.2
Laborers	146,000	.5	4,375	46.7
Service	6,271,000	22.0	3,875	38.7

workers with rote, repetitive jobs. In fact, the major difference between women and men is the almost total absence of a true professional and managerial sector. Many of the "professional" jobs women hold, like medical lab assistants, are really more comparable in training and skill levels to the highest male skilled workers' jobs.

However, the most important fact is the profound difference between the salaries of men and women. In every category, women receive thousands of dollars less than men for jobs which are at approximately the same skill level.

The low wages paid to these women workers have two important consequences. First, for the 58 percent of married women who are married to blue-collar workers as we saw, it can make the difference between almost literal poverty and a less than adequate, but tolerable, life. Although some commentators with an unshakeable optimism have seen the startling growth of women workers as a result of "widening horizons," a desire to find self-expression, careful studies show that economic necessity is the more probable cause.[33]

Second, the low wages paid to these women are the margin of profit for many industries, such as clothing or electronics which are hard pressed by cheap foreign imports. Women factory workers often get a starting salary of $2.15 or $2.25 in these industries, which would be below the poverty level for a man. The same is true for occupations like salesgirls, who often receive less than $90–100 a week.

These figures indicate that, although the women's liberation movement has, up till now, received far more publicity for its personal and social grievances than for its economic discontents, there are very serious issues involved. Although very different from blacks, both blacks and women have been shunted off into separate occupations and industries with the lowest wages, and so the more visible injustices of racial and sexual inequality conceal the general issue of class inequality. But the economic position of women, like blacks, is clearly part of the general question of work and inequality in America. And, if only because so many blue-collar workers' wives are working today, the condition of women workers is inseparable from the standard of living of the American working class as a whole.

As we have seen, every one of the three points in the professor's lecture, which began this chapter, is painfully wrong. The majority of Americans are not white-collar, or well off. Thirty percent of blue-collar workers are poor and another 30 percent cannot earn enough to reach the very modest government definition of a middle-American standard of living. In comparison with the middle class, the chasm of inequality that separates them is comparable with the split between blacks and whites, and there is a wide economic and social gap in life-styles and comfort between workers and the middle class.

American workers are a class apart with real and legitimate problems and discontents. And unlike the abstract paper coalitions of wildly disparate groups which liberals have proposed, they are united by common interests and constitute a majority of the American people.

CHAPTER TWO

The Discontents of Work

SEVERAL MONTHS AGO I got up at 5:00 A.M. and drove over to a small plant to apply for a job as a punch-press operator. The hiring office was small and served as both waiting room and office for the hiring manager, so while I was waiting I could hear him interviewing the man ahead of me. He was a college graduate who had been doing a desk job in some city department. When the hiring manager saw this on his application he told him he was sorry but he was "over-qualified" for the job.

But instead of just leaving the student suddenly snapped back, "You know, that's just unfair. I mean you're just being biased against people who went to college." The hiring manager looked surprised at this outburst for a moment. Then he answered, "Look—we get guys like you coming in all the time and do you know how long they stay?—two maybe three weeks. I mean, we've just found that kids who have gone to college or have sat behind a desk all day just won't do this kind of work. I've got a whole file cabinet full of cases that prove it. The money sounds good. But in general your better educated person just can't do this kind of job. There are all sorts of things he just won't put up with."

Although he is not a noted social thinker the hiring manager quoted above put his finger on the basic issue. While theorists and writers have spent the last twenty years debating about whether workers are alienated from their jobs or are really satisfied, one conclusion has always been clear to people who actually work in America's factories or construction sites. It is that most workers have to put up with a range of very concrete conditions regarding pressure, health and safety, job security, and many others which most middle-class people can't even imagine and certainly never have to tolerate. If there is a huge gap between the social and economic conditions of blue-collar and white-collar workers, the gap between the working conditions of the two is even greater.

The popular notion among intellectuals, that a college professor who is forced to prepare mundane and insignificant papers is a victim of alienation like the factory worker, shows how little understanding there is of the very concrete day-to-day life of a blue-collar worker.

A friend of mine, a young worker studying under the G.I. Bill, once encountered this argument and suggested that the professor would begin to understand how a factory worker feels if he had to type the same single paragraph from 9:00 to 5:00 every day of the week. Instead of setting the pace himself, the professor's typewriter carriage should begin to move at 9:00 and continue at a steady rate until 5:00. The professor's job would be at stake if his typing did not keep up the pace.

For permission to go to the bathroom or to use the telephone, the professor would have to ask a supervisor. His salary, $16,000 for a full professor, would be cut by $8,000, and his vacations reduced to two weeks a year. He could also be ordered to work overtime at the discretion of the company or lose his job. If unlucky, he might have to work the night shift. Finally, if he faced the grim conclusion that his job was a dead end, his situation would then approximate that of an unskilled young worker in a contemporary automobile factory.

In general we will look at factory workers, and to a lesser degree at construction workers. These are two major working-class environments, and two whose conditions and discontents are largely unknown to all but those who work in them.

II

It took me about fifteen minutes to learn the job at the can manufacturing factory. I was stationed between two machines. The machine behind me cut long sheets of aluminum into rectangles the size of paperback novels and deposited piles of them in eight little trays. The machine in front automatically rolled them into cylinders and passed them through a furnace which sealed one edge to the other. My job was to take each pile of aluminum rectangles from the trays where they fell behind me, straighten them out like a deck of cards, and put them in the tray in front of me, which automatically fed them to the machine.

There were, of course, some tricks to learn. For one thing, the piles of aluminum were slippery. The first time I grabbed a handful of about one hundred they slipped through my hands and fell to the floor. Also, a pile eight inches thick weighs ten maybe fifteen pounds, and you have to keep them neat when you put them in the feeder, which means squeezing them tightly. It feels something like trying to pick up a heavy brick covered with vaseline.

The machine in front of me operated continuously and, if there weren't any aluminum sheets in the feeder, a light would automatically "fink" on you.

There was one other thing I had to do—keep an eye on the cutter behind me, and turn it off when the piles got high enough—and back on when I had used all eight. Aside from that, it was just picking up the stacks of aluminum, straightening them out, and putting them in the tray.

The first couple of days on a job like this are the worst. You haven't learned the tricks and muscles get sore in places which you don't ordinarily use but which the job forces you to exercise.

But most of all it's the rhythm you have to catch. At first you fight it and try to beat the machine. You try to lift two piles at once or find a better way than the one the foreman showed you. But finally you stop trying to beat the machine and go along with it. When you get that feeling you're more free, you just let your mind wander, and you don't feel the exertion the same way.

A lot of guys like to say they think about sex all day while they do jobs like these, and maybe they do. But a lot of times I think guys just start thinking any crazy thing that comes into their head. One thing I did was to try and imagine a machine that would do my job. It was a kind of robot on wheels with two pinchers. It would clamp down on the stack of aluminum, wheel around in a perfect half circle, and drop the rectangles exactly into the tray. I don't know why but the image was pleasant to think about.

There was a lot of time for day dreaming like that because the noise was tremendous and the nearest guy was ten feet away. In fact, can factories are among the worst for noise because there are several thousand cans banging together on a half dozen conveyer belts that run overhead. The clattering doesn't recede into the background the way some other factory noises do. I literally couldn't hear someone even if he shouted. A lot of the workers wore ear plugs to block out all sound.

The factory ran three shifts, the first starting at 7:00 A.M. If you got to sleep by 10:00 P.M. you could get up by 6:00 A.M. and feel okay during the day. But for most young guys it's hard not to break out once in a while and go drinking until 12:00 or 1:00 A.M.

The effect of too little sleep or a hangover is awful the next day. It's not like high school or college where you can sit and pretend to listen. You are on your feet all day long and you have to keep up the same speed as usual. At about 10:00 A.M. the lack of sleep hits hard. You can't tune out the noise and the work, and you can't keep the rhythm going without thinking about it. You start looking at the clock every three minutes and figure you'll survive if you make it until lunch.

But more than anything else you feel furious that you can't slow down the pace, or make any kind of change in the work, until you feel a bit better. I suspect that it's at times like this, when a guy has missed two hours sleep or feels sick, that he gets so mad that he walks out or socks his foreman. You feel the whole setup is penalizing you for wanting to have some little break in the routine.

One day, after a night drinking with a guy from the plant, I met him taking a break at about 10:00 A.M., alone in the tiny lunchroom. He pulled a half-pint bottle of cheap bourbon out of his pocket and offered me a little "medicine" for my hangover, something that always seems like a good idea at the time, but never is. I got a Coke and sat down next to him. We sat for a while, just talking and drinking. I told him that I couldn't figure out why they didn't get a machine to replace me. He said they probably couldn't find one who wanted the job. The image struck us both funny and we were still laughing when suddenly the foreman came in looking for us. He saw the bottle and started giving us hell. He didn't even threaten to fire us, though. He was in his forties and he spent so much time dealing with guys smoking joints or worse that the sight of two young guys with a bottle probably made him feel positively nostalgic for the good old days.

At least that's my guess. I actually didn't hear what he said too well. The lunchroom wasn't well insulated and the clatter of the cans drowned out every second word he said.

When people speak of the discontents of blue-collar work the thing they think of first is the nature of the work itself. Obviously the thing all working-class jobs have most clearly in common is the manual, often hard, physical labor, which does not allow for much creativity or individual expression.

Usually the wide range of conditions and problems of blue-collar work are compressed into a single phrase like "hard, dull, repetitive, dirty, and boring jobs." Or else the auto worker is chosen as typical and an example given, such as the man whose job it is to fasten four bolts to each car as it passes by. But, though there are deep and profound sources of discontent in blue-collar work, one should be wary of any argument based on typical workers. There are problems and conditions which are widespread but there are no typical workers or typical jobs.

For example, there are jobs which are simply dull or repetitive without being physically arduous. The routines of nonindustrial workers like doormen, gas station attendants, guards, watchmen, and parking lot attendants fit this description. In industrial environments there are many similar monitoring jobs, some of them high paying, in power plants, petroleum, chemical plants and highly automated production plants.

Other jobs are primarily "heavy dirty work," but are not boring in the way in which an assembly line job is boring. Longshoremen, laborers in construction, the men who carry the bricks and wood, garbage collectors, the thousands and thousands of men who unload trucks and stack boxes in warehouses are all in a very different environment from the automobile assembly line worker if only because they are not tied to the rhythm of a line.

In the lowest skill level of industry, however, jobs like the auto workers are widespread. Classical assembly lines are often found in canning and the food and dairy industry as well as in the auto industry. In other industries devices like conveyer belts or simply high production quotas, produce the same kind of pressures and deadening routine. In the textile industry, spinners and weavers watch over a large number of machines and are kept constantly occupied running from one to the other, quickly replacing or adjusting the spindles of thread. In electronics, assembly workers may take small parts from bins and perform a series of simple operations like soldering some wires or a resistor, working to fulfill a daily quota. The same pattern exists in many industries at the least skilled levels.

At a slightly higher level than these workers are, for example, machine shop workers, who are assigned specific jobs by their supervisors and use various machines and techniques to complete a particular task. In the long run there is a boredom or routine that they encounter, but not of the same kind as the unskilled assembly line worker. Truck and bus drivers also fit into this category, as do thousands of skilled or semiskilled machine operators for whom each job is different.

Finally, there are the skilled craftsmen, the carpenters, electricians, auto mechanics, etc., who have considerable knowledge and whose jobs involve a good deal of independent judgment.[1]

So any simple notion of what working-class jobs are like is unfortunately going to be an oversimplification. But despite this, these jobs do have certain things in common, things which are profoundly different from the occupations of the middle class. While many scholars use terms like alienation or estrangement, workers themselves describe it with elegant simplicity as being treated like a machine and not a man. If there is one sentence that captures the difference between working-class and middle-class jobs it is this.

First there is the effort to control the rate and rhythm at which a worker performs his task. In assembly line or conveyer belt jobs the attempt to make men imitate machines is brutally direct. Time study engineers select a very competent worker and measure the time it takes him to perform an operation or series of operations, and foremen are expected to enforce that rate with all future employees. From then on it doesn't matter if a worker sprained his finger slightly or if he was up late, or if his wife is sick. The line moves at the same pace and he is expected to keep up with it. Quotas are also set in accordance with the engineer's design, and the worker only has the freedom to work a bit harder in the morning, for example, in order to take it a bit slower in the afternoon. But if his quota is a thousand units he is always expected to have them done by 5:00 P.M. One study shows that only 5 percent of office workers are subject to work measurement standards in contrast to 80–85 percent of production workers.[2]

A union official described one case that he encountered in his work:

Three young workers, ages twenty and twenty-one, were hired on the second shift to clean the offices. One evening the foreman caught one of the young janitors doing his homework (he went to school during the day), another was reading the paper, and the third was asleep with his feet on the desk. The foreman exploded and gave them a written warning. The workers filed a grievance protesting the warning. "We cleaned all the offices in five hours by really hustling and who the hell should get upset because we did our own thing? . . . What more do they want?" The steward replied that the company has the right to expect eight hours work for eight hours pay. "They're spacing it out nicely now and everyone is happy," he says, satisfied to have settled the grievance within the understood rules. The young workers, however, are not so happy.

They want the same freedom as professionals to operate within those same eight hours however they see fit.[3]

The very institution of the time clock and the distinction between hourly wage workers and salaried workers points up the difference between blue-collar and white-collar. It assumes a steady mechanical rhythm of work: that blue-collar workers are being paid not for quality or for doing the job itself but for a certain output of work per hour. It is a standard set for a machine, not for a man.

Another aspect of blue-collar work is loneliness. Many working-class jobs are very consciously designed to keep people apart. In many factories the noise level alone prevents any conversation beyond a shouted remark or two. In others the work stations are far apart or the job too difficult to permit any real communication. Rules against talking are also common, either written down on paper or delivered by the supervisor. The attitude is that if you're talking you're probably not doing the job. Only where the work is necessarily done in teams, like construction work, is there any opportunity for real contact, and for many workers like truck drivers, or nonindustrial workers like guards there is no opportunity at all. Their jobs require them to be completely alone all the time.

One aspect that is often overlooked is the complete isolation of most workers from women during their working hours. In many cases this is a conscious strategy of the company. When I once applied for a job in an electronics factory, which had mostly women for the assembly work, the hiring manager said very honestly that they didn't like to hire men because they tended to "create disturbances." I replied as a joke that I wasn't in the habit of assaulting women unless they asked me to. But he answered very seriously that "that wasn't the problem." He said, "It's really that just the presence of the opposite sex tends to make people think of the job as a place to socialize instead of as a place to work."

This attitude is in stark contrast to the world of the middle class. On college campuses, in offices, or among professionals there is frequently the opportunity for a man not only to just talk, but to work with and get to know a woman.

Many psychologists have noted the destructive effects of total sexual segregation in all-male environments like prison and the army, but none have extended this to the factory, even though for five days a week workers have the same situation. Aside from the obvious pressures that total isolation, like prison life, generates, the partial isolation of workers has less dramatic effects. For a few it results in what the psychologists call a "lack of social skills," an inability to relate to women simply for lack of practice. But more generally it makes a worker's relations with a woman superficial. Men who never work with women seldom get the opportunity to socialize with them, or just get to know them as people. If the cliché image of college students is one of earnest discussions over coffee about life and philosophy between a boy and a girl, and the sexual style one of living together, for the worker it is a bunch of guys in a pickup truck going from bar to bar looking for a quick score.

One of the more repulsive examples of middle-class condescension is in this area. Workers are scorned by middle-class people for their rough manners with women, for the way construction workers whistle at girls who walk by or by the crude way they attempt a "pickup." Eminent psychologists write articles finding the roots of their behavior lying in all kinds of neuroses and deep-seated sexual insecurities.

But if you work in a factory all week, the only time you can meet women is on Friday or Saturday nights, and it was businessmen, social scientists, and time study engineers, not blue-collar workers, who decided that workers would never see a woman during the day. And yet, no one argues that company presidents and personnel managers are latent homosexuals or male chauvinists; that attack is reserved for the workers themselves.

In many ways, this lack of contact with other people, both male and female, is more boring than the job itself. It means that the working hours feel like stolen time, time taken away from the nonwork hours when one can really live. It means that the days Monday through Friday are experienced as a long routine of work and preparation for work. Workers get up at 6:00 A.M. or 6:30 A.M., eat breakfast, get dressed, and go to work. They watch the hours go by until lunch, which is often only twenty or thirty minutes. At 5:00 P.M. they get off and maybe go for a drink. For most workers, the work is tiring, so they go home, eat supper, and watch an hour or two of TV. Most nights they go to sleep by 10:00 or 10:30 P.M. at the latest.

All these pressures are intensified for the many factory workers who are forced to work overtime or moonlight on a second job to make ends meet. A study done in 1966 reveals that almost 21 percent, nearly a quarter of all American workers, worked forty-nine or more hours per week. For operatives it was 19 percent. This means that about one out of every five factory workers is working not eight but ten hours per day and some even longer.[4] In the auto industry, in the summer of 1973, many workers were putting in more than nine hours a day, six or seven days a week. In human terms it means leaving the factory at 7:00 P.M., not 5:00 P.M., or driving a cab in the evening after work; it means getting home at 8:00 P.M., having dinner and having at most one hour of "leisure" time before going to sleep, day after day, month after month.

To those millions of workers all the talk about the problems of "leisure" time and what to do with it sounds like a cruel joke. Anyone familiar with the situation has heard the many complaints of wives who describe their husbands coming home and falling asleep in front of the TV only minutes after finishing dinner.

It is also worth remembering that the family income figures we saw in the last chapter included overtime and moonlighting. The average salary of $7,636 for operatives included those who worked ten hours or more per day.

Another group for whom the problem of loneliness and isolation is profound is the factory workers who work the second shift, from 4:00 to 12:00 in the evening, or the "graveyard" shift from 12:00 to 8:00. The number of these workers is often underestimated. But in the Northeast it is about 23 percent of all factory workers.[5]

These shifts pay 10–15 percent more, but again this is included in the income totals we saw in the last chapter. Shift work means disorganized family lives and a cycle of work that cuts them off from everyone except those with whom they work. One complaint that workers on the 4:00–12:00 shift often voice is that they never get to see their school-age children. The children wake up and leave home before their fathers are awake, and the men come home long after their children are asleep.

Thus, behind the simple cliché of "boring work" lies a range of concrete conditions that color the whole life of a b ue-collar worker. Although there are middle-class people who face some of the same problems, there are no middle-class occupational environments that systematically impose these conditions the way they are imposed on blue-collar workers in entire industries or occupations.

And this is only part of the story. There are also the

problems of job safety, job security, and fringe benefits, and lastly of the authoritarianism and petty control exercised over workers on the job. This last-named factor could have been included here but it is so important that it demands a separate section of its own.

III

The engine plant where I worked for a while was one of a whole row of smaller factories that were packed together for the better part of a mile. They faced a wide stretch of railroad tracks on the other side of which stood a huge steel plant that must have been over a quarter of a mile long.

I had tried some of the bigger plants before I came to this place but none of them was hiring. It was very tight all around for jobs at that time, so when I found this plant, I took the job. It paid $106 per week starting salary, which is not the worst you can do, especially in the South.

The plant took old used motors, gutted and then rebuilt them, using mostly new parts. I was in the first section where the old motors were taken apart. There were about eight guys taking care of one or another part of the job. The motors came to me on a conveyer belt that was just a series of rollers. The guy who did the first part of the job would push the motor halfway and I would pull it the rest of the way in front of me until it sat on a special bench.

By the time the engine got to me the cover had been removed and the engine flipped upside down. So what I saw in front of me, inside the engine, was the crankshaft which looks like the backbone of some prehistoric animal, and below it the six pistons which were attached to the crankshaft by a series of small clamps. They sat in six cylindrical holes in the bottom of the engine block. My job was to remove the crankshaft and pistons, leaving only the metal case itself. I had to take out some twenty-five screws from the various clamps which held the crankshaft in place, and then lift it out and pass it down the line. Then I had to force the six pistons, which were now exposed, down through the holes and pass them along to another worker.

This section was known as the grease pit and for obvious reasons. The old motors came in caked with a thick layer of oil and grease. And there was no way to avoid becoming quickly covered with the stuff.

The first part, taking off the clamps, was usually easy. Hanging overhead was an automatic wrench, called an airgun, that removed the nuts very quickly. All I had to do was put on the right socket and lean on it as it turned. But if the pistons had rusted, which they had most of the time, I had to use a small one-hand sledgehammer and sometimes a full size one to knock them out. Sometimes a few hard blows with the hammer and wedge would do it. But sometimes I had to smash the ceramic and metal parts of the piston before it would come loose and fall through to the floor. There was one big guy who was given some of the worst engines to dismantle. He was kind of crazy, and he would take wild swings with the sledgehammer and send the wedge he was using flying across the room. They finally transferred him to another section after he took a particularly wild swing that missed the wedge, broke the sledge, and sent the hammer's head flying through the air, just missing another guy's groin.

The job wasn't boring in the same way as putting four screws on a passing car is boring. The rhythm was different. I was wrestling with the engine, not mechanically putting some screws on it. It was routine and frustrating work, but not precisely boring. But everything about the job actually hinged on one fact: we were expected to do fifty-four motors per day, about one every ten minutes.

At 7:00 in the morning when work started and I was

fresh, if the motor was not particularly rusty, I could turn out a motor in ten minutes. But to turn out fifty-four motors a day meant keeping up the pace all day long. It meant that if I stopped to go to the bathroom or to get a Coke from the machine, I had to push harder when I got back. It meant that one especially rusty set of pistons that took more time to remove set me back and forced me to hurry to catch up. The existence of the quota fundamentally changed the nature of the job. It was no longer just hard work, it was tense work. Only during the twenty-five minutes set aside for lunch did I feel that no one was looking over my shoulder.

The supervisor didn't seem like a bad guy. One day I gashed my finger on the sharp metal edge of one motor and went for first aid. When he bandaged it we were alone and I was feeling sort of light-headed, so I forgot the first rule of factory life, and tried talking to him as if he were an ordinary person. He asked me something about how the work was going, and I answered with some joke about my secretary not being pretty enough.

As soon as I said it, I knew I should have kept my mouth shut. They don't pay foremen as much or more than the highest-paid craftsman in the plant for them to laugh at some employee's cynical wisecracks about his job. He went into a long speech about appreciating a decent job when you find it and he mentally marked me down as a malcontent.

I wasn't the only one, though, or the worst. There was constant turnover in the grease pit. A lot of guys didn't stay for more than a week.

There was one older guy, a big man of about thirty, who came in one day and started work. The very next morning about 10:00 when everyone started feeling irritable and looking forward to lunch, this guy suddenly threw down his sledgehammer and said in a thoughtful but loud voice: "You know—fuck this shit." And at that he turned around and marched out.

The foreman came over to ask what had happened and to go look for the guy. But before following him, he stopped and told the young guy next to me to try and fill in to keep everyone from being idled. The young guy looked up for a moment, smiled and said, "You know—fuck *that* shit."

The rest of us were in hysterics by this point and the supervisor was looking at us like the whole world had just gone crazy. He finally did get someone else to fill in, though, and the line never had to stop.

The next day, after buying a hamburger from the lunch wagon, I sat down on a gas barrel to eat. In small plants like this, one thing they often do not have is a lunchroom, or even chairs or tables. I was looking out at the sun, thinking what a pretty day it was.

The whistle blew and everyone started back to work. I was looking at the guy next to me and I could see that we both had the same idea. We ran to our cars and drove off as if we had just broken out of Folsom. It was a wild feeling, like playing hooky from school, only better. It must have been a funny sight, because I was still covered from head to toe with grease, but at that point I was enjoying myself too much to care.

In the 1960s when students began to rebel against the authoritarianism and paternalistic policies that governed their universities, they often saw the issue in terms of winning the same independence and responsibilities that other adults have.

At that same time, in America's factories and workshops, blue-collar workers were in the grip of rules and policies that made the universities look like hippie communes by comparison. It is difficult to describe the situation simply because there is nothing in the work experience of the middle class that remotely corresponds to the authoritarianism and lack of freedom that exists in working-class America.

First of all, there are the work rules themselves. An article in *Fortune* magazine aptly summarized the situation with the comment, "At some plants there are sternly detailed work rules that would make a training sergeant at a Marine boot camp smile with pleasure. The rules prohibit such offenses as catcalls, horseplay, making preparation to leave before the whistle sounds, littering, wasting time, and loitering in the toilets." [6]

This by no means exhausts the list: using abusive language, distracting the attention of other employees, and (several years ago) merely having long hair were bases for disciplinary action by the company. And when one considers the wide range of activities that can be covered by terms like insubordination, carelessness, careless workmanship, and loitering, it becomes clear that almost anything can be construed as meriting a temporary suspension from work (called "disciplinary layoff" or DLO for short) or even permanent dismissal. For most workers, it is an axiom that if the boss wants to get rid of you he will find a way.

The cutting edge of these rules is the foreman, a figure who has absolutely no counterpart in middle-class society. Salaried professionals do often have people above them, but it is impossible to imagine professors or executives being required to bring a doctor's note if they are absent a day or having to justify the number of trips they take to the bathroom. In middle-class life, if the work is done that is all that is required. In union plants the degree of power the foreman has and the kind of discipline he can enforce is complexly defined, but for the millions of nonunion workers it is brutally simple; you do what the foreman says or lose your job. One fact that makes the tremendous power and authority of the foremen in nonunion establishments clear is that, in the South even in the 1960s, in some towns and industries foremen were automatically made special deputies to allow them to wear pistols and presumably to use them.

A black union organizer I know told me that one of the first and most deeply felt demands that one group of workers he organized raised was that the foremen be prohibited from carrying guns. As he said, "The workers had to be terrified. The foreman not only could fire you, but arrest you, or even shoot you, and almost certainly get away with it." Admittedly this is an extreme case, but the fact that such things could occur is in itself significant.

But even in union shops the situation is still essentially undemocratic. Union contracts specify hours, safety rules, and other in-plant issues, and the worker has the right to file a grievance through the union, protesting a suspension or firing, if he feels that it is unfair. These grievances are either acted on by the union and company or brought before a "neutral arbitrator" from the Federal Mediation and Conciliation service. But at every stage of the process the cards are heavily stacked against the worker.

First of all, in a fundamental sense the grievance procedure is one-sided. The fact is that a worker is guilty until proven innocent. As one writer has noted, "If the company disciplines a worker the penalty is put into effect immediately and the individual grieves for it. For example, a worker given a three-day suspension for 'bad work' gets the three days off without pay. He protests this through the grievance procedure. If the case goes through arbitration, it can take over a year for a final ruling, even those decisions reached before arbitration usually take over six months to resolve." [7]

In the union papers, one occasionally finds stories of workers who were unjustly fired and who finally won reinstatement six months or so later. On rare occasions, they get all their back pay, but usually it is lost. And in the interim, their income and their whole lives have been disrupted.

On the job itself, a worker must follow all orders given by a supervisor, even if they violate the union contract or, more surprisingly, the safety rules. His only recourse is to file a grievance after he has actually done what was demanded of him. In one case two workers were given two-day suspensions for refusing to work overtime, even though the union contract had specified that overtime was voluntary. They filed a grievance protesting their suspension and the case went to an arbitrator. The arbitrator admitted that they were in the right, but their suspensions were still justified because "the correct procedure is to work the overtime under protest and later submit the problem to the grievance procedure."

In another case, the issue was far less prosaic. A worker was ordered by his supervisor to pour pails of a dangerous chemical by hand, although, for safety reasons, it was usually done by machine. He refused and was suspended for ten days. He submitted a grievance about the suspension, but when it went to arbitration, the suspension was upheld, although reduced to three days. In other words, the worker lost three days pay, say $90, for refusing to follow an order that was both wrong and dangerous.[8] It is clear that the grievance procedure limits the absolute authority of the foreman, but it does not come close to providing an equitable situation.

Petty abuses and injustices abound. One worker at the Chevy Vega plant in Lordstown described the following incident.

Last week someone up the line put a stink bomb in a car. I do rear cushions and the foreman says, "Get in that car." I said, "If you can put your head in that car, I'll do the job." So the foreman says, "I'm giving you a direct order." So I hold my breath and do it. My job is every other car, so I let the next one pass. He gets on me and I say, "It ain't my car. Please, I done your dirty work and the other one wasn't mine." But he keeps at me and I wind up with a week off. Now I got a hot committee man who really stuck up for me, so you know what—they sent him home too. Gave the committee man a DLO. See it's just like the army—no it's worse 'cause you're welded to the line. You just about need a pass to piss.[9]

Another example of the fundamental advantage the company has over the worker is found in an incident from another plant. In the course of an argument a worker had with his supervisor about the amount of work he was required to do, he expressed himself in what is usually known as "shop talk" and he received a warning from the company. (A warning is less serious than a layoff, but does go in a worker's work record, and can seriously affect his future.)

His protest was answered by the company in the following terms, "Insubordination and abusive language will not be tolerated. Whenever such an incident does occur, discipline will follow." But when workers in the same plant filed a grievance against a certain supervisor for swearing at an employee, the company only replied, "It is not the company's intent for management to use profane language to hourly employees." No suspension, no warning, no action at all was taken against the supervisor. The point of this is, of course, not the language but the double standard that exists.[10]

In fact, the situation has become worse in recent years. The grievance system is slow and cumbersome at best, and sometimes there are literally thousands of grievances which have piled up, so many that a good number will probably never be seriously dealt with. Because there is no quick and efficient system of industrial justice, grievances often become pawns in collective bargaining arguments, with unions facing the uncomfortable choice of getting a better wage settlement if the grievances are put aside.

Many liberal and left-wing critics have criticized the unions for an excessive focus on the bread-and-butter issues of higher wages, a criticism which is in many cases quite valid. But that alone is not sufficient explanation for the reasons why these problems are getting worse. One writer in one of the industrial relations magazines provided another aspect of the situation.

In the typical company throughout the 1945–1955 period, there developed a whole series of informal relationships between union and management. Grievances were often handled on a "problem solving" basis without much reference to the specific terms of the contract. Foremen and stewards, superintendents and committee men were permitted and even encouraged to reach private, unwritten understandings or "agreements" which, in effect, modified the contract.

Without question unions learned to use this flexibility to their advantage. When an impasse was reached in formal negotiations, they had a host of weapons they could use to strengthen their position—wildcat strikes, slowdowns, over-literal compliance with rules, and even sabotage. The foreman had weapons too—refusal to grant overtime, strict discipline which kept the men to their jobs and which hindered union officers in their activities. But on the whole, this was a type of guerrilla warfare in which the union had all the advantages of terrain. Recently, efforts have been made to strengthen management's position at every step of the grievance procedure. Two personnel managers reported that they refused to consider any grievance, formal or informal, unless the foreman has had ample opportunity to study it. In one instance a new personnel director inaugurated his regime by insisting that all

witnesses in arbitration proceedings be sworn, in sharp
contrast to previous practices. In several instances personnel
directors were able to win contracts which made the grievance
procedure more rigid.[11]

Except in cases of safety rules, these issues may seem
unimportant and frivolous, but they are not. Issues like these
are often the crucial difference between having a sense of
elementary security and dignity in one's job and being
completely at the mercy of the employer. There have, of
course, been great changes since the turn of the century when
companies would post notices saying, "If you don't come in
Sunday—don't come in Monday," or in the thirties when
supervisors would literally follow workers into the toilets to
make sure they weren't just loitering. But the lack of fairness
and democracy in the workplace is still a crucial source of
discontent for working-class Americans.

IV

There is a bar near where I live where young guys go
after work to have a beer or two during the Happy Hour
from 5:00 to 6:00 when the prices are low. On one
particular day, we were sitting around listening to one of
the guys who had just started on a new job in a small
warehouse and was already having his troubles with the
supervisor. It was one of the first days of spring and
everyone was feeling pretty good. As this guy kept on
talking about what a son-of-a-bitch his supervisor was and
how he wasn't going to take any B.S., everyone else began
to chip in stories about the worst jobs that they ever had
done. All these guys were young workers and the only
skilled guy was a twenty-six-year-old master carpenter, so
the competition was pretty stiff. One friend of mine pretty

much won the contest with a story about shoveling chicken manure in a poultry plant and then with the temporary job he did in a milk-bottling plant. The milk bottles went swiftly by on a conveyer belt and his whole job was to stick a glued label on each bottle as it passed by. The details made it sound even worse, and since he got $1.65 per hour for the job, we got ready to raise our glasses and to tell him he had won.

But a young married guy who usually didn't talk too much suddenly spoke up. He described what happened to a friend of his in a small, low wage paper plant. He had been working overtime in the cutting section and got his hand caught in the machine that cut the paper into $8\frac{1}{2}$ by 11 inch sheets. The machine cut his hand off neatly at the wrist. To make it worse, he had just been married and his wife was already pregnant when it happened. This married guy said his friend was trying to get compensation, but since it was a small nonunion shop, he was having trouble and might not get anything at all.

One of the guys at the table tried to pass it off with a cynical joke but the rest of us were silent. The story did not come as a shock since everyone at the table knew some horror story about someone who got messed up in a factory. But we couldn't get back the feeling we had before. We broke up early and went home that day and forgot about it. Since then nobody has wanted to ask if everything turned out all right, probably because they knew the odds are that it didn't. You tend to forget things like that if you can't do anything about it. It's easier to say that it will never happen to you. I didn't think much about it at the time, but later I realized that little things like easy conversations in a bar at 5:30 or a sudden moment of silence can really tell you something that you can't find in polls or studies about work and workers in contemporary America. No one has invented an opinion poll that can measure something like that silence or the fear behind it. It is something you have to feel in order to understand.

In 1911, in Jack London's book, *The Iron Heel*, the hero, Ernest Everhard, took a middle-class lady to see a man who had lost his arm in a factory as the most dramatic way of shattering her condescending complacency about the conditions of workers at that time. If London were writing today, he would use the same tactics. More than sixty years later, nothing has changed the reality that many working-class jobs kill and maim on a scale the middle class cannot even imagine.

For example, in 1970 a Ford glass plant machinist's left hand was cut and badly mangled in his machine. His cries for help went unheard because all of his co-workers were wearing earmuffs to guard against an illegal noise level of over ninety decibels. Only under the threat of a strike did the company knock down the noise level to seventy decibels.

In Hazelton, Pennsylvania, Robert Fernandez, a beryllium refinery employee, fights for his life by taking oxygen four times a day. His doctor's prognosis is that he is probably close to the terminal stages of an increasingly common lung disease, chronic berylliosis, and in addition the doctor says that his violent coughing spells could cause a hernia.

Daniel Maciborski, a laborer who works with asbestos, has mesothelioma. He has been told to expect death any day now after a malignant tumor hardens and encloses his stomach, making it impossible to eat. In the last eight years at least sixty of his co-workers have died of this disease, in addition to one wife who merely washed her husband's asbestos-covered clothing regularly.

A female electronics worker suffered forty attacks of gripping chest pain, fever to 104 degrees, sweating, shivering, sore throat, and difficult breathing for nine months. The cause was microscopic teflon particles in the factory air that contaminated every pack of cigarettes she opened during her lunch hour.[12]

This list could go on and on with case after case of mangled hands, blindness, decapitation, and other injuries, making a list so unpleasant some readers would be forced to stop reading. But these things happen all the time. Fifty-five men die every day and twenty-seven thousand are injured by such conditions. In the year 1970, 14,200 workers died from accidents, ten to twenty million were injured, and at least 100,000 died from occupationally caused diseases. This makes the factory twice as dangerous as the highway and the number one killer in America.[13]

Reading a list of occupational diseases one begins to feel, in fact, as if one were a general scanning casualty lists in some epic war.

BLACK LUNG: A lung cancer of coal miners which comes from inhaling coal dust. 300,000 are exposed and 150,000 have already got the disease.

BROWN LUNG: A similar disease for textile workers who are forced to inhale cotton dust. 819,000 a year are exposed—17,000 are seriously disabled, and perhaps 100,000 are suffering in some degree.

ASBESTOSIS AND MESOTHELIOMA: Cancers that affect laborers in factories, shipyards, anywhere where this material is found (asbestos). It can take twenty years for symptoms to show up. 350,000 are exposed every year—the number affected is unknown.

BERYLLIOSIS: Again, it can strike twenty years later and suddenly kill you. A half million workers are exposed. The number who have died cannot be estimated.

GAS AND FUME POISONING: In auto factories it is

carbon monoxide—in other factories, trichlorine, a common industrial solvent. In aerospace it is "exotic fuels" inhaled by the workers. The number exposed to some form of this is probably in the millions. The total number of victims is hard to estimate.

DESTRUCTIVE NOISE LEVELS: Can cause deafness or hearing impairment. In some cases it also can cause high blood pressure, heart attacks, psychological disorders (including sexual dysfunction). 17,000,000 workers are estimated to be exposed to some degree of excessive noise.

ACCIDENTS: Construction workers, machinists, longshoremen, and butchers are particularly affected. Accidents include explosions, electrocutions, falls, and many other kinds of dangers. Accidents are often undercounted as 2.5 million in 1970, by dubious definitions about what is a "disabling" accident. Labor Department studies, however, suggest that it could be as high as 25,000,000 accidents a year.[14]

All the clichés and pleasant notions of how the old class divisions and injustices have disappeared are exposed as hollow phrases by the simple fact that American workers must accept serious injury and even death as a part of their daily reality while the middle class does not.

Imagine for a moment the universal outcry that would occur if every year several corporate headquarters routinely collapsed like mines, crushing sixty or seventy executives. Or suppose that all the banks were filled with an invisible noxious dust that constantly produced cancer in the managers, clerks, and tellers. Finally, try to imagine the horror that would be expressed in every newspaper in the country if thousands of university professors were deafened every year or lost fingers, hands, sometimes eyes, while on their jobs. Nothing exposes the profound class injustices that still exist in America like the simple facts of occupational health and safety.

This callous disregard for American workers carries over into Workman's Compensation. As Frank Wallick says in his book, *The American Worker: An Endangered Species*:

> It is cheaper from a business standpoint today to risk a thousand-dollar workman's compensation payment to a disabled or dead worker than to invest in better equipment and better work place ventilation, or optimum work place environment for workers. This, unfortunately, is the grim legacy of a political trade-off a generation ago when workers gave up the right to sue an employer for negligence in return for which they got a state schedule of workman's compensation payments.[15]

These payments vary greatly from state to state. A union lawyer told a Senate Labor Subcommittee hearing in Jersey City, "In Mississippi a finger is worth less than what it is in Pennsylvania, and in Pennsylvania a finger is worth less than what it is in California. There is no uniformity in terms of what the equal protection laws are. Is there anyone in the room today who would take less than $10,000 for the loss of an eye? In Pennsylvania you receive $60 a week for 150 weeks which is a $9,000 total or the same as for the loss of a hand." [16]

A study of workman's compensation appeared in late 1972. An editorial in *The New Republic* summarized its findings in a terse paragraph:

> Despite improvements in many states the commission reported that today the maximum weekly benefit for temporary total disability in more than half the states does not equal the national poverty income level for a non-farm family of four. Maximum weekly benefits for permanent total disability in most states are inadequate, and in nineteen states can be cut off completely before the disabled worker's death. 15% of the

work force is still not covered by workman's compensation; nine states still do not provide full coverage for all occupational diseases; and fifteen states still do not provide full medical benefits for disabled workers.[17]

Thus, more dramatically than any other topic, the issue of health and safety draws a line between working class and middle class, and exposes the magnitude of the injustice which exists in blue-collar America.

And when we turn to the problems of job security and the fringe benefits that have supposedly helped to eliminate the discontents of previous years, we will see neither alters the basic conclusion that the American working class gets a raw deal from 9:00 to 5:00 and are second-class citizens when compared to those who write about them.

V

Even in the last few years, as joblessness has risen sharply, unemployment has rarely been given much attention in all the articles about the "blue-collar blues" or the discussions of the problems of American workers. It is, of course, mentioned, but it is quickly dismissed as a major problem. After all, even at the worst point in 1971, unemployment affected only about 6 percent of the labor force, and it did not take a great deal of mathematical knowledge to recognize that therefore 94 percent were not laid off. When the energy crisis emerged as a serious source of joblessness in 1973–74, estimates of its final impact ranged from 5 to 8 or at most 10 percent of the labor force In comparison with the thirties, it certainly did not sound like a major crisis.

Liberals did criticize these figures on the grounds that they excluded certain groups from the unemployed, like "discouraged" workers who had given up looking for work, and people who could only find a few hours work a week but wanted to work full time. Conservatives replied by noting that the 6 percent included women, students looking for summer jobs, workers who quit their jobs, and other people for whom unemployment did not have the same impact as it does on the male "breadwinner" of a family who is suddenly laid off by the company. In February of 1972, the rate for married men, they noted, was only 2.8 percent.[18] Since blacks also constituted a disproportionate number of those who were out of work, most writers concluded that for the "typical" worker, unemployment was not a real problem.

To most middle-class people, this sounded quite logical. They did not see bread lines, and having no personal contact with workers it was easy to imagine 94 percent of them secure in their jobs and no more worried about unemployment than white-collar workers.

The problem is this, the unemployment "rate" which everyone watches so closely is a rather confusing measure, like the "rates of increase" we saw in the last chapter. If, instead, we ask the simple question, "How many people were unemployed last year?"—"How many workers lost their jobs and spent weeks or months looking for another one?"—the answer is striking. In 1969, which was before unemployment had even become a major issue, 18 percent, almost one out of every five operatives was unemployed for some period of time. In 1970 the figure rose to 23 percent, almost one out of every four. In that year, their unemployment lasted on the average for over three months.[19] *

* The reason the unemployment "rate" gives such a completely different picture is that it only counts the people who were unemployed on the day of the survey. The census takers ask a sample of people if they are working or not, and the results are counted up. What this reveals is what percentage of people on a certain day were without work, but not all those who were unemployed before or will be afterwards. The "annual unemployment rate" is simply

The following chart tells the story (since unemployment rose dramatically in 1970, figures for 1969 are also shown):[20]

TOTAL UNEMPLOYMENT IN 1969 AND 1970

	1969	1970
Middle class		
Professional and Technical	5.7	6.5
Managers, Officials, and Proprietors	4.3	5.2
Clerical	10.2	11.5
Sales	9.7	10.8
Working class		
Craftsmen	12.7	17.5
Operatives	18.1	23.2
Service	12.1	13.6
Laborers	22.6	25.7
Construction workers	24.4	30.7

The conclusion is simple. Unemployment is tremendously widespread in working-class America. Millions of workers are thrown out of work every year, and the fear that it will happen to them is widespread among the remainder. There is no doubt that the majority of American workers, even though they keep their jobs, cannot feel real job security.

It must be noted that a significant minority of workers lose their jobs more than once a year and therefore the total number of workers who are unemployed during the year is somewhat lower than the figures suggest. But neither do these figures include workers who have been temporarily unemployed, such as auto workers during a model change, nor do they count workers who are idled by bad weather, even though they are not paid during that time. Almost all

---

the average of the twelve surveys per year, not a total of all those who were unemployed at some point during the year. These total figures are called the annual work experience data. Although these statistics are far more meaningful than the rates, they are almost never used to judge the severity of unemployment.

construction workers, in particular, lose several weeks or more a year from this cause.

Equally striking is the contrast between working-class and middle-class unemployment. Operatives lose their jobs four times as often as professionals and managers do. Even skilled workers are twice as likely to lose their jobs.

Another part of the picture is how long unemployment lasts. In 1969 about 23 percent of the unemployed blue-collar workers were without work for four months or more. In 1970 it rose to over 30 percent.[21] Four months without work not only shatters a family's standard of living for that year, but creates highly destructive personal and family tensions. It is a depressing period of sitting around the union hall or hustling odd jobs if they are to be found.

For these unemployed workers the lack of job security is, of course, a deep source of discontent. But virtually all workers have to face the fear of unemployment. There are very few plants so stable or specific jobs so fully protected that this fear does not exist. If unemployment itself is widespread, the lack of job security is far more so.

One group for whom this issue is of crucial importance is construction craftsmen. Again and again one can hear the self-righteous refrain, "Those people are making $7.00 or $8.00 an hour or even more . . . that's, let me see . . . fifty weeks or 2,000 hours times eight, why that's over $15,000 a year."

But not even 10 percent of all construction workers actually made $15,000 or over in 1970. The stunning truth is that in America as a whole, a majority of construction craftsmen did not even make $10,000 a year. The median income for construction workers was $9,055, according to the Bureau of the Census.

In part, this is due to lower wage rates for nonunion

craftsmen, especially in parts of the country other than the Northeast. But more importantly it is due to the fact that construction work has the highest unemployment of any sector of the American economy. A quarter of these workers, 24.4 percent, were unemployed some of the time in 1969. In 1970 the figure rose to over 30 percent. On a typical day in that year, more than one out of every ten construction workers was without a job. The duration of their unemployment is also striking. In 1970 more than a third of the unemployed spent four months without work.[22]

So the "scandalous" wages skilled construction workers receive are not so outrageous after all. If construction workers were paid the same wages as factory workers, their income would fall below the "lower poverty budget." As it is, $9,055 is below the "intermediate budget" of that year. Some, with the highest union wages and with a full year's work, can make affluent incomes. But for most, unemployment cut it down to the same scale that skilled workers in other areas got—$9,000 to $10,000 a year.

In Kenneth Lasson's *The Workers*, a nonunion brick layer from Boston described his situation this way.

During last summer from June to October I would bring home an average of $225 a week, but during the spring and fall it was $150 to $200 a week, and almost a month and a half without work in the winter. This summer if I get $200 a week I'm lucky, and the fall and winter I don't even want to think about.

And later he says:

A lot of people get the impression that the blue collar man is making a shitload of money but that's not always true. Sure, some construction workers, union men, are getting six or seven dollars an hour. But . . . people don't realize that we're out of a good five weeks work a year because of bad weather. Another thing that misleads them is when they have spot jobs around their houses. You get a "brickie" for example to fix your steps and he charges you a full day's pay for four hours work. He does it because he has to bring in an extra man and a truck maybe, and for him he loses a day's pay. The little guy who foots the bill figures we make $10.00 an hour all the time, that we're living high when we're not. Look at some of the white collar workers. Take an accountant come tax time, you go into their offices, spend an hour, and they cream you, they kill you—they sock you good for their seasonal living.[23]

Unemployment insurance does help the situation to a certain degree, but only 70 percent of the labor force is covered and unemployment falls disproportionately on those who are not. In 1968, 64 percent or almost two-thirds of the unemployed were not able to collect any benefits. Some state laws require a certain period of employment and a waiting period. In addition, many employers hire consultants to challenge the unemployment insurance claims of their workers because a low layoff record enables the company to pay lower taxes for the program.

Finally, in many states, the benefits were similar or worse than welfare payments for aid to dependent children. Only a few industries such as auto and steel provide private supplements that give 90–95 percent of normal pay for three weeks if a worker has a year's seniority, and a year for seven-year employees.[24]

The political implications of this are enormous; and although we will deal with them more fully in a later chapter, this belief, that workers do not have serious problems in employment and job security, has been at the base of such a depressing number of liberal misjudgments that something must be said.

The environmental movement, for example, in the past has taken a complacent "well, there are other jobs around" attitude to the question of shutting down factories that pollute. But there are *not* just loads of other jobs around. Otherwise 22 percent of operatives would not have been unemployed during 1970.

Since it is periods of unemployment that can rob a worker of the money he was saving for his child's education, or even make him lose his house, it is clear that he has to fight back, even if he too wants clean rivers and air. All too often liberal ecology proponents spoke beautifully about alternative employment and new jobs for blue-collar workers, but when it came down to real life, the attitude was "shut down the factory now and later we'll figure out something for the worker." Usually, the something turned out to be nothing at all, which is not only unjust but politically stupid.

Equally, the attitude of many liberals toward the construction trades' exclusion of blacks is often based on the idea that there are enough jobs for all and the "hard hats'" opposition to integration is just pure racism. In all too many cases, the racism is indeed present. But so is the specter of unemployment, and it is also very real.

Myra Wolfgang, the international vice president of the Hotel and Restaurant Employees, made the point that "When 22 percent of the members of your union are unemployed, as is the case with the carpenters in the Detroit area, this isn't the best time to say to them you should share with blacks. The blacks and whites who are building tradesmen would all be working if the Administration met the needs of housing in this country." [25]

This is endorsed by Jesse Jackson, the nationally known

black leader. He said, "I don't blame the white man for not wanting the black to get his job. And I don't blame the black man for wanting to get that job. I want to see a policy under which they can both have jobs." [26]

Unfortunately, opinions like these are for the most part ignored by liberals on the basis of the 6 percent unemployment mythology which "proves" that working-class concern over jobs is just a "smokescreen" for simple racism. But working-class unemployment is very real and destructive, and only when this is recognized can any serious progress in either of these areas be made.

VI

Steve, one of the young guys I know, has done a lot of construction work. We talked and I just put down what he said.

One place I worked for a while was in the Virginia area outside of Washington, a development and very fancy. There must have been fifty of us putting up fifteen to twenty of these houses. The cheapest one must have gone for $85,000, and the best for $300,000. They had everything: picture windows, intercoms, fireplaces, mahogany bars, and even a couple of indoor swimming pools. Like I said, they were real fancy.

The job itself—well I was doing light framing work with the head carpenter. I suppose you could think it's just hammering in nails all day, but really it's a very complicated thing and you really have to know a lot of skills. You have got to be able to read blueprints, do calculations, and have the whole house in mind when you're working. If you don't lay out the floor plan exactly right, you'll have a chimney coming up through the bathroom. There is this one carpenter I know who's gotten so good at figuring things out in his head that he'll bet a guy five bucks he can do some really big calculations in his head faster than the other guy can do them with paper and pencil, and he always wins. It's just because he's doing it all day long when he works.

Basically the framing carpenter's job is putting in the floor and building all the wall frames, the main beams which support the walls, then the walls themselves, and finally if it's a one-story house, the roof. With the walls, you put together the frame for one wall on the floor. Then, when the whole skeleton is ready, you lift it up all at one time and you've got to get it exactly vertical. Then you put in some stabilizing braces to hold it. On a big house you can have twenty wall frames you've got to put in this way. Then you use some different kinds of braces to connect the walls to each other so the whole thing is self-supporting. Then you take off the angle braces.

With the roof, it's more complicated (unless it's designed like a pillbox with a flat roof) because you've got all sizes and shapes you have to build. You've also got to be an acrobat half the time. Guys who can really move around and work while they're balancing up there get nicknames like "monkey" or "spider," because that's about how agile you have to be.

There is pressure, but it's not at all like a factory. A contractor knows how long the job should take and if he sees one wall frame up when you should have had all of them ready, he knows something is wrong. In fact, this one contractor I know had this huge book that said exactly how long this or that particular operation should take. And he used it when he estimated his costs.

But the whole problem rarely comes up because a carpenter or some other skilled worker feels very differently about his job. They've spent years becoming real craftsmen and they feel like they're getting better money because they do good work and they want to do a good job. If the house falls down when they've finished, it's like their fault and you can't really say the same thing for an auto worker. Of course, for a lot of guys who work with small contractors, they want to do a good job just so he'll hire them again. But basically their attitude is that they're getting a good wage, they're willing to do a good job.

It's dangerous, there's no question about that. I've had a ramp collapse on me when I was carrying wood one time and nearly got wiped out. Another guy in our crew lost a piece of his left thumb because a plank fell on his back while he was using a circle saw. Then, of course, there's falling. I'll work on a roof of a house or something like that, but to tell you the truth, I sure as hell couldn't go walking around on a beam twenty stories up in the air. I mean, that really is risky! I don't know if it's still true, but I heard they used to use American Indians for those high jobs because they just seemed to have a better sense of balance or something. You sure as hell need it, that's the truth.

The biggest worry, though, is how much work you'll have. It's a real feast or famine kind of work. You can go for a year working all the time and getting good money and suddenly you can have a long period with very little work. I once was talking with this architect and he told me that when they announce a change in the interest rate or "discount" rate, that same morning his phone is ringing. He starts getting orders or cancellations inside of an hour. So that's how this business is. For me, it's not too bad because I'm young and single. But I know one married guy who hit a run of luck and started thinking he had it made. So he started living high and spending everything he got. Then a bad period hit and he was really up the creek with debts and no savings and a second kid on the way. It's that kind of thing that really hurts and makes a guy mean. It's like you almost have it in your hand, but you're always worried it's going to slip away.

Another demoralizing and agonizing fear for workers is the fear of an old age spent in poverty. Unlike executives and many professionals who often can make investments while they are young or continue working on up into their seventies, blue-collar workers face a sudden and total change when they grow too old to work. Since their jobs are often hard, physical labor, the time when they can no longer do them comes sooner, and they become completely dependent on the income from Social Security or, in some cases, additional private pension plans.

Even with the combined income from both these sources, the total is significantly below the worker's preretirement income. But this fact alone does not come close to capturing the real dimensions of old age poverty for the working class. Even with the large expenses of raising their children behind them, for the majority old age is still a time of literal poverty.*

The central fact is that about half of all blue-collar workers are employed in occupations or industries without any private pension plan at all. These tend to be in nonunionized smaller plants or unskilled jobs which also pay the lowest wages. Thus this half of the working class is also the least likely to have any savings. (One estimate is that savings only provide 15 percent of what workers need to live on in a year.)[27] Thus, they are completely dependent on the monthly Social Security check in order to live.

Here are the basic weekly Social Security payments workers who worked in 1971 received:

---

* The statistics in this area can be complex. But a study by a top economist of the Bureau of Labor Statistics fortunately focused directly on the Social Security and Private Pensions benefits of, as he says, "rank and file workers in the private economy." The statistics exclude retirement plans of highly paid professional or managerial workers and pensions in the public sector—for example, the army, government, etc.

WEEKLY SOCIAL SECURITY PAYMENTS IN 1971*[28]

	All private industries	Manu-facturing	Con-struction	Service	Retail trade
Single worker retiring at age 65	$56.60	$51.85	$54.02	$44.77	$39.05
Married couple both retiring at age 65	$78.90	$77.77	$81.03	$67.16	$58.57

For many people it will be hard even to imagine a life on this income level, $77.00 a week for a factory worker and his wife, $81.00 for the married construction worker who does not have a union pension plan.

Many workers simply cannot live on this income. They are forced to continue working, in many cases, or become a burden on their children. Some go on welfare to add to their Social Security checks. If the house wasn't paid for, it goes. Often, the last years of their lives are spent in furnished rooms and "residential hotels." It is a bleak and depressing prospect.

More than half the employed male factory and construction workers, however, are working in places which are covered by private pension plans, and they can imagine retiring on a significantly higher level.

But the tragic fact is that under the current laws, from one-third to one-half of those workers might never receive a single penny from their pensions. Every year thousands of workers suddenly discover that they have been totally cut off from their benefits. The private pension system represents, in

* Social Security benefits improved after changes were voted in late 1972, but no systematic data are available. And considering inflation, the data here only slightly understate the situation.

the words of Ralph Nader, "The most comprehensive consumer fraud that many Americans ever encountered." *U.S. News and World Report* notes that many critics describe private pensions as a "cruel hoax." [29]

Take, for example, the case of a man who worked for thirty-two years in a refrigerated butter warehouse. The company shut down the facility when he was fifty-two years old, three years before he reached fifty-five, the minimum age for getting a pension. He received nothing. The same thing occurred to an Anaconda copper worker who got caught up in company cutbacks. Forty-eight years old and thirty years on the job, but he received no pension at all.

In addition to age or length of service requirements, pension funds (whether company or union) are not insured or protected. If there is a financial failure or a merger and there is not enough money in the fund, the workers lose their pensions. When the Studebaker Automobile Company went out of business in 1963, four thousand workers aged forty to sixty got only 15 percent of what the company owed them. Many received no pension at all.

The list goes on and on: A widow received no survivor's benefits from her husband's pension plan when he died, because he was fifty-two years old, not fifty-five. A worker covered by a union pension plan is transferred outside of the union's jurisdiction. He loses his pension. A large food store chain admits that two-thirds of its employees since 1950 forfeited their benefits. A telephone company estimates that 70 percent of its workers lost their pensions including some who had worked there for fifteen years.[30]

It is, in fact, possible that a majority of even the workers covered will receive only a fraction of what they sacrificed in wage increases. It stands as one of the sickest examples of cynical disregard for working people's basic and simple needs in the whole postwar period.

Finally, even for the minority who do receive both Social Security and the full value of their pensions when they retire, the results are modest at best. Here is a list of nine pension plans for thirty-year employees that is representative of various industries.

SELECTED PRIVATE PENSION PLANS IN 1971[31]

Company	Weekly pension income for thirty-year employees	Weekly total income— Social Security average for individuals and pensions for a couple 65 years old
Armour	$45	$102
Detroit Edison	58	115
Ford	45	103
ILGWU	16	73
Int'l Paper	39	96
N.Y. City Carpenters	72	129
Southern Bell	40	97
U.S. Steel	49	106
Western Conference of Teamsters (Truck and Warehouse)	47	104

The totals for a married couple would be higher than these combined figures above, because Social Security, as we saw, increases for a married couple. But, at the same time, more than half of American workers will not receive private pensions.

To many older workers, retirement virtually constitutes a return to the standard of living they sacrificed so much to escape. Many American workers end up thirty or forty years later in conditions all too similar to those in which they began. And like unemployment, this fact of life does not affect the older, retired worker only, but also his children and every man who thinks about his future as he works in the factories or construction sites of blue-collar America.

Although far less profound in their impact, the other blue-collar "fringe" benefits are also worth considering and comparing with those of white-collar earners. In the area of paid vacations the advantages of office workers are clear.

PERCENTAGE COVERED BY PAID VACATION
PROVISIONS IN 1970[32]

Benefit	Plant workers	Office workers
2 weeks or more paid vacation after 2 years of service	54%	95%
3 or more weeks vacation after 10 years service	66%	81%
4 or more weeks vacation after 20 years service	50%	62%

In general, two weeks and rarely three, is the typical working-class vacation. Their paid holidays are also fewer. Workers get an average of 7.1 days, and office workers get 8.4 days.

Health care provisions and insurance benefits, on the other hand, vary widely. A majority of workers in large plants get hospitalization and surgical insurance paid by the company. But the "better" benefits like Major Medical coverage and paid sick leave are far more common for office workers than for plant workers. Only 37 percent of factory workers have Major Medical expenses paid by the company. For office workers it is 45 percent. For sick leave, only 21 percent of factory workers get full pay and no waiting period; 64 percent of office workers, however, do.[33] Once again, the constant pattern of inequality between working-class and middle-class America is clear. It is necessary however to correct one distortion which inevitably creeps into any survey such as this, that basically focuses on the problems and discontents of working-class jobs. These conditions and problems can seem to suggest an image of factory workers as joyless robots— zombies who never laugh or smile on the job. If one goes, for example, on a quick tour of a plant, it is very easy to imagine that this is the case.

But this is, in a way, as much of a distortion as the "happy worker" was in the fifties. Despite the obstacles noise and pressure often create, deep friendships are formed, jokes are told, and all sorts of activity goes on. In construction or other jobs that involve teamwork, friendly cooperation is almost always the rule. Even the worst environments can't prevent workers from finding ways to "beat the system." A friend of mine and his co-worker who work together on the assembly line, aligning wheels, used to play checkers while they worked, making one move in the few moments between each car. Only a novelist who spent years in a factory could adequately capture this part of working-class life; the way friendships grow, or the way "hidden" activities—like betting on the numbers racket (which is common)—go on. Or even something as simple as the way a message may be passed through three people from a guy in another section of the motor plant asking for a couple of pieces off the next Chevy engine which he needed for his car. In return, he offered spark plugs, whenever they were wanted.

But perhaps the wildest example of the "unknown" side of factory work is the prostitution that goes on in the parking lots of some large plants. In one case I know, the women come in a VW van during lunch and return again when the day is over. In one sense there is something mean and sordid in this, but at the same time there is a crazy kind of self-assertion. For all its lack of emotion, it is a way of announcing that one is not a robot or a machine, but a man.

The point of this is simply to give some hint of the things that a quick survey misses. As was stated in the beginning, there are conditions and problems that are common, but the only way to understand the problems and discontents is to know individual workers and particular working-class jobs.

CHAPTER THREE

The Discontents of Community Life

MILLIONS OF WORDS have been written about the social and economic discontents of blue-collar workers or the "middle Americans" as they are most often called. Many have been written by liberals who are sympathetic to workers' complaints and who have tried to explain their discontent to middle-class America.

But for the most part, they have failed. Most people, it seems, still have a sneaking suspicion that blue-collar workers really don't have any profound or legitimate problems. After all, they are in the "middle," neither very rich nor very poor, and they seem to be getting by. They are often described as "confused" and "frustrated," but almost never as the victims of real and pervasive injustice. What, in fact, could seem more fair than to be in the middle?

Of course, in economic terms, blue-collar workers are not "in the middle." The majority are closer to poverty than to affluence. The median income for blue-collar workers is thousands of dollars below the middle class and very significantly below the Bureau of Labor Statistics' standard for a modest but adequate life.

But even the basic facts of family income fail to capture the real issues involved. Although the term injustice is rarely used, it is the only word which indicates the fact that workers' discontents are not the product of some psychological frustration or paranoia about blacks, but in a large part a valid protest over real issues that deserve respect and attention.

America made a promise after the Second World War, the promise of a "fair deal," an end to a society divided into classes where only the rich could live a full and comfortable life. It was not a promise that workers could live like company presidents, but that they could at least share equally in the "American Dream."

In the years directly after the Second World War, GI loans and the development of relatively low-cost housing in suburban areas like Levittown, made it possible for many workers to own a house and hope that the "fair deal" for them and their children was on the horizon.

But in America of the seventies the "fair deal" has still not come to pass. In every area of life, social, political, and economic, blue-collar workers remain second-class citizens in America.

II

It was only about four-thirty when I turned off the main avenue and on to the block where Dave lived, so I figured he'd still be at work. A couple of kids on bicycles were weaving down the center of the street, and only when I honked did they part and let me pass. One of them made a face, but there was no real malice in it so I just smiled.

The block was part of a new largely blue-collar housing development between Baltimore and Washington, and the houses were better than the usual for such a community. Dave's, which was in the middle of the block, had a garage, a lawn in the back which was larger than the postage stamp dimensions that are common, and a semifinished basement he was turning into a sort of den. The layout and architecture were also nicer than usual. Instead of the "crackerbox," the unadorned square or rectangular "ranch house" styles, it had a solid, individual quality including a good deal of ornamental metalwork across the front.

I had only been to the house twice before and I had to slow down several times to check the numbers on the passing doors.

We had been friends several years before when he was still a single, free-wheeling "gypsy" truck driver running trucks all over the country. It was entirely illegal, since among other things, he would go for fifteen and sometimes twenty hours straight in violation of the safety laws, but the money was good and paid in cold cash, and so none of it went to taxes.

Since then, however, he had married, had a kid, and settled down with a factory job in the Baltimore area.

But his car was in the driveway as I pulled alongside his house. I parked in the street and wondered to myself if he were sick or if the seven-year-old Mustang had finally broken down.

It was Dave himself, however, who answered the door. It took him a couple of seconds before he reacted.

"Oh, hey, come on in, you SOB. What are you doing here?"

"I'm on my way to New York and thought I'd stop in and say hello."

"Well, great. Come on in. It's great to see you."

The words came out correctly but his face didn't match. And then, the look his wife gave me as I entered, told me I'd walked into the middle of a fight. She wasn't in tears, but she was close.

"Hey, look," I said, "I guess I should have called. If I've come at a bad time . . ."

"Naw, hell," he interrupted. "We've got this thing right now but it'll be settled in a couple of minutes."

His wife snorted angrily and retreated toward the kitchen. I offered again to leave but he insisted I stay for dinner.

"Finish your talk," I said, "I'll go sit in the yard."

I took a paper and went out through the back door. I started to read, but the kitchen window was open and I couldn't have avoided hearing them if I'd wanted to.

"Call him and tell him you've changed your mind, please," his wife said, a tense rising note sounding in her voice.

"And do what instead? Take the $120 at the plant? We can't live on that.

"It's not forever."

"There are twenty guys in my section and we all have priority," he said, sneering the last word. "Somebody isn't going to make it up the ladder. That's just a fact of life."

Dave's wife was silent for a moment. You could almost hear her thinking, looking for a different line of attack. From what they had said, Dave's section had been closed down and he was going back to gypsy trucking—if she would let him. The plant was apparently offering him an entry level job, but with nineteen others in the same position, there was no way of telling when, or if, he'd get a job like the one he had.

His wife broke the silence. "It's just no good, we can't live that way."

"I did before."

"You weren't married before. I mean, what if you get into trouble?",

"You're a hell of a one to talk about that," he snapped suddenly.

There was a sudden pause and then she exploded with a viciousness that was startling. "Oh, Jesus Christ, shit," followed a moment later by a slamming door.

A few moments later Dave came out.

"Let's go out for a drive."

I agreed and we got in the car. As Dave gunned the engine and as we began to accelerate the gears slipped from second to neutral with a snap, a mechanical problem that Dave had jokingly called his "automatic" transmission.

"I see you've still got your luxury option," I said trying to break the silence.

"Yeah," was all for the moment and then, "I guess you heard it all."

"Yeah."

"What do you think?"

"I don't know. The other job is just out of the question?"

"Yeah, you don't even know the whole of it."

I didn't know, but from his last remark and her reaction it wasn't hard to guess. "She's pregnant," I said.

It wasn't a question, but a statement.

He didn't say anything at first but then he said softly, more to himself than to me, "What the fuck am I going to do?"

He didn't expect an answer, even if he had, there was none I could give.

It is not surprising that the economic problems workers face have not excited the imagination of many socially conscious people. While many recognize that workers do not make "affluent" or completely comfortable incomes, the gap between workers and the middle class is often treated as a matter of quantity, a slightly smaller house, a less elegant car, or perhaps a black and white TV instead of color. But the income gap between working class and middle class does not only lead to differences in the style and quality of their possessions. It divides them on the most basic issues of economic security and the quality of life itself. Despite all the changes and improvements that have occurred, blue-collar life is still permeated by profound economic insecurity and a life-style based on "just getting along," rather than advancing. There has been a great increase in the quantity of goods a worker may own, during the postwar period. But, in these two central areas, the classic discontents of blue-collar workers are still agonizing realities. Only for the upper levels of the middle class have such problems truly become a thing of the past.*

The most logical figure to use for dividing the upper middle class from the lower middle class is about $15,000–16,000 (using 1970 figures, today it would be higher). This is the "higher" (affluent) standard budget of the Labor Department for that year, and it also divides the white-collar group roughly in half (once one excludes the misclassified manual workers in the clerical and sales category).[1]

This is a less than precise way of defining lower and upper middle class since it ignores the significant factors of salaried versus independent, and intellectual versus managerial. But at least it separates the $70,000 a year psychiatrist from the $10,000 a year high school teacher, and the president of General Motors from the man who has a Chicken Delight franchise.

The clearest measure of economic security is savings, and the facts in this area are startling. Data about the majority of the American people, both working class and middle class, from the Michigan University Survey Research Center indicate how profound that lack of security really is. Most

* In turning to the social and economic problems of blue-collar workers, it is necessary to separate the very affluent business executives and independent professionals from the clerks, high school teachers, and other salaried employees who often make no more than blue-collar workers. Although their job conditions are usually better and their income generally a bit higher than an equivalent blue-collar job, their economic problems and discontents are often identical with those of workers.

workers simply do not have any meaningful savings. A person with the typical working-class income only had eight or nine hundred dollars in all liquid assets in 1969.[2] This means he could afford nine days in a hospital, less than half of a Volkswagen Beetle, or a couple of weeks in college for his son without going into debt. In contrast, a person with the average middle class income had assets of about $4,000 and $1,000 in savings accounts alone.*

In terms of the country as a whole:

In 1969, two-thirds of American families could not pay for their child's tuition and regular expenses at a public university without going into debt. 83% could not afford the total amount.

67% could not pay for major medical expenses of over $2,000 without insurance. The majority could not even pay $1,000.

42% of the American people could not afford a two-week vacation (at $30 a day for the whole family) without borrowing the money. In fact, the majority of Americans took no vacation at all, not even a short trip to Disneyland or some national park, much less to Acapulco or Europe. Most spent their vacations in their living rooms.[3]

What this means is that for most workers a single economic crisis can wipe out the work of a lifetime. The cost of caring for an aging parent, for example, is difficult for all but the most well-to-do. But for a worker it can literally drive him back into poverty. An on-the-job accident can also literally mean a

---

* Liquid assets include savings and checking accounts, certificates of deposit, and savings bonds. The actual amount of savings would, in fact, be much lower than eight or nine hundred for blue-collar workers, since much of the money workers have in checking accounts is already committed to expenses or bills. (As an indication, nearly half of the people making $9–10,000 a year have no money in savings accounts at all.) The upper middle class, on the other hand, has a range of investments which the term liquid assets does not include.

return to grinding economic want. Even something as simple as a set of braces for an adolescent's teeth, a cost that is rarely thought of as a major burden for most middle-class families, is often postponed for years or even rejected as too expensive in the lower half of working-class America. A medical student I know in a south Wisconsin industrial center once described a twelve-year-old girl brought to the emergency ward of his hospital with a severe cut on her lower lip. She was painfully embarrassed by her buck teeth and had cut herself trying to fashion a coathanger into braces. The upper middle class may not have the "inner beauty" poets have ascribed to common people, but at least their teeth are straight.

But, in addition to the long-range insecurity, the day-to-day lives of workers are often an economic treadmill where one must run hard simply to stay in place.

One personal experience brings this clearly into focus. When I began working at the canning factory, one Tuesday I arrived with only a twenty-dollar bill. At lunchtime, when I discovered this and tried to get change, it turned out that none of the forty men in my section had twenty dollars in any denomination in their pockets nor did anyone in the next section. In fact, their attitude was frankly incredulous. As one said, "Man, it's been so long since I had twenty dollars on a Tuesday that I can't even remember the last time I did."

In contrast, there is probably not a single office building, university campus, or other middle-class environment where someone is not carrying more than twenty dollars. In fact, many middle-class people would feel uncomfortable not to have substantially more on their person.

A central factor in the extremely tight day-to-day economic situation of workers is the stunning growth of credit. In the two decades from World War II, consumer indebtedness as a whole has grown from six billion to *eighty-six* billion dollars.

The rate of growth has, in fact, been twice as fast as financial assets.[4] In personal terms, it means that for a family earning an average working-class income, two-thirds, two out of every three, are in debt. One out of every three owes more than a thousand dollars to some company or credit agency.[5]

The result is a profound difference in the daily life of workers and that of the upper middle class (as well as many lower-paid professional and intellectual workers who do not purchase cars and homes on credit). Simply, for many workers the entire paycheck is already committed when they walk out of the factory gates. Between the money that is set aside to pay the bills and the money for food and necessities, there is almost nothing that remains for leisure.

Often, in order to be near a factory or other well-paying job, a worker will be forced to buy a house beyond his real means, and even though he is earning twelve or thirteen thousand dollars a year, he will surreptitiously check his wallet before suggesting even a trip to the movies with his family. Often that same choice of housing makes a second car vital for his wife, although in many cases they can't afford it and the blue-collar wife becomes a virtual prisoner in her house until her husband gets home from work.

Much of what is parochial and limited in working-class life comes out of this fact. Many workers, in the elation of the first days after their honeymoon, lock themselves into a lifetime of debt when they buy a house and furniture to add to the payments they are already making on their car. From then on, their freedom to travel or try a new job, or just engage in a range of activities outside work is taken from them by the structure of debt in which they are enmeshed.

For some, the house becomes a focus of attention—the single symbol of affluence amid the daily life of severe economic pressure. It is this that explains the sometimes irrational fury with which workers react to threats to their neighborhood or home. It is not simply a piece of property, but something which has absorbed so much of their income, so many hours of work, and closed out so many alternatives, that losing it is like making all the sacrifices futile. Add to this the fact that, unlike professionals or intellectuals, many workers do not enjoy their work or find real fulfillment in it, and the meaning of economic sacrifice becomes clear. One night I sat with an older worker who had just made the last payment on his house. He suddenly became fascinated with the question of how many days he had worked to pay for it. He figured with great care the exact number of days and even hours. When he got the result, he sat back with a look of awe on his face. He was literally seeing his adult life pouring out into the house he had bought twenty years before.

The continuing misunderstanding between workers and intellectuals also has its roots in this reality. The intellectual, for example, drives past the home of a skilled worker and easily concludes that they live on a far higher level than he. But the worker sees the bearded sons of the middle class carrying knapsacks and boarding planes for Europe, or college students with expensive stereos or sportscars. He can't afford first-run movies, good restaurants, shows, vacations, eight-track tape decks, Gibson and Velasquez guitars, in short, all the items which the middle class consumes. From his point of view, it is true that even the professional lower middle class is far more affluent than he. The single family home he has is his only example of affluence.

Thus, from day to day, as well as from year to year, blue-collar workers are still caught up in a web of economic insecurity and persistent scarcity. The gulf that separates them from the affluent is not the size or color of their televisions, but the quality and structure of their lives.

What still remains to be shown, however, is that workers are not only less affluent than the middle class, but the victims of systematic injustice in the economic policies and practices of contemporary America.

Taxes provide the most glaring example. Literally every tax in America is regressive and exacts a greater sacrifice from workers than from the middle class. In 1972, *Business Week* magazine calculated the percent of income taken by all the taxes and transfers levied on Americans. The results showed that the percentage of income taken from someone making $4,000 a year was virtually the same as for someone earning $6,000 or $8,000, or in fact anything up to $50,000.[6] In their book, *Blue Collars and Hard Hats,* however, Patricia and Brendan Sexton made allowances for the loopholes and tricks available to the rich and offered these figures:

Family income	% of income taken by all taxes[7]
$3,000	34%
5–7,000	33
7–10,000	32
15,000 plus	28

Considering that workers often receive inferior public services for their money, as in the case of schools, it becomes difficult even to find words that capture the magnitude of the injustice involved.

More than any other issue, however, the injustices of the tax system have finally received attention, and therefore a very quick look will suffice.

Federal income taxes: There is a maze of inequities in the tax system, and in the glaring loopholes corporations enjoy in comparison to the individual taxpayer, but the central issue is the "triple standard" which taxes wages far more heavily than other sources of income. One particularly lucid description is given below.

"For example, a worker earning $10,000 a year and supporting a wife and two children pays a federal income tax of $905. His next door neighbor who decides to take the year off and sells some corporate stocks at ten thousand dollars more than he paid for them (capital gains) is subject to a federal tax of only $98. Another neighbor receiving the same $10,000 income from interest on municipal bond holdings pays no federal income tax at all."

State and local taxes: Although higher personal exemptions make these taxes more progressive at lower income levels than the federal ones, they also favor the affluent.

Social Security taxes: The most obviously regressive of all taxes. After $10,800 a year they take a smaller and smaller percentage of income. To put it dramatically:

Income	Amount to be paid in 1973
$ 7,433	$438.83
$ 10,800	631.80
$ 100,000	631.80
$1,000,000 plus	631.80

Property taxes: *Business Week* quotes one executive as follows: "The property tax is the most regressive tax . . . in the United States because housing is so large a component of spending for lower income families." Also, another author notes that "In the kinds of places for which blue collar workers leave the central city . . . property tax increases (during the sixties) have been especially marked." Even workers who live in apartments are affected because landlords frequently include the tax burden in the rent. As much as 20–25 percent of the rental price of an apartment can be going to pay the owner's tax bill.[8]

Inflation, also, is not merely a problem for workers but is in many ways as directly inequitable as the tax system. Its impact on a factory production and maintenance worker has certainly been profound. Between 1965 and 1971, his real after-tax earnings were virtually at a standstill. Wage increases in those years at no time outdistanced rising prices. In constant 1967 dollars the situation looked like this:

TAKE-HOME PAY AFTER TAXES—WORKER WITH
THREE DEPENDENTS (CORRECTED FOR INFLATION)[9]

1965	$102.41
1966	102.31
1967	101.26
1968	102.45
1969	101.49
1970	99.66
1971	102.42
1972	108.41

Only in 1972 did factory workers actually have an increase in their real take-home pay. Even construction workers who were able to win far better wage increases only increased their take-home pay by about $20 a week over the six-year period, from 1965 to 1971. And for the millions of workers who did not get any wage increases at all or the retired workers on pensions, inflation cut deeply into their standards of living. Certain kinds of vital goods and services like medical costs, in fact, increased astronomically in recent years making first-rate health care impossible for many workers to afford.

But although a great deal has been written about inflation, one point that has often been overlooked is that inflation is essentially regressive. Inflation has the same effect in the supermarket that a regressive sales tax would have. The punch press operator's wife and the executive's wife both must pay the same increase for a steak that used to cost $1.85. The effect on the living standard is far more agonizing for blue-collar workers and others who live on a very tight budget than it is for the affluent. The middle-class person will pay the increase, but the worker has to switch to hamburger.

An additional element of injustice was added by all the programs that were designed to deal with the problem. The wage-price freeze controlled wages far more stringently than prices, and profits were subject to no controls at all. The tax provisions of the program, such as accelerated depreciation, were indeed, as labor described them, "a bonanza for big business," and "Robin Hood in reverse." [10]

It is not surprising, however, that many writers have overlooked the intrinsic unfairness of inflation and downgraded the inequities of the freeze since they were busily announcing to the nation that "excessive" wage increases were what was causing the inflation in the first place. For example, until the stunning increases in food and gas prices made it clear that workers were victims of forces beyond their control, even many liberals were persuaded that inflation was arising mainly from blue-collar greed.

But just asking for more money is not "inflationary." To "cause" higher prices, wages must rise to the point where they make the product more expensive so a company must raise its prices or accept a lower level of profits.

From 1960 to 1965, however, labor unit costs (the amount it costs the company in wages to produce an item) declined. Yet, the wholesale price of manufactured goods still rose slightly.

Nor did workers grab a disproportionate share of the economic pie in those years. Profits increased 50 percent, dividends 43 percent, and a worker's take-home pay only 21 percent.[11]

Even if workers had made substantial gains in the second half of the decade, it would only have corrected the previous imbalance. And yet, as we saw, in no year between 1965 and 1971 did workers' real income outrun prices. Only by pretending that American economic history began suddenly in the middle of 1965 could the proponents of the greedy worker thesis make it seem convincing.

One final area of clear economic injustice workers face is the credit system. Its basic unfairness is usually not mentioned because without it most workers would never be able to own a home nor could a substantial number afford even a car.

But the price it exacts is high. Credit means very simply that the worker will pay far more for the same goods than a well-off person who pays cash—$350 for the $250 TV set, and $500–600 more for his car. Even though heavy mortgages are not confined to workers but extend to most middle-class people as well, it is still worth looking at the effect of buying a home on credit for a worker. A new house which costs $22,000 cash will cost $38,678, or almost twice as much with a $17,000 thirty-year mortgage. In fact, the worker will work *three and a half years* just to pay the interest.[12]

Thus, taxes, inflation, and credit are all part of a pattern. In the realm of economics, blue-collar workers face not only insecurity and deprivation, but systematic injustice as well.

III

The snow was starting to fall when I got my first good look at the steel mills that run for miles along the southern shores of Lake Michigan. I was standing on a slab of concrete that let me see all along the coastline. Sharp crystals of ice began to whip my face and forced me to turn my head away from the offshore wind. My black companion, a steel worker who had just got off work, was pacing back and forth, eager to get back into the car and get home.

The vantage point was perfect. The dock where we stood was on a small peninsula and I could see from the Gary Steelworks, where we were, all along the coast through Hammond and East Chicago, to, in the far distance, the soft halo of light from Chicago itself, reflecting on the low-hanging clouds.

But along the lakeshore, all one could see was factories—steel mills, rolling mills, foundries, massive building upon building, running along the edge of the water. Years before, I had driven through the Andes Mountains of Peru and seen the vast plateaus; the lunar landscapes of the altiplano at twelve thousand feet above the sea, and although it was very different, I had the same sense of awe, like staring at the surface of some huge alien planet. Before my eyes was a series of plants in an area about a mile deep and ten miles long, and that was only what my snow-blurred vision could see. Beyond it were miles and miles more. These were steel mills of the Calumet region, lining the southern shore of Lake Michigan.

"Come on, let's get home," my friend demanded, rubbing his hands together to keep the circulation going.

I tore myself away and got into his car.

"This is where I work," he announced suddenly, as we drove past one enormous building, an aluminum shed that stood four or five stories high. A door was open and I caught a quick glimpse of huge rolls of steel, like enormous spools of thread.

He turned a corner and we passed a very small red brick building hidden by two large buildings on either side.

"That's the lunchroom," he said. "They used to have a cafeteria that served hot meals but now they put in those automatic vending machines that just give sandwiches and soup. Some guys want the union to ask for hot meals again, but the machines do have their good points."

"What?" I asked.

"Well, if you know how to monkey with them, you can get back your money. It's lousy food but it's free. They probably don't fix the machines 'cause it's cheaper for them this way than it is to run a cafeteria."

I nodded and agreed it probably was something like that—it usually is.

As we headed down the main avenue of Gary, Indiana, I looked back and found it hard to repress a smile. Gary is basically a company town, planned, built, and financed by U.S. Steel at the turn of the century. Its physical layout is typical of that era, when big business had not yet learned the value of a "low profile" and captains of industry splashed their mansions along New York's Fifth Avenue, rather than discreetly hiding them away from the public eye.

Looking back, I saw the center of the city—the major banks and stores and government buildings all lining the main avenue.

But the avenue dead-ended in one of the major entrances to the mills, and as the shift changed, I could see the lines of buses and cars backing up along the avenue as they entered the plant that stretched across the horizon. The municipal building and the city hall sat on either side of the avenue, just before the factory gates, and it was hard to avoid the image of the two decorative statues of cats that guard the entrance to an Egyptian Pharaoh's tomb.

Since 1968, however, Gary has had a black mayor and the physical layout no longer corresponds to the political reality. Since then, on a number of occasions, those previously loyal cats, the mayor's office and city hall, have, in fact, been seriously at odds with the company that lay beyond them.

"All this is black," my friend said suddenly, breaking off my daydreams. We had turned off the main avenue and were traveling along one of the streets of Gary's central city.

It was, in a way, like looking into the past. The houses that line the streets of urban Gary were once filled with Poles, Slavs, Greeks, and a mixture of other ethnic groups, purposely thrown together in the hope that ancient national feuds would impede any attempts at union organization.

But today, these districts have become predominantly black, and the aging buildings house the black population, while the white workers live miles to the south. As we drove slowly down the street, zigzagging to avoid the deep cracks and holes, I watched the procession of condemned, vacant apartments pass by—the weather-beaten signs announcing that this store or that lot was for rent. It was the sad vision, not of black indifference or neglect, but simple economic reality—poor people cannot buy enough to support nice stores and fancy restaurants. So there is no profit to be made in serving them. Business and consequently economic health go where the money is and in Gary it is not in the oldest and poorest section of the black community.

But farther on we came to the homes of black steel workers. We passed house after house that looked like the homes of unskilled and semiskilled workers anywhere. The simple boxes and rectangles, without new paint or garage, but clean and neat.

"Here we are," my friend announced, pulling into a driveway, setting the emergency brake, cutting the engine off, and opening the door.

I knew he had dinner waiting so I said good-bye and walked over to my rented car, parked where I had left it hours before.

I continued south, leaving the black area and crossing the "little Calumet River," the unofficial dividing line between urban Gary and Glen Park, between black and white. Some older white workers still live downtown and one can see black and white children playing stickball together only blocks away from the plant. But the river is the real division and below it is the core of white, blue-collar Gary.

It was getting dark, and looking back as I headed to my room I could see flames outlined against the darkened sky, that were leaping from the smokestacks of the mill, giving it a particularly diabolic aspect. The old poem by William Blake about the "dark, satanic mills" of eighteenth-century England seemed very apt. It was, in one sense unfair, since the modest but certainly decent houses of many steelworkers had been made possible by the wages the steel industry pays, but if the devil ever ran out of brimstone and had to use carbon monoxide as a substitute, he might very well come to Gary for a look. It is said to be one of the most polluted cities in America and staring at the forest of smokestacks, I saw no reason to doubt that it was true.

The other thing I wondered to myself was how many of the children I was seeing on the streets, even the white ones, would ever be able to go to college, or at any rate escape the life of their fathers, working in the mill until finally they are too worn out to continue. It is a question that wage scales or income levels alone could not answer.

Unlike the economic pressures and injustices that workers face, it is hard to sum up the problems that exist in the community itself, for workers live under a wide range of conditions—from overcrowded, cramped trailer parks to some highly desirable communities.

But for the majority their neighborhoods are profoundly inferior to those of the affluent suburbs. Black and white workers in cities share many of the same community problems, though the ghetto inevitably has them in greater degree.

Here, for example, is Peter Binzen's description of a white working-class community near Philadelphia in his *Whitetown, U.S.A.*:

> Kensington's air is polluted, its streets and sidewalks are filthy, its juvenile crime rate is rising, its industry is languishing. No more than a handful of new houses have been built there in the last third of a century. Its schools are among the oldest in the city. Its playgrounds—the few that it has—are overrun with young toughs. Industry is moving out. Social workers and clergymen often give up in despair (a Protestant minister has written of his five years in Kensington: "There is nothing here that I wouldn't like better someplace else.")[13]

This may seem an extreme case, but similar descriptions apply to ethnic communities all across America. Certain issues, in fact, reappear again and again.

For one thing, blue-collar neighborhoods generally get second-class treatment from community services and city government. In urban working-class areas, both white and black, there are often no decent parks or places for recreation. Health services are inadequate and often even garbage collection is less frequent. Inadequate public transportation is rarely confined only to the ghetto, but is equally poor for the adjacent white working-class communities.

One resident of such a community described the problems as follows:

> This neighborhood could be an ideal place to raise children if we were supported by the agencies of the city whom we support with our taxes . . . When we asked the city to replace trees that died this request was ignored.[14]

This failure of city services is echoed by a worker in another blue-collar community:

> [This] could be a nice place to live if our area was given the same consideration as other areas. Our swimming pool was closed for four years because it had a crack in it. If this was west, north or south Philadelphia, it would have been repaired right away. We had to wait four years.[15]

Private interests also get away with practices in blue-collar neighborhoods that would not be tolerated in middle-class areas. A community action group in Gary, Indiana, for example, organized a protest and finally won in a struggle with contractors over the flooding of workers' homes which occurred because of bad sewerage planning.

> For years [the workers] had put up every spring with the flooding of their homes, when a nearby river overflowed its banks and inundated the storm sewers that backed up into their basements.
> . . . the solution was simple enough—and inexpensive. Sewer covers were cemented over and a faulty storm sewer system was repaired. The contractors had ignored the people because they had anticipated that the working class home-owners would remain passive . . .[16]

But perhaps the most clearly unfair way in which working-class communities have been penalized by special interests is the trend of expressways to avoid disrupting middle-class communities and to plow instead through blue-collar neighborhoods where workers have lived all their lives. As Binzen notes:

> Rarely do you see new businesses or industries in White-town. Often, though, you see new expressways plowing

through its heart. In many cities freeways criss-cross the old ethnic neighborhoods enroute to the expensive housing, fancy shopping centers, and modern industrial parks in shining suburbia. Not only do these freeways destroy the unity of America's Whitetowns, but they also hasten the exodus of white owners, thus undermining what little stability these old ethnic neighborhoods have left. The federal government rarely spends a nickel to help Whitetown, but it has put billions into expressways.[17]

In this area especially, blue-collar workers are clearly aware of the class bias involved. In Chicago, where a community-based protest group sprang up in response to the threat of displacement, a reporter noted that:

> To Mike Stolarczyk [the leader] and his friends, it looked as though their way of life was being threatened so that affluent suburbanites could get home for dinner quicker.[18]

In the Brookline Elm section of Cambridge, where a similar group appeared, one young worker was quoted as saying:

> "There are alternate routes—Memorial Drive, Albany Street—but they figure they're going to step on the little guy . . . it's just a kick in the teeth these people around here don't need." [19]

There are no national statistics which pin down all the ways or the exact number of times working-class communities have been victimized by practices like these. But in the case of the schools, perhaps the most important community institution of all, the evidence is precise and unambiguous.

The educational system, which is supposed to be the great avenue of social mobility, in fact, systematically discriminates against the working-class child, black or white. The working-class child's chances of going to college are far smaller than a middle-class child's, *even if they have the same academic ability.* One study in 1966 showed that a working-class high school student, even with above average test scores, only had about a 30 percent chance of going to college. A middle-class child with the same amount of measured aptitude had a 55 percent chance. Thus the odds were better than even for the middle-class student and about two to one against a student from the lower economic half of the population.[20]

The reason is not only economic. There is really a dual school system in America. Not only are most high schools in middle-class areas better than those in working-class districts, but even in a particular school there are "special progress" classes for the middle class and "vocational education" for many working-class children.

The "objective" tests which send working-class children down these dead-end paths are, in fact, little more than paper and pencil versions of the English "old boy" system. If advancement in turn-of-the-century England depended on whether one's father had an Eton tie or not, "objective tests" today really elicit the same information, but in a roundabout way. Stripped of all their pretensions they are, in essence, vocabulary tests (the vocabulary section of the IQ, for example, is the most predictive section for college success), and the young child of college-educated parents obviously will have had better preparation in this regard. Far from giving every student an equal chance, regardless of background, the system of testing and tracks, simply ensures that those who start with an advantage continue to hold and increase it.*

* There are, of course, claims made that the IQ test, in particular, can measure innate "intelligence" and conclusions drawn from the results as to the inherent ability of social classes and races. The critique of these views, certainly as applied to blacks, are familiar enough to make it unnecessary to repeat them at length here.

Even without such formal mechanisms as testing and tracks, a teacher's unconscious favoritism can, and often does, have the same effect. Many of the criticisms that have been made of black, inner-city schools, in fact, also apply to the schools of white worker communities. One author, for example, notes that: "The 'morbid, desolate, crumbling' school of 'rank smells' and pervasive gloom that Jonathan Kozol in *Death at an Early Age* found destroying the hearts and minds of Negro children in Boston's Roxbury section, exists in white Charlestown, too." [21] The way in which the school's tax money is collected and allocated by particular districts ensures, in fact, that the discrimination in funding is basically by income level rather than by race, per se.[22]

The result is that many working-class high schools are often little more than training grounds for the factory. As one author has argued:

> Socialization in such a [working-class] school comes to mirror that of the factory. Students are treated as raw material . . . there is a high premium on obedience and punctuality and there are few opportunities for independent, creative work or individual attention by teachers . . . [the teacher] may be compelled to resort to authoritarian tactics whether she wants to or not." [23]

This view of blue-collar schools is supported by the fact that while many factory jobs now require a high school diploma, there is nothing in the job itself that makes one necessary. As one set of studies indicated:

> ". . . During the 1960s many employers raised minimum job qualifications to high school graduation for blue collar work . . . The shift upward was not based on any demonstrated superior capability of high school graduates compared with

non-graduates . . . Rather management simply believed that those who 'stayed with it' were more reliable." [24]

The effects of this class bias in the educational system can be seen in the figures on school enrollment:

% MALES ENROLLED IN SCHOOL[25]

Age	Blue collar	White collar
16–17 (high school)	80	92
18–19 (entering college)	49	73
20–24 (continuing college)	20	43

If more detailed statistics separating two-year colleges, four-year colleges, and graduate school existed, they would show an even more distinct process of attrition. A significant number of workers' children do attend "college," it is true, but many go to two-year community colleges which teach essentially skilled working-class jobs like auto and air-conditioning repair, printing, and electrical trades. The number of workers who can afford to finish a four-year college course are far fewer, and, in a final irony, for many the degree now no longer guarantees a good job as it once did. The university system expanded in the sixties to accept more than just the sons of the elite, but the labor market did not. In 1971, four-year college graduates had an unemployment rate of 8.5 percent and more stunningly, fully half the employed said that their jobs were not related to their college training. The preponderate reason was that the unrelated jobs were the only work they could find.[26]

The statistics on mobility bear out the failure of the schools. Despite the rapid expansion of white-collar jobs in the fifties, the most comprehensive study of mobility, done in 1962, showed that two-thirds of American workers saw their children enter working-class jobs and many of the others saw only slight advances for their children, into clerical jobs or small, often marginal, businesses like franchise operations. Only 10 percent of the sons of manual workers, they note, entered the professional and technical "elite." [27] The percentages have undoubtedly changed since then, and, to be sure, there is significant upward mobility in America. But there still is nothing even approaching a fair deal in education for the young blue-collar worker.*

The final community issue which must be considered brings up the whole problem of black America. Years ago, it would have been possible to deal with the legitimate injustices of class separately from the reality of race and racial segregation. But crime and violence in particular have erased the simple division between the legitimate neighborhood problems of workers and the racial attitudes of the community. The fear of crime is a central and legitimate problem. But it is also inescapably tied up with the question of race as a whole.**

At first glance, it may appear that crime, like pollution, is a problem for every American and is not a special discontent of the working class.

But while in some geographical areas, like Manhattan's East Side, the upper middle class lives right next to the ghetto, in national terms white working-class and lower-middle-class communities are disproportionately victimized. One study, for example, in the Presidential Commission's Report on Civil

* While a more precise statement of the patterns of occupational mobility might seem of interest, it is unfortunately impossible to say much more than the above without an extremely long discussion of definitions, and the explanation of some highly technical mathematical statistics.

The deceptive census categories alone make it difficult to arrive at "common sense" answers and since the only statistics that fully deal with the complex factors of age, region, farm migration, and so on, are over ten years old, more precise data will not really tell us anything vital that the figures above do not already indicate.

** The broader issues of working-class attitudes toward blacks and issues like busing will be considered in the next chapter and again in the later ones.

Disorders gave the following comparison of the two white communities:

CRIME RATE PER 100,000[28]

	High income	Low middle income
Number of index crimes against persons (homicide, rape, aggr. asslt., robbery, burglary, grand larceny, auto theft)	80	440

This means the white working-class neighborhood had a rate of serious crimes five and a half times as high as the affluent area. (For the black community, the number was far higher, an astronomical 2,820 in one district and 1,615 in another.) Like many other areas, while blacks suffer the worst conditions, white workers are far worse off than the affluent middle class.*

While the nature of the problem crime and violence creates is obvious, there are several points which need to be stressed.

First, crime and violence have become the number one problem for many Americans. Gallup polls show that in the large cities 21 percent chose it as the major problem, with drugs and transit tied for second place at 10 percent and 11 percent respectively.[30]

Second, the problem of crime in many peoples' minds is fused with the rise of black militancy, especially in its extreme forms like ghetto riots of the sixties or terrorist activities. As a result, an act like the robbery of a house seems far more threatening than it did years ago. One woman who purchased a handgun after years of rejecting the idea, said quite seriously, "They might be coming to kill my children." This reflects a

---

* The years since 1965 when this study was done have seen a growth in suburban crime, but the latest studies indicate that this general relationship still holds.[29]

growing feeling that black crime is now essentially a kind of terrorism like the Mau Mau of Kenya rather than basically economically motivated.*

Third, crime, especially violent crime, is the work of a very small group of recidivists. In Philadelphia, for example, one study showed 627 youths were responsible for some 5,100 crimes during a single year.[31]

However, though the number of violent criminals is not large, their impact is tremendous, in part because they are rarely captured. To a large degree, unfortunately, the more emotionally charged the crime, the more difficult it is to catch the culprit. An attempt can be made to at least trace burglarized goods or stolen cars. But the rapist or mugger, the most deeply feared criminals, are almost immune to capture except in unusual cases. This incapacity of conventional law enforcement methods creates a highly dangerous situation. Just as the "invisibility" of the Viet Cong made all Vietnamese peasants appear like potential enemies, so the invisibility of the violent criminal leads to a fear and suspicion of all young blacks.

But the central point about crime is that, like the other community discontents workers face, its impact falls disproportionately on them, and the urban part of the middle class. The more affluent suburbanites are far less likely to suffer its impact.

IV

One of the things that everyone hears somewhere in the first years of school is that only in America can a poor boy rise

* Although there is no solid evidence, I suspect there is an unfortunate element of truth in this fear. While most crime remains economic, in certain cases there is an unnecessary brutality or even murder involved in muggings that cannot be ascribed to rational economic motives. On the other hand, the fact that most street crime by blacks is still not racial is proved by the fact that it is perpetrated against other blacks.

up in the world and become President. But unless one is especially naïve, long before one graduates, one realizes that the odds against it are somewhat worse than the Irish Sweepstakes. Not only the Presidency, but virtually every position of political power in the United States is held by people drawn from the upper reaches of society. In the years between 1947 and 1957, for example, only 1 percent of senators were blue-collar workers at the time of their election, 99 percent were drawn from the upper or middle classes.[32]

While everyone knows that this is the case, it has never seemed like an important issue because, as the textbooks explain, America is a "pluralist society," which means that every interest group has ways of making its demands felt and translated into legislation.

While it is recognized that this is manifestly untrue in the case of blacks or other minorities, it is also untrue for blue-collar workers. Like the economic system, the political system also fails to deal justly with the pressing needs of working-class Americans.

This fact is often overlooked because of the undeniable influence the unions have, both as a lobby in Washington, and as a source of funds and support for political candidates. Since 1960, in fact, their role has grown tremendously and unions now have a significant voice in the Democratic Party, as well as a sophisticated lobby in Congress. In 1968, they spent some 5 million dollars on politics, registered four and a half million voters and had close to a hundred thousand of their members working on Election Day. Rather dramatically, a *Washington Post* series on labor's political influence concluded that "labor is not only competent and powerful [in Congress]. It is feared." [33]

But despite this appraisal, even if the labor movement had twice the influence it does today, the American political system would still be decisively biased against the average worker. Although blue-collar workers are a majority of the population, in Washington their interests are treated as those of a "special interest" group.

The injustices of the tax system provide the best example. Labor may lobby for certain reforms and they may support candidates who are in agreement with them on this issue But the tax structure itself, as it was designed and has been applie< during the whole postwar period, has been biased against workers. Labor's influence has been at best an effort to mitigate the worst features of the system. They certainly never had the opportunity to determine the basic form of taxes and make them fair from the outset.

Equally, unions have struggled against the Taft-Hartley Act, which severely restricted their power for twenty years. Yet to date they have at best fought a defensive battle preventing even more harsh limitations from being imposed.

Labor's power is, in fact, defensive. They can prevent antilabor legislation from passage or win certain improvements in existing programs, but they cannot determine the basic shape of legislation, or ensure the passage of any bill by themselves alone. As one writer in *Fortune* magazine noted, "As labor knows, it is far from strong enough in Congress to dictate the terms of major legislation. It wins its battles instead by joining its strength and influence to those of other groups." [34]

On some parochial issues of interest to only a small group of workers or to the unions alone, this would be understandable. But even when it is a basic social program, in the interests of the vast majority of workers and all Americans, labor's power is often insufficient to overcome the influence of special interests, and pro-business forces.

Here, for example, is one major union's, the Communication Workers, terse summary of the 92nd Congress's action on bills that affected workers.

> "National health insurance, the C.W.A.'s (Communication Workers of America) and organized labor's number one legislative priority died in committee. House anti-worker forces blocked final action on the urgently needed increase in the minimum wage with administration support. Pension reform and tax reform also go on the list of the 92nd Congress' failures."
>
> It then continues on the "plus side" listing one point, "members of the House and Senate increased Social Security payments by 30% during the 92nd Congress. They also enacted other needed improvements in Social Security benefits . . . but Congress failed to respond to Labor's proposals to use general revenue payments to pay the benefits instead of the taxes on workers' pay checks." [35]

Three failures and one very limited success, and this for a "pressure group," labor, which represents more people than every other lobby in the country combined.

But even this assessment severely understates the problem by equating organized labor's legislative goals with the basic and long-range needs of American workers. Labor, for the most part, has taken a broad view of its role and has not confined itself to the issues of importance only to the unions themselves. But their legislative goals and lobbying activity are highly practical, chosen on the basis of what is possible at a given moment and not broad statements of what needs to be done. When one looks at the way the political system responds to the key issues which workers face, the massive indifference and often injustice workers suffer become clear.

Take for example the issue of occupational health and safety. During the entire postwar period, there has probably been no area where legislation was more desperately needed or could do as much for the average American worker. But until 1965 there was virtually no action at all.

The chronology below charts the way the political system has responded to this need since then (mine safety legislation has been treated separately by Congress and therefore is not dealt with here):

1965   The first study, the Frye Report, is issued, describing the more urgent occupational health problems and possible corrective measures. It called for a national expenditure of $50 million for occupational health.

1967   Two years later a bill is introduced to deal with workers' "on-the-job" health and safety.

1968   The bill is killed by a flood of employer mail opposing it.

1969   *The Nation* magazine, in describing the limitations of the existing protection, notes that "States hire as many fish and game wardens as occupational health and safety inspectors."

1970   A study by Labor Department mavericks reveals that the disabling accidents rate may be ten times what the reported rates suggest. The Labor Department and Nixon attempt to first suppress and then shelve the report. Jack Anderson gets a copy and breaks the story.
        At the end of the year a compromise bill, the Occupational Health and Safety Act of 1970, is passed empowering the Secretary of Labor to set national health and safety standards for workplaces,

to impose fines and seek court actions against employers who violate standards. Workers are given the right to refuse work without any pay loss where dangerous toxins are concentrated and to obtain chemical analyses of these toxins from the Department of Health, Education and Welfare. The act also provides for unannounced federal inspections and prompt disclosure of the findings. Among the weaknesses of the act is a provision that even if an inspector finds a dangerous machine, he cannot shut it down on the spot. A commission on state workmen's compensation created by the bill has only three representatives of labor out of a total of eighteen members.

April
1972   Ralph Nader charges the Labor Department with a "frantic rush to turn the Occupational Health and Safety Administration [which enforces the law] into a farce." He notes that "With 500 compliance officers . . . by June 1972 there will be one inspector for every 7,200 establishments." *The New York Times* notes that the Labor Department also emasculated the law by nonenforcement and reinterpretation, such as simply eliminating four cancer-causing substances from the standards of the new act.

June
1972   Congress votes to cut off funds to enforce the law on firms with fifteen or fewer workers, putting five out of every six firms outside the inspection orbit.

August
1972   President Nixon vetoes the appropriation for the act. Three million dollars is cut from the budget of the O.H.S.A.

January
1973   Part of the law requires states to submit plans at least as tough as the federal standards by the end of 1972. Only four do, so the Labor Department extends the deadline six months, saying Congress had made a mistake in only giving the states two years to submit plans. The AFL-CIO gets a court injunction against the extension, but the Labor Department appeals.

1965–73 During the seven years between the first study and today, well over 500,000 workers have died on the job in America. The law as it stands is still not sufficiently strong, nor adequately enforced.[36]

Pension reform is another example. A commission, in 1961, pointed out the need for laws to protect workers' pensions. A year later, a special committee was appointed to study the issue. Its report came out in 1965, but as we noted in the last chapter, in 1972 there was still no law to protect workers from losing their retirement money. During that session of Congress, the Senate Labor and Public Welfare Committee put aside pension legislation because of administration pressure to move ahead on emergency antistrike legislation. It is a bitterly ironic commentary on Congress's priorities. A law to help thirty million workers on a vital issue gets put aside in favor of an antilabor measure.*

The root of the problem is something that black leaders recognized years ago about their interests. There is a profound difference between being represented by someone who is "sympathetic" to your interests and having someone who will champion them. There are thirteen members of the "Black

---

* Although several bills were introduced into the '73–'74 session of Congress, even the best (if it were passed without compromise, which it would not be) did not fully deal with the inequities of the current system.

Caucus" in Congress, and that is still far fewer than what is just. Yet there is no blue-collar-workers' caucus at all. Labor can lobby and try to influence legislation, but there is no one in Congress whose first question about a bill is "What does it mean to American workers?" When one looks at the halls of Congress, or state and local governments, one rarely sees a politician with whom an American worker can identify. Politics is, without question, a rich man's game, and all too often it is played at the expense of American workers.

It is an unfamiliar figure who has emerged from these pages. The blue-collar worker of the clichés, the satisfied middle American with his house and car has turned out to be a false caricature, concealing genuine problems and a pattern of profound inequality. And when a worker finally looks to the political system for solutions, he finds instead the same pattern of indifference and disregard, often in the most important areas of his life.

It is hard to disagree with the generalization that workers are, indeed, the victims of genuine injustice, and are second-class citizens in their own land.

CHAPTER FOUR

Working-Class Political Opinion

MY NEIGHBOR Al's house has a small backyard which faces away from the city. The lot next to it is vacant and on a summer night you can easily feel as if you are in the country, especially after the rush hour traffic has come and gone.

A friend of mine, on vacation from college, had come to visit and we were both cooking some steaks with Al and his brother. Al and I had put the grill together ourselves months before, and one of the three wheels of the tripod which supported it was completely out of line with the others, which had led to disaster the first time we had used it. Turning the brazier to catch the wind, we succeeded in dumping $4.00 worth of spare ribs and half our bag of charcoal on the single patch of flowers which his wife had painstakingly planted in the spring. It took several weeks before she could laugh about it and there was still coal dust visible where it fell.

We told the story to my friend and Al's brother, exaggerating the amount of food we lost and the destruction it caused, as one always does with a story like that.

I had warned my friend that Al and his brother seemed like Archie Bunker types when you first met them. Al calls the black community "Niggertown" and to this day he is convinced that the single black-owned bank in the city is somehow supported by his taxes.

But he also has an unusually deep friendship with Charley, a black co-worker. They often go for a drink after work, or sometimes visit at each other's houses. I realized the full depth of their relationship when Charley went into the hospital and Al visited him nearly every day.

Many people who know workers have had this same kind of confused reaction at one time or another. Robert Coles, the psychiatrist, expressed it more clearly than anyone else in an article he wrote. After giving a long quote from a worker he knew, he said:

The longer I know this man, and the more I hear his talk, the harder it is for me to call him this or that and in so doing feel halfway responsive to the ironies and ambiguities and inconsistencies I hear in his words and, more important, see expressed in his everyday deeds, in his situation and life. He speaks about times, about blacks and students and college professors, with . . . anger and contempt. . . . He can be irrational, mean, and narrow-minded, and work himself up into a spell of mixed racism and jingoism that would only please some of the very people he chooses to attack later on, the rich and powerful.

He can also be seen working beside black men, talking easily and warmly with them, sharing food with them, offering advice to them, or taking advice from them—on what kind of gas to buy, where to get a household item, a gadget, an article of clothing. . . .

We had all gone to the auto races that day and the cool air was a relief from the humid day. So we sat just enjoying the evening.

The question of the elections came up and Al's brother who had just returned from Vietnam, expressed his fury at the idea of amnesty for deserters and draft dodgers in no uncertain terms. To hear those few phrases, was, indeed, like reading of the typical "hard hat" or Archie Bunker.

But moments later he was saying something startlingly different.

"The guys who went to jail," he said, "Now, I respect them a hell of a lot. I didn't want to go over there any more than they did, but I didn't have the guts to go to jail. I respect a guy who was willing to do that. But not these guys who want it both ways. I mean, a guy like Martin Luther didn't try and get out of anything," he continued, using the shorthand version of Martin Luther King's name that many southerners do. "If he broke the law, he was willing to take his medicine."

I could see my college friend's eyes reflecting the surprise he was feeling. He was discovering that Al and his brother are complex. They grow and change and struggle like anyone else to live up to their ideals unlike "Archie Bunkers" or the "typical hard hats," who are nothing more than fleshed-out versions of an overheard remark on the street or a quick image seen on a TV news program.

Late that night, back in my apartment, as my college friend and I lay awake waiting for sleep to come, he suddenly said, "You know, they're really not such bad guys. They're just, well, different."

In recent years, most of the discussions about workers' political opinions have revolved around a series of images, like the "typical hard hat" or the "Archie Bunker" vote. The mental picture one has is the guy with "support your local police" and "Bomb Hanoi" bumper stickers on his car, or at the extreme, a hate-filled construction worker assaulting students.

While some liberals accept these images quite literally as accurate representations of American workers, even those who reject them as inadequate stereotypes rarely challenge the underlying conception that workers are now a basically conservative force in American society. As A. H. Raskin, a labor reporter for *The New York Times,* puts it, "The typical worker—from construction craftsman to shoe clerk—has become probably the most reactionary political force in the country." [2] It is almost never asserted today that workers are not more racist or militaristic than the middle class. And the idea that workers are actually more liberal in certain important areas, is absolutely unheard of.

Yet, when one looks at the hard national data from votes and opinion polls this is exactly what one finds. Opinion polls for the most part suggest only a small and by no means consistent difference in racism and militarism between social classes. And elections and other votes, even in 1972, indicate that workers are still one of the most "liberal" forces in American politics.

There are good reasons, however, why the distorted image is so compelling. The image of workers presented in the popular media, as well as in the academic community, has been consistently negative and essentially endorsed the "Archie Bunker" kind of clichés. This pattern is so widespread that no one can escape having their view of workers negatively influenced.

In the mass media, in addition to Archie Bunker, there have been other TV series that pictured blue-collar workers— Jackie Gleason's "Ralph Kramden" and William Bendix's "Life of Riley." All three were ridiculous comic figures, overweight, unintelligent, and in two cases, arrogant domestic tyrants. They never show the world of work, the factories or shops, and the genuine problems they faced.

Films also reinforce this image. Although there were also positive portrayals, especially in the fifties and early sixties, such popular films as "Joe," "Straw Dogs," and "Easy Rider" all presented a wild image of workers as homicidal maniacs. And in the last few years, these films have far outnumbered in audience and popularity the positive films which have been made.

This alone would not be a decisive influence. But it is reinforced even by the very terms applied to workers by the academic community. In just one article often assigned in college classes all of the following phrases were used: Workers have "a fixed and rigid perspective," "Absence of a past and future," "Inability to take a complex view," and finally, "They do not have a rich, inner life, indeed their imaginative activity is meager and limited." [3] Descriptions such as these were hardly calculated to inspire any respect for workers as human beings.

Theories also echo this view. The most widely known analysis of workers' political attitudes is Seymour M. Lipset's notion of working-class authoritarianism. This theory, originally developed to explain the rise of fascism in Germany, became specifically applied to workers in his interpretation. It argued, on the slim basis of a few opinion polls and on a pencil-and-paper questionnaire (the "F" scale), that workers were particularly prone to intolerance, antidemocratic feelings, as well as a number of other "conservative" personality traits. For many years this and related theories went largely unchallenged and frequently found their way into the popular press as well as scores of textbooks and studies. Only recently have systematic critiques appeared pointing out that much of the existing opinion poll data actually contradicts the thesis, that the methodology of studies like these have large subjective elements and that the whole notion of the authoritarian personality is in fact "too elusive for measurement, if indeed it is a clinical entity." As one critic noted, such things revealed more about the biases of the writers than of their subjects.* [4]

Finally, public opinion of workers was influenced by the 1970 news reports of several hundred construction workers assaulting students in downtown New York. Other examples of clashes between workers and blacks or students occurred and since one did not see several hundred professors or businessmen engaging in physical violence, the conclusion that workers were more reactionary seemed obvious.

But there are undoubtedly thousands of businessmen and even college professors whose hostility toward demonstrators was just as deep as that of the hard hats. What stopped them from engaging in physical violence was not their greater liberalism, but simply the fact that in middle-class America and especially in the academic environment, hitting people for any reason is condemned. Thus, while the political attitudes of many businessmen, for example, are far more conservative than that of most workers, they appear "tolerant," simply because they would be embarrassed to break the social norms against force that exist for their social group.

* It is hard for people unfamiliar with sociological research to realize how easy it is for bias and subjectivity to enter those impressive-looking studies with their imposing-looking statistical tables and jargon. But take, for example, the case of several researchers who began a study of social class and prejudice with the assumption that lower-class people were more prejudiced. They admitted that only three out of five previous studies supported their hypothesis, but they dismissed the two heretics as follows: "There is just too much independent evidence that prejudice toward negroes is inversely associated with current occupational status for us to contemplate seriously the possibility that the . . . Elmira data are substantially correct." And as for the second, "This curiosity has no obvious explanation and makes us as suspicious of the data as we were of the Elmira studies above."

But then their own study also failed to show that workers were more racist than the middle class. Thus, there were three studies for the hypothesis and three against. However, they resolved this by saying that their own results were "possibly attributable to faulty data . . . since other studies have shown that socioeconomic status tends to be inversely related to prejudice." [5]

But the facts about workers' attitudes, as we shall see, suggest a very different picture, more complex and also far more optimistic.

II

The streets near the factories of an industrial town are one of the loneliest places to walk between the change of shifts. There are few stores and fewer people. The bulk of the factory casts kind of an invisible gray shadow along the streets and the neon signs of the bars and pool halls call out like warm campfires in a frozen forest.

I went into the nearest pool hall and sat down. Beside me were two older men with long Slavic faces and ski jackets. At the pool table a black man stood, cue in hand, watching his white opponent execute a difficult safety that left a tight cluster of balls in the center of the table, offering no opportunities for sinking any ball with ease.

"Nice shot, you mother," the black said appreciatively.

"Just call me Minnesota Fats," the other replied.

In the file of articles in my bag were dozens of descriptions detailing the tension and hostility between black and white workers in many areas of the country. One described the case of a black auto worker in Detroit who shot three white workers in a burst of rage. Another, by one of the most thoughtful and well-informed labor reporters, said that blacks and whites at best tolerated each other in silent hostility. A third was about opposition to residential integration. A fourth about the antibusing protest in Pontiac, Michigan. It was a list that would make anyone despair of any change between black and white workers in America.

Yet, in that pool hall, a black and a white man were relating to each other in a way that contradicted everything I had read.

I turned and watched them again. The black man had just made a difficult shot, and sunk one ball into the pocket while opening up the cluster in the center. He would probably run the rack and win the game.

"Ooh—you son of a bitch," the white said jokingly—"I should have messed you up on that shot."

They playfully pointed their cues at each other, pretending to use them like clubs. No one looked up, no one took them seriously. They were a couple of guys playing pool on a weekday afternoon, before they went on the late shift at the plant.

A few notes from the pad I carry in my back pocket, notes that do not add neatly to a simple conclusion, but which suggest pieces of the vast puzzle that neither the popular clichés nor neat rows of figures can provide:

Riding with a young guy from the Gary car rental agency, driving me out to where I can pick up my rented car. He tells me he worked for several years in the mill and suddenly pauses to note that "The center of town is dying."

I have learned enough to know that a direct question about blacks will almost ensure a dishonest answer, so I told him about one job I did and described a totally imagined racial incident, only then asking him if he had any difficulty relating to blacks on the job.

"No," he said, "nothing like that. We just got along. I mean we did the work and got paid. No hassles or anything."

Nighttime on the road, heading into another industrial town in another state. I landed in Chicago and took the limousine, a yellow VW bus, since no planes fly to many industrial towns and many, like Gary, do not even have airports.

The guy driving was a factory foreman, moonlighting two nights a week as a chauffeur. We talked a bit about the north, and the south, from which I had just come.

"Anyplace I can get a drink?" I asked, as we entered the center of town.

"There's a bar in the hotel," he says, "But you'll be the only white man in it."

"Makes no difference to me," I said, "Does it bother you?"

"Oh, hell, no," he replied, with complete honesty. "I go there myself. It's just that you southern guys seem to be bothered."

I told him I was born up north and he seemed to nod in agreement, as though now everything made sense.

My first day on the job at the motor rebuilding plant. The lunch whistle sounded and we ran out to buy a hot dog or sandwich, from the lunch truck. I sat with the guy who was teaching me the job, but I quickly saw that I was in the wrong crowd. The older white workers sat along one wall of the plant, the young workers at another point, and blacks in still a third. Three cultures as separate as islands from 12:00 to 12:30.

But 5:00 and washup brings everyone together—blacks and whites stand side by side washing the grease from their hands and faces. These are white men from the Deep South and ten to twelve years ago this would have been impossible. But now it is accepted as an everyday thing.

I went to buy some cigarettes at a gas station in the South. An older guy with a beet-red face was handling the pump. He was filling up a car which had a black girl and white man. As they drove off, he turned and said, "You know, that really burns me up, a black and white together like that."

"Doesn't burn me up," I said, absently, thinking about other things. "If they like it, it's OK."

"Well," he replied, "That's true too, I guess."

I was in a foul mood anyway, having spent half the night without getting a word down on paper.

"Make up your mind," I snapped, "Either it burns you up or it doesn't." He was a bit startled and responded with an honest look of surprise.

"It depends on who I'm talking to, I guess."

"Well, when you talk to me remember that it doesn't burn you up," I said, irritably, turning away and walking off, still thinking of the unfinished work that lay before me.

I walked a few paces and began to feel a bit bad for being so unfriendly. Gas station attendants get lonely and I realized his initial answer had been very honest. He was just looking for conversation and figured that would be a good way to start. He probably didn't know himself how he really felt about that particular couple in that particular car. They were just a way of starting some conversation on an empty Tuesday morning.

In one section of that massive line of mills on Lake Michigan's southern shore, I rode with a black union official and watched him as he chatted with workers leaving their jobs at the change of shifts. We had been driving along with the windows shut when someone shouted his name. He stopped, rolled down the window.

"How ya doing," an older guy asked.

"Just fine," he replied, "The wife is due anytime now."

"I hope it's a boy," the white man shouted. "See you Thursday."

There was genuine affection in the voice and eyes, not only of that man, but his two companions.

A final factual point. In union elections in the United Auto Workers, and some other unions as well, black men are routinely elected as stewards, vice-presidents, and presidents by predominantly white locals. And this is not in one or two exceptional cases, but all across the country. The area said to be filled with tension and hostility simultaneously is the most democratic and tolerant sector anywhere in America.

The nature and extent of the prejudice and racism that exist are the most important questions about working-class political attitudes. Many people have come to believe that, while white racism has always been a part of America, today workers' attitudes have become steadily worse, in a "backlash" against black demands, and they are now far more intolerant than the middle class. These presumed changes have shattered the liberal dream of reestablishing the "new deal" coalition of blacks, white workers, and liberals, even on the limited basis which at least elected Roosevelt to the presidency and allowed the unions to organize. Instead, tolerance is now supposedly a middle-class characteristic.

One source of evidence is public opinion polls. While it is correct to have a healthy skepticism about how well a poll predicts actual behavior, if one takes them at face value, as nothing more than what people say about the issues, they still are quite useful. One would have to ask a lot of questions all over the country to get a similar input of information about what workers are saying.

But the real problem is that not enough careful studies have been done. The Harris poll does not even break down its data by occupation and the Gallup polls include black and white, male and female workers together in their "manual" category. Since these polls are also small, and comparisons between occupational groups can be off by 6 or 7 percent simply because of the laws of chance, this is no way to extract from them any solid information.[6]

Fortunately, there are a few studies which overcome some of these problems. The best, and in fact the only book-length examination of workers' political opinions is Richard Hamilton's *Class and Politics in the United States* which was published in 1971.*

Taking the North (or more precisely, non-South) first, here are Hamilton's data for what could be called general equal rights attitudes, which he calculated from a 1968 University of Michigan Survey Research Center study.

CIVIL RIGHTS ATTITUDES OF NON-SOUTH WHITES[8]
BY CLASS IN 1968
(Married White Respondents, Head Economically Active)

	Percent in favor			
Question	Operatives, laborers, and service	Skilled	Lower middle	Upper middle
Government should see that Negroes get fair treatment in jobs	49	44	43	45
Government should see that Negroes can go to any hotel or restaurant.	67	62	64	65
Government should see that white and Negro children go to the same schools.	55	40	48	47
Negroes have a right to live wherever they can afford to.	82	88	85	82

* Hamilton divides the upper and lower middle class by income for the reasons noted in the previous chapter. He also examines the North and South separately, for as he found, the two regions have very different patterns of racial attitudes. The 1968 data incidentally are not from the book itself, but from two articles he wrote soon after.[7]

The conclusion is evident. There is simply no significant difference between workers and the middle class. In fact, workers appear to be a tiny bit more progressive, although the difference is insignificant. And these questions not only involve simple democratic feelings, but support for government programs to enforce equality in the key areas of jobs and schools.

A series of somewhat similar "equal rights" questions was also asked in 1968, by a different polling organization, the National Opinion Research Center. The opinions of non-South manual workers vs. nonmanual workers are shown below.

CIVIL RIGHTS ATTITUDES OF NON-SOUTH WHITES BY CLASS, 1968[9]

Question	Blue-collar	White-collar
Do you favor fair employment laws that make white people hire qualified Negroes, so Negroes can get any job they are qualified for?	89	88
If a Negro with the same income and education moved into your block, would it make a difference to you (percent given is those saying no difference)?	83	88
Negroes have a right to live wherever they can afford to— just like white people.	85	84
Should black and white go to the same schools or separate schools (percent saying same)	80	89

It must be granted that some of these responses have probably changed for the worse in the years since 1968, under the impact of the issues like crime and quotas. Also, on more intimate issues like interracial dating, there is far less tolerance (6 percent of workers are favorable, 13 percent of the white-collar group). Finally, these questions are clearly posed in the least provocative way, making them harder to disagree with.

But even so, these responses are in stark contrast to the common wisdom. If blue-collar workers are, indeed, so much more racist than the middle class, one would expect at least some indication to appear. Yet, on broad social issues like these, the difference cannot be found.

CIVIL RIGHTS ATTITUDES OF SOUTHERN WHITES BY CLASS, 1968[10]
(Married White Respondents, Head Economically Active)

	Percent in favor			
Question	*Operatives, laborers, and service*	*Skilled*	*Lower middle*	*Upper middle*
Government should see that Negroes get fair treatment in jobs.	50	22	19	44
Government should see that Negroes can go to any hotel or restaurant.	47	13	38	52
Government should see to it that white and Negro children go to the same schools.	35	14	20	34
Negroes have a right to live wherever they can afford to.	55	37	49	67

In the South the general levels of tolerance were lower for every social class, but what stands out is the gap between skilled workers and the rest of the working class. The Operatives, Laborers, and Service workers, as can be seen, were just as tolerant as the upper middle class and better than the lower middle class on three issues, and only on one was there a significant difference in favor of "elite" tolerance.

The huge gap between skilled and unskilled, however, is very different from the North. What is especially interesting about this is that many union leaders and other observers of the South have always felt that poor southern whites seemed to often be highly tolerant of blacks and got along with them quite well from day to day. Many writers felt that the reason was that the low wages and status of the "poor white trash" did make them an oppressed group to a much greater extent than the northern white workers. This study gives concrete support for such a view. (As we will see, in strikes and actions across the South there are examples of interracial unity among workers occurring today.)

Other studies of working-class attitudes, although by no means as careful and systematic in their methods, have shown the same pattern. Another large study in 1968, by the Michigan University Survey Research Center, shows no class differences on questions like "do you favor civil rights legislation?" or "do you favor interracial contact?" The study notes that "The racial orientation of white people at different occupational levels differs very little." [11]

But all this is based on opinion polls and it is easy to suspect that workers will act far differently than the middle class when it comes to real life. The vote for city referenda on open housing is about as "real life" as one can get, and studies have been done on how people voted in the middle sixties. In two cities, Berkeley and Toledo, the authors of one study drew the following conclusion:

> "In neither city were blue collar workers in toto far from the Caucasian mean and they exhibited *less* intolerance than white collar workers, exclusive of professionals who are sui generis (i.e., a special case). In fact the most intolerant segment in Toledo was white collar workers with incomes below $7,000, whose rate of support was 3%. . . . In Toledo the support rate of unskilled and semiskilled was slightly above the city mean, whereas the least support was among white collar and skilled workers." [12]

Another study during a Detroit Open Housing Referendum concentrated on voting by income. The results showed lower and lower middle income people gave 32 percent of their vote in favor, middle income 21 percent, the upper middle 24 percent, and only the upper income group was higher than the low paid with 52 percent.

In summarizing these three cases, plus an additional California referendum, the author of the study concludes:

> "The highest incidence of antagonism to open housing is among white collar low income workers, not the [white] working class . . . [their] *support for the laws in the referenda somewhat exceed that of their bosses and social superiors, the business proprietors and executives.* . . . Skilled workers are one of the most antagonistic sectors whereas other blue collars matched or slightly exceeded the white mean." [13]

This alone deals a rather heavy blow to the myth that workers are the worst racists in America. But there is other evidence as well.

Another investigator looked at the white voting in segregationist referenda in fifteen southern cities about a decade ago. He found that in eleven cities there was no voting difference between lower socioeconomic status groups and upper status groups. In three, the lower groups were more liberal than the rich, and in only one of the fifteen did workers seem to be any worse than the middle class.* [14]

More recently Professor Chandler Davidson studied the voting patterns in three southern cities, and Memphis in particular, looking for evidence that the lower class voted in a more racist way than the upper strata. He looked at twenty primary elections in which there was a clear choice between a candidate who was a liberal on the issues of race and economics and one who was conservative in both areas. The results were quite clear. In every single vote lower-income groups tended to be more liberal than those of higher socioeconomic status. Even in six nonpartisan elections or referenda, where there was no possibility of straight ticket voting, the results showed only one case of greater working-class intolerance—two of greater middle-class intolerance and three with no difference.[15]

Thus, "real life" votes on open housing or segregationist referenda and elections between liberals and conservatives, show that workers have been, if anything, slightly more progressive than the middle class. The belief that workers are all reactionary while the middle class is "tolerant" on issues relating to blacks is clearly a myth. While the popular image of workers has been based on a few dozen or sometimes a few hundred workers involved in demonstrations, the evidence

---

* It is not really correct to call these groups "workers" and middle class since this and the following studies used income, not occupation, and therefore low-paid white-collar workers get mixed in about one quarter of the time. But if anything, the previous studies suggest that low-income white-collar workers are less tolerant than blue-collar workers and therefore should make the "lower socioeconomic" group look more racist, not less so, than blue-collar workers alone would be.

here is based on the behavior of *hundreds of thousands* of blue-collar Americans. And along with the opinion polls it clearly shows how wrong the stereotype is.

Some recent opinion surveys which ask questions like, "are blacks pushing too hard?" or "asking for special treatment?" however, reveal a very real hostility among white workers. One 1970 study, which asked the two questions above along with a third about whether "blacks deserve the things they are asking for," found that 70 percent of blue-collar workers took a "racist" view on all three questions. On the other hand, only 42–43 percent of the middle class selected the hostile view on all three.[16] Other studies have shown smaller, but similar, effects.

But despite these new areas of antagonism, the paradoxical fact is that white working-class racism, even in the North, was much worse in the forties and fifties than it is today. If there was no George Wallace on the national scene in 1956, nor other anti-integration demonstrations at that time, it was simply because there was no pressure for change. There is more obvious tension today, but that is because the crisis of the ghetto and consequently the nature of black demands has grown at a much faster rate than the white responsiveness. It is nonetheless true, however, that the white worker of today has less difficulty accepting black demands than did his counterpart of the fifties.

As many black leaders have noted, the much touted "tolerance" of the North in the fifties and early sixties, especially among workers, was in large part based on a rigid system of de facto racial segregation.

The phrase "don't go through south Jersey" for example was known to every northeastern ghetto black in previous years because black people just passing through that area were subject to harassment. Even in New York, blacks who ventured to Times Square in the late fifties were often told to "get the hell back to Harlem where you belong" by a policeman, unless they were delivering messages or sweeping out an office.

In literally scores of working-class neighborhoods across the North, a black man found after dark was in serious danger of being beaten up unless he could justify his presence. While schools had some black students, they frequently walked home in a group, especially if the hour was late. And if a black dared to move into a white neighborhood, on more than a few occasions some men with shotguns smashed every window in the house. Many northern plants had separate lockers and washrooms and a system of segregation just as thorough as Mississippi's.

When this is recognized, it is clear that a real change has taken place. In some areas, the unofficial discrimination still exists, and even de facto segregation in the plants. But clearly the average white worker today has much more contact with blacks and accepts the elementary rights of blacks to a far greater degree than before. Residential integration is still not accepted, but there has clearly been a change. Working-class racism has been a constant reality since the beginning of America. But in historical perspective it cannot be said to be becoming worse.

Opinion studies from the forties, fifties, and sixties confirm this view. As Hamilton notes, "A comparison of studies which asked identical questions in 1942, 1956, and 1963, with insignificant and fragmentary exceptions, showed an immense and continued shift toward more favorable attitudes." He also notes that even the data from 1968 "indicate a continuation of the trend." [17]

But there is one final point that helps to explain the seeming contradictions in working-class attitudes, the combination of real tolerance in some respects, together with areas of clear hostility. While liberal intellectuals think in terms of black and white and base their concern on an abstract sense of egalitarianism, the positive aspects of workers' attitudes are based on the common problems and sense of injustice they share with working-class blacks. Listen, for example, to a worker quoted by Robert Coles:

"I get sick and tired of welfare cheaters and worse are the hippies who sit around doing nothing, but they call up Daddy if they run into trouble, and the Niggers always pushing, pushing. But what the hell, who really is in charge of this country? Who is calling the shots, and who is raking in the money? Not the poor colored people. I'll tell you, it's not them. What have they got for themselves out of this country for all the damn back-breaking work they done since they got picked up in Africa by guys with guns and sent over here like cattle." [18]

Or listen to a Chicago steelworker interviewed by Studs Terkel:

". . . I can't really hate the colored fellow that's working with me all day. The black intellectual I got no respect for. The white intellectual I got no use for. I got no use for the black militant who's going to scream about 300 years of slavery to me while I'm busting my back, you know what I mean [laughs]? I have one answer for that guy—go see Rockefeller, see Harriman, see the people who got the money. Don't bother me, we're in the same cotton field, so just don't bug me[laughs].

"It's very funny, it's always the rich white people who are screaming about racism. They're pretty well safe from the backlash. Did you ever notice it's always 'go get the Klans-

men,' 'go get the honky,' 'go get that Polack,' 'don't touch me
baby cause my name's Prince John Lindsay, Park Avenue,
Lake Shore Drive . . .

"How the hell am I going to hate the colored fellow when
he's sweating and I'm sweating. We're both working hard.
When a strike comes I carry a picket sign, he carries a picket
sign . . ." [19]

Where workers see a common working-class issue, they
respond "tolerantly." But when the issue poses the needs of
blacks as a whole against all whites, workers often become
incensed at being lumped together with the affluent and seeing
their problems ignored. Many workers genuinely accept the
demands for simple justice being made by black workers. But
few can relate to the liberal intellectual's focus on issues like
improving welfare benefits or seeking to understand the black
criminal. Where "racism" appears most dramatically among
blue-collar workers is in those aspects of black protest that pit
the needs of what used to be called the "lumpenproletariat,"
the disorganized families of the unemployed, against those of
workers.

But, as we have seen, all workers, black and white, have
profound problems and pressing grievances that demand
solutions. It is now also clear that the stereotype of workers as
the worst, hopelessly racist sector of American society is just
another in the string of myths about working people that must
be put aside. There are, of course, deep currents of racism in
working-class America. But the notion that only the middle
class is capable of tolerance and change is nothing more than
an elitist fantasy. The facts about workers' opinions paint them
as something less than the proletarian saints intellectuals made
them in the thirties. But they also suggest the outlines of a
strategy that could free the progressive movement from the

stalemate between black and white that has held it captive in recent years and allow it to begin moving forward once again.

Richard Hatcher is the black mayor of Gary, Indiana. He is a short, good-looking man with a style that alternates from easygoing to intense. When he is describing events which have occurred in the years since his first election in 1968, he leans back in his chair and speaks easily, with frequent flashes of a cutting wit. But when he turns to the broad issues facing black America, he sits up and his eyes fix on the listener and one feels his deep desire to convince you—to make you see what he is trying to say. His office is small and intimate, and curtains that cut out the light make the conversation seem less formal than in some huge office with sunlight streaming in the windows.

I did not know Mayor Hatcher's feelings about the relations of the black and white steelworkers who make up the population of Gary when I met him. But considering the obstacles he had faced in the election, I suspected that he had seen the problem at its worst.

The democratic machine had fought him bitterly, and he had only a handful of white allies.

Wild allegations of Communism were made all during the campaign, and Hatcher was accused again and again of being a violent revolutionary or a black powerite. Some people who worked in his campaign were followed home and threats and actual beatings occurred. Hatcher himself received death threats and a tremendous hysteria was whipped up.

The struggle came to a head a few days before the election, when a white woman went to Hatcher and revealed a massive vote-stealing plot. Only the intervention of the Justice Department, under the pressure of some liberal Democrats on the national scene, prevented the plot from being a success.

These things ran through my mind as I asked him about black and white workers in Gary.

"To begin with," he said, "I think I and my administration started out with a false premise, based on the election returns, that 100 percent of the white, blue-collar workers felt the same way the very reactionary city councilmen and commentators did. (I guess it was similar in a way to the judgments many whites make about black people.) And so during the first few years of my administration, we did two things. First, we tried to overcompensate by bending over backwards in terms of city services and so on. For example, when there was a snowfall, the trucks went to Glen Park first (the white working-class area), and then worked their way back to the central city. This had absolutely no impact on the problem, because the political representatives simply exploited the issue by saying, 'See what I did for you. They didn't really want to do it, but I made them do it.'

"But basically we assumed that the blue-collar workers themselves did not really want to communicate with us, and did not really want to work with us. I used to walk down the streets of Glen Park and people wouldn't even speak to me. They, of course, knew who I was and after that sort of treatment you really start getting gunshy, so to speak.

"But a crisis developed when one councilman, along with some other people, decided he would get a movement going to disannex an entire section of the city. That really forced me to try and overcome some of my own reservations. If that particular area of the city was able to disannex, then I could just see other sections of the city doing the same thing, so it obviously had to be stopped there.

"So that's when I first began to really talk to people, even people who didn't want to talk to me. I found some people who really weren't concerned about me but felt that if the disannexation went through they would have to pay higher taxes. They agreed to hold meetings in their houses. So for a period of about six or seven weeks I was going to three, four, five meetings an evening in that area and meeting and talking directly to people out there.

"I found out that, contrary to what I had assumed, there were varying shades of opinion about the whole issue of black-white relationships. Some people had a kind of 'take it or leave it' attitude. Some were really hostile, you could feel it and hear it in their voices. Others were very positive. You know, 'I've known black people all my life and I don't have any problem working with them.' They stop short of inviting you to marry their daughter, but they have no problem with coexistence. That was extremely helpful to me.

"The whites, in turn, I think for the first time, found out the truth about the rumors that they had always heard, such as that I was in favor of killing all white people. Some people really asked me questions like that, and they would be amazed when I would say, there was a 'degree of inaccuracy' in that statement. But the result was that they would leave those meetings and would start calling friends and say, 'You know, I just met with the mayor last night and he said . . .' It just started spreading, and it was so successful that it just killed the whole disannexation movement, which was very hot at the time. Not only that, but the councilman who started it tried to run for Congress and suffered a smashing defeat at the hands of a liberal. He did not even carry his own precinct, and he certainly did not carry that district. Winning that victory required an enormous amount of work and energy, but it showed that such battles can be won."

III

Several thousand students slowly filed past the shops and buildings of the downtown area. It was 1969, in a midwest city, and the issue was the war in Vietnam.

My Nam vet neighbor from blue-collar Milwaukee was near the front, marching under the banner of the "Vietnam Veterans Against the War."

A big young man, about twenty-six or twenty-seven, wearing paint-spattered overalls and with a pair of work gloves hanging from his back pocket was shouting at the passing demonstrators. His face was livid with rage and the veins in his temples stood out clearly as he cursed the passing marchers. He was literally screaming that he had "been there" and he knew the truth.

Most of the marchers moved to the center of the street to avoid him, but my neighbor walked right up. During the Tet offensive he had faced a Viet Cong suicide charge that had overrun his position and ended in hand-to-hand combat, so it was unlikely that any one man could intimidate him.

"First Cav?" he asked.

The guy looked for a moment and replied, "Yeah."

"Me too, around Hue during Tet."

"Yeah?" the guy said, looking more closely.

They began exchanging the names of CO's and others they knew in common. After some more idle reminiscing my neighbor suddenly said, "Look, we were over there— we know what was going on."

"Damn right," the other replied.

"Well, hell, you know we should have never gotten in there in the first place—you know we didn't belong there."

"Yeah," the other guy said dubiously.

"Well, that's all we're saying," my friend replied.

"Yeah, but I just can't take them damn kids who don't know what we went through, saying we're all a bunch of killers, and that the Viet Cong are all saints."

"I got six ounces of lead in my ass that shows that's not true. But I just don't want anyone else killed in that mess."

"I agree with you on that, but I just can't stand these hippies."

"Well, maybe you'd like to join the vets against the war—we all were over there too."

I listened to all this in stunned silence. In five minutes my neighbor had changed a guy who looked like a borderline psychotic into not only a reasonable man, but was suggesting he join the march. And, although the guy refused to join, the change in him was astonishing. There was clearly more going on than the issue of war and peace. In a very basic way the issue was class and class distinction. Looking at the rows of students passing by, that counterdemonstrator was furiously hostile. With a guy whom he recognized as a peer, both as veteran and worker, what appeared like inflexible reaction was converted into a viewpoint not so very different from that of the people marching by. Once again one's easy assumptions turned out to be wrong.

Liberals have tended to lump together blue-collar hostility to students—a reaction to "radical" tactics like the occupation of buildings, and flag-burning—with blue-collar feelings about the war itself. But this is profound error. As we shall see, the working-class hostility to hippies and flag-burning is not based on the same assumptions as their attitudes toward the war in Vietnam.

At the beginning, in 1964, opinion polls indicated that blue-collar workers were probably more "antiwar" than any of the higher status groups. Even studies that attempted to prove the opposite—that workers were the most reactionary—had to admit that this was the case. There was a small group of liberals who criticized our involvement, but the main source of opposition was not from the middle class. It was, in fact, very similar to the range of attitudes held during the Korean War. At that time, also, blue-collar workers were more likely to want an end to the hostilities.[20]

As the war continued, however, it became impossible to find any valid studies of working-class opinion. The results of different questions, the failure to separate blacks and whites, men and women, or North and South made it possible to support almost any interpretation one wished. Not one systematic study has ever been done of class and the opinion "data" on the war in Vietnam.

Just as an example, however, of the opinion polls that do exist, a 1970 study, which at least confined itself to northern white workers, showed the following:

PERCENTAGE OF NORTHERN WHITES IN FAVOR
OF IMMEDIATE WITHDRAWAL[21]
(OR WITHIN 18 MONTHS), 1970

Working Class	48.9%
Middle Class	40.9%

There are many other studies which have shown similar comparisons, but while they look impressive, the fact is that a competent researcher could drive a small truck through the gaps in the data. There is, for example, evidence that workers tend to choose the "extreme" positions, both hawk and dove, while the middle class is more susceptible to appeals to "support the President." [22]

But one thing the various polls do not support is any image of workers as having been all prowar and the middle class as antiwar. By the seventies it was clear that most Americans, of all social classes, were fed up with the fighting and wished we had never become involved in the first place.

Again, one can doubt whether or not opinion polls tell the real story. But referenda, this time on the war, provide some indication of "real life" behavior. Six referenda have been studied and the results are as follows:

In three cases (Dearborn, in 1966 and 1968, and San Francisco, in 1967) working class communities were more likely to support the anti-war referenda than were middle class neighborhoods. Only in the case of San Francisco did blacks constitute a significant factor.

In two cases (Beverly Hills, Cal., and Madison, Wisconsin) there was no measurable difference between the working class areas and the middle class one, except for skilled workers in Madison, who tended to be somewhat more hawkish.

In only one case (Cambridge, Massachusetts) did the results fit the popular stereotypes. In that city the professional and managerial neighborhoods did give clearly greater support to the referenda than the working class areas.

The conclusion that the author of this study drew was that "disapproval of the war appeared to be related to working class rather than high status characteristics. In most communities as the proportion of voters possessing low status attributes grew, the vote against the war continued to mount." [23]

Thus, on the war in Vietnam, also, the stereotype does not turn out to be true. The evidence again suggests that American workers may actually have been slightly less militaristic, not more so, than the middle class.

This conclusion, however, seems hard to square with other indications of working-class opinion like the ostentatious displays of patriotism by many workers, the pasting of flag decals on cars, and the hanging of flags on their front porches.

And, even more difficult to understand is the clear indication opinion polls gave that, while they were not enthusiastic about the war itself, workers reacted to student protests and demonstrations with a fury that was, indeed, frightening.

The following polls from different sources, although typically inadequate for any real precision, are probably not too far wrong:

	Blue-collar	White-collar[24]
High hostility to student demonstrations (1970)	50	30
Student protest and demonstrations unjustified (1970)	62	53
Student protest is violence (1968)	43	—
	(union members)	
Draftcard burning is violence (1968)	63	—
Police beating students is violence (1968)	45	—

In this area workers are clearly intolerant, especially in the last two questions where draft card burning is considered violence by a majority while police beating students is not.

The questions these statistics raise is obvious. Why were many workers so hostile to students and student protest while they were also opposed to the war in Vietnam?

Many commentators have focused on the "threat to traditional values" and the "old-fashioned patriotism and morality" as answers to this question, and undoubtedly they play a part.

But there is another factor which is of crucial importance. The year 1968, when this hostility came to a head, was exactly twenty years, one generation, since the announcement of the "fair deal" for American workers. The children born at that time had reached college age only to discover that the promise had been broken. Older workers saw their kids going into the Army or the factories while college continued to be reserved for the middle class. Thus, when students began to shut down campuses or burn flags, workers responded more than anything else to the fact that these weren't "their" kids, but the ones who had kept their children out—the students had 2-S (student) deferments, another middle-class amenity denied to workers, and were therefore safe from the danger. Finally, when they began to call policemen "pigs" it added a final element of class elitism and snobbery.*

One worker described his feeling toward students in the following way:

> I've got one son, my youngest, in Vietnam. He didn't have a chance. He couldn't get out of it by going to college. He says that all the men there are in the same boat. They come from average families just like ours and a lot of them are bitter as hell about being picked to go over there and get killed. They just don't get the same breaks as the college kids.
>
> Of course, my son's willing to do his duty to his country if he has to. And I feel the same way. But we can't understand how all those rich kids—the kids with beads from the fancy suburbs—how they get off when my son has to go over there and maybe get his head shot off. They get off scot free . . . and when they see they're going to graduate from college, and maybe get drafted, they raise such a stink.[25]

* The popularity of the word "pig" as an epithet for policemen among students in the sixties was a fascinating example of the class prejudice which is still very real in America. Although most student "radicals" in the sixties would deny that they were engaging in middle-class elitism against all workers by using that term, workers clearly recognized it for what it was.

The word "pig" has always been an upper-class insult to deride the poor, based on the image of pigs as living in filth, eating slop, and being tremendously fat from an excess of carbohydrates.

None of these characteristics have any relation to the real criticisms students have of police behavior. It is not an accident that during the thirties, when striking workers clashed with police, both public and private, they called them "goons" or "thugs" or "hired gorillas," but never "pigs." Equally in other countries like Mexico when peasants and workers sought a metaphor to describe the vicious paramilitary forces of the government, they chose the word *halcone* or vulture. These images captured the real criticisms common people had of the injustices of the official authorities. The word "pig," however, related to none of the transgressions of the policemen. It is an insult that an elitist will use to refer condescendingly to the lack of education and "culture" of the classes below. Students may have deluded themselves as to their motivations but workers were fully aware of what was going on. Policemen were often their neighbors or relatives, and if policemen were "pigs" so were they. (Ghetto blacks also used the word "pig," but the word has a fundamentally different significance when applied by the poor to someone above them on the social ladder, e.g., the cliché of the "rich pig.")

Thus the issue of class is again tangled up in this area of working-class "reaction." Workers were "reacting," but in significant part to the fact that their kids went to Vietnam while middle-class kids went to college. And no one seemed to mind that particular piece of injustice except them.

IV

The 1972 elections have also been cited as proof of the conservative tide raging among blue-collar workers. The clear appeal of George Wallace and Nixon's significant inroads into the blue-collar vote have both been noted again and again as showing a basic shift to the right in workers' political stance.

A full discussion of the 1972 elections and why they had the results they did must wait for a later section. But far from being a simple question of workers' attitudes somehow automatically "drifting to the right," the growing discontent of blue-collar workers, the changing structure of the labor force, and liberal strategy itself all played a part in the Wallace and Nixon phenomenon. The last issue especially, errors in liberal strategy, is a crucial element in the way working-class political attitudes have changed.

But there are several other points which must be made in this chapter simply because the real changes that the election signified have been wildly exaggerated in some segments of the liberal community, creating a hysterical picture of a fascist threat from working-class America.

One writer, for example, summarized the election as follows:

. . . [McGovern] could hardly have been McGovern and been accommodating too—in terms of issues at any rate—so long as the "middle" stuck heroically to its segregation, its militarism, and its indomitable defense of corruption and other low forms of governmental life. Some prophets, notably John Gardner, had been announcing the end of the middle's apathy, but on the dark days before the election it looked as though the apathy was over only because it was being replaced by something worse, namely the positive assertion of all the middle's worst vices.[26]

But is this true? The vote for Nixon and Wallace are cold facts. But the conclusion that workers have all become reactionary is not. Certainly the data we have seen up till now contradict this interpretation. While it has shown substantial racism, nowhere can the "reactionary worker" and tolerant elite be found.

George Wallace's vote, for example, was indeed a sign of reaction, but even in 1968 it was recognized that in addition to racism, he skillfully blended in a "populist" or more precisely a "class-conscious" appeal to the discontents of workers. He said:

> Now what are the real issues that exist today in these United States? It is the trend of pseudointellectual government where a select elite group have written guidelines in bureaus and court decisions, have spoken from some pulpits, some college campuses, some newspaper offices, looking down their noses at the average man on the street, the glass workers, the steel workers, the auto workers, and the textile workers, the farm workers, the policemen, the beautician, and the barber, and the little businessman, saying to him that you do not know how to get up in the morning or go to bed at night unless we write you a guideline . . .[27]

Also while commentators focused on his inroads in the North, his working-class support in 1968 was still overwhelmingly southern. (He received only about 8 percent of the northern working-class vote, his biggest support coming from the small towns and rural areas of the South.)[28]

Scammon and Wattenberg, in fact, note that Wallace's real problem was being perceived as so far out on race that it hurt his class-based appeal. They say:

> . . . as the campaign drew to a close, Wallace was increasingly perceived as a regional candidate, and one who would not handle the law and order problem effectively. Wallace, in short, went over the far side of the social issue—if the American people wanted order and an end to discombobulation, they do not want it from a man perceived as an extremist or a racist." [29]

This squares with the responses one heard from northern workers, that while Wallace "said some really good things," he was "too far out" to actually receive their vote.

In 1972, however, before he was shot, Wallace did seem to be far stronger than in 1968. Although no really precise calculations have been made, he did win majorities, or more often, substantial minorities in working-class districts.

But although there is no evidence that deep in his heart Wallace changed his segregationist opinions, his public rhetoric was very different in '72 than it was in '68.

He scrupulously avoided overt segregationist or even "racist" rhetoric ("racist" in the pure sense of claiming that blacks are genetically inferior or do not deserve elementary democratic rights instead of sophisticated ploys like referring to unnamed "criminal elements"). During the campaign he asserted that he was opposed to busing, but also claimed he accepted nondiscrimination in the schools. When blacks in Pittsburgh tried to get into the skilled trades, he defended the exclusionist unions by saying that they are aware "that people of every race are entitled to work," and they "adhere to a national nondiscrimination policy of employment." He was only concerned, he said, about the problems of "unqualified" workers.[30]

This of course did not alienate his racist constituency, who knew that "ol' George" was just playing politics when he used such subterfuges.

But it allowed him to reach out to the far larger body of workers who considered the Wallace of '64 or even '68 "too far out" in his views. Consider the following description from *The New York Times* of one blue-collar Wallace voter in 1972:

> . . . Dewey Burton is twenty-six years old, short and thick, with a gravelly voice and gap tooth grin . . . His job begins at 5:52 A.M. as the first car moves past him on the assembly line. He calls the black man, who is the president of his local union, the "best president we've ever had." He has no qualms about his son, David, going to school with blacks, and if a black family moved on his block he would not object. He bets they would take better care of their home than the white folks on welfare down near the corner, whose conduct scandalizes him.
>
> But he is violently opposed to busing. Even one-way busing that would bring black children into his son's school three blocks away, saying "my child will never be bused into Detroit or anywhere for integrational purposes. Busing, that's the only issue I'm interested in. That's the biggest issue in this campaign . . ."
>
> . . . But he also insists "If a black mama and daddy buy or rent a house here and send their kids to David's school and pay their taxes, that's fine."
>
> . . . In 1968 Mr. Burton voted for Hubert H. Humphrey as a union man "coming from a long line of F.D.R.

Democrats" . . . His mother-in-law, Violet, was leaning toward Mr. Wallace as the third party candidate, but Mr. Burton persuaded her to vote his way, calling Wallace a "racist."

. . . Mr. Burton, never a soldier, does "not give a damn about the war."

"It has never concerned me," he said. "People getting killed concerns me. When this war is over, there will be another one. Maybe it's just because it keeps big industry going, keeps people employed."

"We're fighting a civil war, you see. You see thirty Vietnamese running down a road in the newsreels and you don't know if they're friends or enemies."

Burton voted on November 7. He reluctantly chose George McGovern. "I really don't think McGovern will win. But maybe if we vote for him we can show Nixon what we want, what the working man wants." [31]

Dewey Burton is without doubt not a "typical" Wallace voter, but there are millions of workers like him who gave Wallace his increased vote in 1972, workers who are not wild racists or militarists and who are not asserting "middle America's worst vices."

The blue-collar vote for Nixon also can't be treated as proof that workers are now terrible conservatives in comparison with the "liberal" middle class.

Much of the shock and horror that was expressed at Nixon's inroads into the working-class vote is really based on a variant of the "workers are stupid" bias of many commentators. It is assumed that the middle class makes up its mind on the issues in every election, while the workers are "traditionally Democratic." (Translation—too unintelligent to read the papers and decide who they want for President once every four years.) So the very idea that workers would stop voting Democratic was seen as cheating. Workers are supposed to keep quiet and vote the ticket, because they are "traditional Democrats."

But everyone makes a choice on election day, and workers do choose who they want for President every time they vote. So the real question is: who gave the most support—who were the real conservatives?

The question answers itself. Nixon received the vote of a little more than half, 54 percent, of union families, according to the Gallup polls. The upper middle class, however, the professionals and businessmen, gave him 69 percent of their vote. Even the college educated, the "tolerant" liberal elite who are always portrayed as an island of reason in a sea of prejudice, gave Nixon a whopping 63 percent of their vote. Even when one calculates in the fact that there is a greater proportion of blacks in unions than in the higher categories, it does not reverse this basic relationship between class and support for Nixon.[32]

Finally a fact noted by many commentators must be repeated. The "conservative" blue-collar vote for Nixon did not extend beyond the presidential race. When they turned to the candidates for Congress and state office, workers still voted for liberal Democrats, showing that it was the candidate and not the general principles of liberalism that were being rejected.

An October, 1972, Gallup poll in fact revealed that had Edward Kennedy been a candidate, he would have received over half the blue-collar vote. McGovern, in that survey, had 44 percent, while Nixon had 49 percent. In a Kennedy-Nixon contest, however, Kennedy had 53 percent of the working-class vote and Nixon, 41 percent. Since blacks voted almost unanimously for McGovern, this entire 12 percent point change was the result of white workers indicating their continued willingness to vote "liberal," if the candidate suited them.[33] Although using a different analysis, pollster Louis Harris also concluded that:

> The post-election evidence is simply not there that Nixon's mandate mirrors a deep and abiding desire on the part of the voters to rally to the roster of the so-called middle American "social issues," centering on crime, permissiveness, and resistance to change.[34]

V

The evidence in this chapter all adds up to one conclusion. The vision of workers as the most conservative sector of the population, like working-class affluence, is fundamentally a myth. While racism and militarism do exist, workers are no worse and perhaps even better than the middle class on many issues, and none of the problems which pitted them against blacks or students results from any "inevitable" conservatism. We have postponed for later   more precise discussion of the elections, but it must be noted that, while they were a disaster for Democrats, the real danger is that the wrong lessons will be drawn from them.

At this moment, it appears that this is exactly what is happening. The Democratic Party is currently warming up for a fratricidal struggle over how to regain their lost blue-collar support. But the issue is being posed in terms of "how far to the right must we move to win back blue-collar workers, how far do liberals have to retreat from their goals of aiding blacks, and opposing war in order to get a Democrat into the White House next time?"

Everything we have seen in this chapter shows that this is wrong. Workers are not blindly reactionary on the issues of race or militarism. More than anything else, they are becoming fed up with having their legitimate needs ignored. As we have seen, the real issue is class injustice, the systematic way that American politics has given them a "raw deal."

So rather than trying to move to the right of Nixon, which workers are too sophisticated to accept, and which verges on the impossible anyway, the opinion polls and the referenda all suggest that what is needed is not to retreat, but to move ahead. Workers will respond if liberals deal with the needs of all working people, black and white, on the job and in the community instead of blindly endorsing programs that often penalize white workers and let the affluent off scot-free. Equally, there is no need to send troops or money to every banana dictatorship on earth in order to win working-class votes. Workers are as opposed to that as the middle class is. Instead, end the extremes like calling their neighbors "pigs" or supporting the victory of the troops who are killing their children. And most important of all, if liberals deal with the issues we saw in the last two chapters, the data show that workers will give their support. Senator Fred Harris put the issue very succinctly when he said that "The blue collar worker will continue to be progressive so long as it is not progress for everyone but himself." [35] This has been the major source of blue-collar discontent, and will continue to be until it is changed.

Professor Davidson, who was quoted earlier, summed up his findings with the following remarks which apply to all of America as well as the South where he did his study:

In the last analysis then the shape of southern politics in the future depends largely upon what the candidates have to offer. We have shown that many less affluent whites will vote for the same candidates as do blacks when appeals are made to their economic interests as well as to their sense of justice. A large part of the white southern electorate is presently receptive to progressive change. And the candidate who fails to take account of this fact has no one to blame but himself.[36]

CHAPTER FIVE

The Influence of Unions on the Working Class

ONE WAY OR ANOTHER, unions will be a key factor in determining the role workers will play in the coming years. Although they have never been able to dictate to workers what they should think or do, no other institution can even remotely approach the influence unions have on the lives and opinions of their membership.

At one time, this influence was seen by liberals as basically positive. Although there was much to criticize in the unions of the thirties, liberals viewed the labor movement, and the CIO unions in particular, as one of the most progressive forces in the society. But this attitude has obviously changed in recent years. A variety of issues, from the loss of the "idealism" of the thirties, to the corruption, the lack of internal democracy, and the patterns of racial discrimination within the unions has led many to lose faith in that positive view.

The criticisms liberals make are, in large part, valid. The issues mentioned above are not condescending myths like the notions of "affluence" or "authoritarianism," but harsh realities, and some of the strongest condemnations, in fact, come not from outside labor but from progressive unionists themselves.

But these failings, along with other events like the support unions gave the war in Vietnam, have led many people to conclude that the unions have not simply fallen short of their ideals, but decisively shifted from the side of progress to that of reaction.

As the authors of a *Washington Post* series on the unions note:

> To liberals and the Left, the unions are often regarded as one of the most reactionary forces in America, a special interest group concerned only with money and defending the status quo.[1]

This view comes out in assertions that labor and management have become essentially similar. Jeff Greenfield and Jack Newfield in *The Populist Manifesto*, for example, announce that "Indeed, watching labor and management is sometimes like watching the pigs and the people in Orwell's *Animal Farm*, you can't tell one from the other." [2]

This view clearly identifies unions as a basically conservative force in American society. Its proponents often hedge that bitter conclusion with statements of respect for the "best traditions" or "basic ideals" of unionism. But if one cannot even distinguish business, which progressives agree is conservative, from the unions, then obviously the labor movement is a basically conservative force.

If the facts supported this view, the prospects for the future would be considerably dimmed. But fortunately they do not. One can be sharply critical of the failings of American unions and fault them for falling short of their own ideals, while at the same time totally rejecting the idea that they are objectively conservative or reactionary. Granted, anyone seeking an American counterpart of the Chinese Red Guard will be deeply disappointed, but in a realistic and practical perspective the role of unions is basically positive both in national politics and in workers' daily lives. In fact, in more than a few important areas, it can be demonstrated that unions are one of the most progressive forces in American society.

Before this can be shown, however, it is necessary to see something of the day-to-day operation of the unions and the impact they have on workers' lives. For, like life in the factory itself, the daily operation of unions is a part of working-class life largely hidden from other eyes.

I was watching TV when Walt, my downstairs neighbor, knocked on the door.

"What's up?" I asked as I let him in.

"They did it again. This time old man Bradley didn't get his overtime check, so I got to call the rep and my phone's out."

His big, grizzly-bear body nearly filled the doorframe, and I stepped aside as he entered. Walt was originally from the Blue Ridge Mountains, and only his sharp eyes and quick, easy laughter belied his hillbilly style.

He was working as a diesel mechanic in a bus company, but it was his position as shop steward for the dozen or so men in the garage that was occupying him now.

"You figure it was on purpose?" I asked.

"Well," he said slowly, "it could just be a mistake, but it's the second time, and I think they may be trying to make me look bad so's they can get rid of the union."

"Lovely people you work for," I said sarcastically.

"Regular bunch of bastards," he replied, picking up the phone.

The "rep" he referred to was the area representative of the union who had responsibility for a number of small

shops like the one where Walt worked. The headquarters of
the union was in another city several hours' drive to the
north, and on a day-to-day basis, Walt was the only
representative of the union in the shop.

Like all stewards, Walt doesn't get a salary from the
union. But he has the right to stop work when a problem
occurs and go up front and argue with the manager or file a
grievance. A voice came on the line and Walt began
describing the problem to the representative, pausing
frequently to listen to the questions he put.

"Hell, no, I can't prove they did it on purpose, but I sure
bet they did. I mean, even if it's an accident, they shouldn't
go fooling around all this time, should they?"

I reached over and pulled the well-worn copy of the
contract out of Walt's back pocket and began thumbing
through it as I listened. When Walt first was elected
steward, I remembered we had spent an evening reading
through it and trying to understand the complex legal
language. Since then Walt had, bit by bit, put cryptic notes
to himself in the margin, like one alongside the section on
his protected rights, which read, "No f with SS." Since SS,
I realized, undoubtedly meant shop steward, I couldn't
control a quick laugh at his terse translation.

Walt had finished his conversation and hung up the
phone.

"What's funny?"

"You should write the next contract," I said, showing
him the section, "I like your version better."

He smiled, putting the contract back in his pocket.

"The rep says he'll stop by tomorrow. That ought to
make them a little jumpy."

"Give them some hell," I said.

"I'll just do that," he replied as he passed out the door and
headed back down the stairs to his apartment below.

A thousand miles away from my downstairs neighbor is the union hall of a large steelworkers' local. The office where I was sitting was fairly large, but four desks and some fifteen workers milling around made it feel somewhat less spacious than a telephone booth. This room is where workers come to seek the union's aid in the battle against management actions that seem unfair.

Sitting across from me was the black vice-president of the local and head of the grievance committee. He was speaking into the telephone, becoming more and more irritable. "Look," he said, "I've got a receipt for the election meeting. A hundred and nine guys showed up and voted, but somebody's got eight hours listed as lost time. Now I don't care if he counts on his Goddamn fingers, it don't take eight hours to add up a hundred and nine votes. I'm taking it up with the executive committee."

The conversation continued, becoming a bit more spicy but repeating the same points. I began to listen in on the men filing along to explain their grievances to the stocky man in charge of problems like theirs.

The first was a young, good-looking guy with blond hair and a goatee. He couldn't have been more than twenty-five and his English was thick with an Eastern European accent.

"I vas three times with the shofel," he said. "When the supervisor, he said that I vasn't doing enough . . ." The rest was lost when someone else opened the door and began a shouted conversation with someone on the other side of the room.

The next in line was a young black, dressed in the long black coat and knitted cap that has become the hip fashion in many areas of the country. The union guy was familiar with his case. The young black had filed a grievance months before and had won the case before an arbitrator. Since then he had become the target for hostile supervisors and had almost been fired on several occasions. Now, in addition, he had found an error in his latest paycheck.

The union guy quietly took notes and then made a phone call. He turned to the young black man and suggested that they first fight the attempted dismissal and then turn to the error in the pay envelope. After a short discussion of which was the better tactic, they agreed, and the young black swaggered out, his dramatic dress achieving its intention and capturing all eyes.

After him came an older white man in his forties, who was dressed in a ski jacket and the thick rubber boots required for some jobs in the mill.

His question concerned an opening for a promotion on another shift and whether or not he was eligible. After a quick reference to two large volumes that sat on his desk, the "griever" agreed that he was, and proceeded to get in touch with the supervisor. The man rose and said, "Thank you," before he left. The union man smiled in return.

II

In theory, everyone knows that unions are not political parties or "cause" groups like the Americans for Democratic Action. But in practice many discussions focus so totally on the political or legislative aspects of union activity that it almost seems as if they are. But unions are essentially local organizations whose basic job is to win concrete benefits for their members. So to understand unions, the place to begin is not in the Washington headquarters of the AFL-CIO, but hundreds of miles to the south in a low-wage, recently unionized plant, and the first man to listen to is not a member of the executive council of the federation, but Walt, the steward mentioned above, as he describes what it was like before they organized the union.

They used to shift people around and give compulsory overtime anyway they wanted. I once worked nine straight days, two shifts a day, because they were short-handed. If they hadn't got someone on that last day, I would have quit.

We had this guy who had been there about ten years and he was dying to get a promotion to mechanic. But when there was a vacancy, the boss put his brother's son-in-law on the job. The kid had knocked up the guy's daughter and had to marry her, so the boss gave him a job.

This is the first contract. It's got lots of things wrong with it that we're going to deal with next time. But at least we got something. Now when they mess around, you can walk right in there and say, "Now that just ain't right," and they got to deal with you like a man. Before the union, if I had said that they would have said, "Get your coat and get the hell out of here." But now they know that if they mess around, it won't be just me but the whole damn shop that will get up and walk out.

The union also negotiated a pension plan and a modest salary increase for the workers. The economic gain was tiny but, as Walt said, "The main thing in a first contract is just to establish the union. The second contract is when you get down to business."

On a national scale, while the gains unions achieve vary widely, generally they do win significant gains for their members when they "get down to business." One Labor Department study, for example, estimated that "Blue collar union members average . . . about $2,000 more than their non-union counterparts." [3] Another comparison, one of the few that ever appeared in the popular press, noted that union members clearly received higher wages than comparable nonunion workers (up to 40 and 50 percent in certain industries). In addition, the article noted that they had better fringe benefits like vacations, better health and job upgrading provisions, as well as the grievance procedures. It concluded that "There seems no doubt that the pros outweighed the cons." [4]

But beyond the specific benefits, there are also the less quantifiable gains like the dignity and independence that comes when "they have to treat you like a man."

Sometimes these things can be more important than the concrete gains. As Myra Wolfgang, International Vice-President of the Hotel and Restaurant Employees, said:

> I have come to the conclusion that those [younger restaurant workers] who joined the union joined because they would like to have someone around who will call the boss an SOB. They are just dying to call him that, but they don't dare because they want that extra money. So they look for a mouthpiece in the union. That is why my public posture has to be one of a general hell raiser. [5]

It was not an accident that the Memphis garbage workers, in whose strike Martin Luther King was killed, chose the slogan, "I am a man," to symbolize what unionization meant to them. The unions are, in fact, the only force that brings democracy into industrial America and keeps workers from being totally powerless from nine to five.

Thus, it must be realized that in their most basic task, winning concrete improvements for their members, unions generally do their jobs, and often quite well. They play a profoundly positive role.

Above the locals are the 185 different national unions in America. While some are huge, the majority are so small that they have little political influence even in the AFL-CIO, the federation to which most belong. Most unions have under 50,000 members while fourteen large and powerful unions have over half of all organized workers in America.

DISTRIBUTION OF UNIONS BY SIZE[6]*

# of Members	Number of unions with this many members
1–50,000	112 ⎤
50,000–200,000	46 ⎬ 47% of all union members
200,000–400,000	13 ⎦
400,000–2,000,000	14 ⎱ 53% of all union members

More significant than size, however, is the difference between industrial unions and the skilled trades. While frequently singled out as the conservative wing of the trade union movement, it is not always made clear that the skilled trades are also a basically different kind of labor organization.

An industrial union organizes an entire factory, shop, or other workplace where workers are already employed. A

* The twenty largest unions and their members are listed below.

TWENTY LARGEST UNIONS, 1971[7]

Unions	# of Members
1. Teamsters	1,829,000
2. United Automobile Workers	1,486,000
3. Steelworkers	1,200,000
4. Electrical (IBEW)	922,000
5. Machinists	865,000
6. Carpenters	820,000
7. Retail Clerks	605,000
8. Laborers	580,000
9. Meat Cutters	494,000
10. Hotel and Restaurant Employees	461,000
11. State, County and Municipal Workers	444,000
12. Ladies' Garment Workers	442,000
13. Service Employees	435,000
14. Communications Workers	422,000
15. Operating Engineers	393,000
16. Clothing Workers	386,000
17. American Federation of Government Employees	325,000
18. Plumbers	312,000
19. Electrical (IUE)	300,000
20. Musicians	300,000

skilled trade union, on the other hand, organizes individual workers with a particular skill, and in addition to questions of wages and conditions, the union must be centrally concerned with ensuring that its members find work.

This basic difference leads to a crucial consequence. An industrial union, by its nature, tends to unite workers and pit them collectively against the company. The demands for higher wages, better conditions, and so on all pose workers' needs against those of the company and not worker against worker. Especially in the postwar period when many companies gave up the use of strikebreakers, and seniority arrangements provided a stable mechanism for deciding which workers were laid off in slack periods, many of the key sources of conflict that existed between workers in the thirties were eliminated.

Skilled workers (and construction workers in particular) generally do not have one permanent job. Instead they are referred by the union for the few weeks or months it takes to complete a project, after which they are once again without work.

Thus, union carpenters, for example, are not united against a large common employer for year after year. Instead, the most direct threat that they face comes from other blue-collar workers. Unemployment, as we saw, is a major problem. In 1970, 30 percent were unemployed at some time during the year.[8]

The result is that instead of finding common interest with other workers, the construction craftsman is often pitted against his fellow workers. In a very real sense, a plumber, for example, has more in common with the owner of a small store than with classic "proletarians" such as assembly line workers.

For many years when there were sufficient jobs, this

conflict was muted by an unofficial truce in which union craftsmen constructed most large buildings (which jobs were more desirable because they ensured a longer period of employment), while nonunion workers did the smaller jobs, including the overwhelming majority of single-family houses.*

In recent years, however, this truce has broken down and many contractors have switched to nonunion labor, even for large projects like hotels and commercial buildings.[9] At the same time, innovations like prefabricated components or paint sprayers have reduced the necessary manpower for certain jobs and eliminated others.

These changes are the basis for much of the turmoil in the construction industry. Although not widely known, serious clashes, verging on pitched battles, have occurred between union and non-union workers. In Florida, where a good deal of construction is going on, there are frightening stories of beatings and serious injury. In Prussia, Pennsylvania, non-union contractors allege that over a thousand Philadelphia unionists participated in an attack against the equipment and buildings of one contractor, causing $300,000 in damage.[10]

The pressure to ensure jobs for their members also leads construction unions to battle against each other. The jurisdictional strikes, where two unions like the pipe fitters and the laborers both claim the right to do certain jobs, arise from this, and there have been clashes between various unions as well as between unions and the "scabs." [11]

This same pressure has led to the highly publicized cases of "featherbedding" where the unions force contractors to hire unnecessary labor to keep their members employed.

In a basic sense, the construction trades still suffer the worst problems of the thirties. The pervasive job insecurity creates

* For this reason, the construction unions are justifiably irritated when people blame the high cost of their houses on the trade unions.

bitter tensions and conflict, not so much between workers and management as between workers themselves. As we shall see, this basic reality influences the racial policies, internal affairs, and politics of the skilled trades.

But to deal with the political role of unions on the national scene, the central force is the AFL-CIO, the federation to which 120 of the 185 unions in America belong.

Perhaps the central point about the AFL-CIO is that, as its name implies, it is a federation, not a union in itself. As one union official noted:

> The AFL-CIO doesn't negotiate contracts or process grievances. Its basic role is political, lobbying for legislation, supporting candidates and so on. It also acts as arbiter in jurisdictional disputes and does research and some other things, but most of its effort goes into politics.[12]

While the largest national unions do operate on their own in the political arena, most unions have a limited involvement. As another official said:

> Unions are really very limited in the political role they can play. Because people have no idea of what unions do, they imagine that we can dedicate all our time to politics, when in fact our resources are really very slim. The primary responsibility has to be the workers we represent, to administer the pension fund and to make sure it is well run, to handle the grievances and contracts, and run the other services we have. Because there is no labor party in America, unions are sometimes expected to fill that role. But they can't, and they never have, not in America or anywhere else for that matter.[13]

This, as we shall see, has a great deal to do with the political stance of trade unions in America. But the first and most pressing issue with which we must deal is the continuing stain of racial discrimination.

III

The evidence of union racism and injustice toward blacks is clear. Like many other sectors of American society, unions have been guilty of serious discrimination against the black population. But to understand the issues involved, it is necessary to look separately at industrial and skilled trades unions.

In industry, blacks have no problem gaining admission to the union. As we noted, industrial unions, by their nature, have to organize everyone in a particular plant or shop if they wish to have any power. Even in the thirties, it was recognized that it was impossible to exclude blacks from membership and still build a viable union. In terms of membership alone, industrial unions are the most integrated institutions in America.

But blacks do have problems in the area of promotion and access to the better-paying skilled occupations. In 1971 only 5.4 percent of the skilled jobs in industry were held by blacks.[14]

The industrial unions have a system of seniority that is democratic in theory. In choosing among several men who are capable of doing a job that requires more skill, seniority dictates that the man who has worked for the company the longest be selected.

But a large industrial plant is most often divided into departments, and upward mobility for workers limited to the better jobs that open in their particular section. The opportunity for advancement can vary widely from department to department, and blacks are very frequently trapped in virtually dead-end jobs which are often the lowest paid and dirtiest as well. In a Bethlehem Steel plant in New York, for example, a federal court of appeals found:

> A microcosm of classic job discrimination in the north. Job assignment practices were reprehensible. Over 80% of black workers were placed in 11 departments which contained the hotter and dirtier jobs in the plant. Blacks were excluded from higher-paying and cleaner jobs . . . the pervasiveness and longevity of the overt discriminatory hiring and job assignment practices are embodied in nationwide agreements, negotiated between company and union in 1963, 1965 and 1968.[15]

While, as the court noted, the discriminatory aspects of the seniority system are codified in joint agreements between the unions and company, it should also be noted that, since the forties, unions have not had any direct control over who is hired into the various departments, and while they acquiesced in racism, it was personnel managers and foremen who made the concrete decisions that resulted in the injustices of today.

In the skilled trades, on the other hand, the problem blacks face is simply getting into the unions. As the chart below shows, in many cases the number of blacks is startlingly small. But it is a common mistake to think that this discrimination is based on a simple desire for segregation and that, for some reason, factory workers can accept the physical presence of blacks while construction workers cannot. The frequent remark, that the "economic" issues are a blind for simple racism, is simply not true.

On most construction sites, you will see black men carrying wood or doing other tasks. They are members of the unskilled Laborers International Union which is heavily black. They get along with whites more or less as factory workers do. The

Skilled trade unions	# Members	% Black[16]
Mechanical Trades:		
Boilermakers	138,000	4.3
International Brotherhood of Electrical Workers	921,000	1.8
Plumbers and Pipe Fitters	311,000	1.2
Ironworkers	177,000	2.0
Sheet Metal Workers	120,000	1.0
Other Trades:		
Carpenters	820,000	3.6
Operating Engineers	393,000	3.7
Painters	210,000	3.7
Trowel Trades:		
Bricklayers	142,000	7.4
Plasterers and Cement Masons	68,000	18.3
Roofers	24,000	16.8
Laborers	580,000	28.5

range of styles goes from very comfortable conversations and banter to occasional incidents of real hostility, the general rule being a cool but tolerant mutual acceptance. In the newspaper descriptions of demonstrations that blacks have held at construction sites one will usually encounter a sentence or two describing the embarrassing moment when black laborers are faced with crossing the picket lines.

As in the industrial unions, though, blacks are kept out of the high-paying skilled jobs and concentrated in the unskilled laborers' union and the "trowel trades," the bottom rank of skilled construction labor. The difference between industry and construction favors the former by only 2 percent. As we noted, 5.4 percent of the skilled jobs in industry are held by blacks in comparison to 3.3 percent in the construction trades. The fact is that the problem of discrimination remains today the saddest failure of American unionism to live up to its own ideals.

But there are three points that must be made to put the issue in perspective. The first, made by Patricia and Brendan Sexton, two progressive trade unionists from the United Auto Workers, is, "Even in the carpenters' unions, among the most exclusionist, black membership is about 2% of the total, higher than black proportions in most northern college faculties." [17]

Second, unless progressives seriously deal with the idea of full employment and government-guaranteed jobs, the question of black representation in skilled jobs has to become a question of throwing a white carpenter, for example, out of work, in order to employ a black, or make a Pole tend the coke ovens while a black gets a better job. The white carpenter will then go on welfare and the Polish worker will get cancer (as coke oven tenders often do) instead of the black.

This is not meant as an argument against racial justice, but an indication of the difficulties. Again and again, as we have seen, the problems of black people are part of the larger problem of class injustice. While racial justice demands that blacks not suffer the brunt of unemployment, complete justice demands that no worker should suffer because the economy does not find him of value. The demand for an end to all forms of racism in the unions is entirely valid. But the struggle for an end to black unemployment and low wages and poverty is a demand that must be made of the American economic system and not the unions alone.*

* In regard to the problems white workers face in this area, some people have demonstrated a capacity for self-delusion and lack of contact with reality that would make the average acid-head green with envy. Hodgson, the Secretary of Labor in 1971, for example, described the "only" effects of quotas for blacks as the "disruption . . . of the expectations of some white employees." [18] Translated into basic English, this delicate euphemism means that a white worker instead of a black one will be stuck with a job with low pay, bad conditions, and in the case of coke oven work, a higher probability of contracting cancer. It is the job that is unjust, and not the color of the man who does it. But "disrupting the expectations of some white employees" gracefully skirts that reality.

Lastly, the role and treatment of blacks inside the unions themselves is strikingly better than their treatment in terms of skilled jobs. Again, as the Sextons note:

> Though their representation is inadequate, blacks have won more influence in unions than in any other social institution. A study of black powerlessness conducted for the Urban League in Chicago and Cook County, Illinois, found that unions had a larger percentage (13%) of black policy makers than any other private institution. In welfare and religious organizations, whose constituents were often largely black, 8% of policy-making posts were held by blacks. Universities (including Chicago, a citadel of radical academic opinion) had a negligible 1% representation . . . Only five out of three hundred and eighty policy-making posts at universities were held by blacks.
>
> In three-fourths of the former CIO locals, blacks were represented in leadership. In two-fifths of the former AFL locals, no blacks were represented, but one-third had leaderships that were fifteen percent or more black. Even the AFL on this study looks better than Chicago's universities, churches, welfare and other organizations. Some of these institutions are learning that they can't cop out by claiming that there "aren't enough qualified black applicants," anymore than the sheet metal workers' union.
>
> In the UAW, . . . about eighty blacks serve as full-time international representatives . . . Perhaps only the NAACP and the Urban League employ a larger body of black policy makers. Two of the twenty-two members of the UAW's international executive board are black, as are the directors of some of the unions' national departments.[19]

None of this absolves the unions from the clear injustices that exist. But it suggests a certain caution in dismissing the unions as "hopeless," unless one is ready to say the same of every institution and force in American society.

IV

The headquarters of Local 1199, Drug and Hospital Union is only a few blocks from Times Square in New York, tucked away between two aging buildings. It represents some 50,000 hospital workers in the New York area, most of them black and Puerto Rican.

In the lobby was an exhibition of paintings and sculpture done by the members of the union. That alone suggested that this was a rather unusual union. In fact, 1199 is exceptional and worth looking at for a moment.

1199 was opposed to the war in Vietnam from the very beginning, and its members marched in every peace demonstration of the sixties. Martin Luther King called it "my favorite labor union," and its headquarters is named after him. Though small in size, it has been one of the most aggressive unions in organizing the unorganized. National attention was focused on Charleston, South Carolina, in 1969 when 1199, working with Mrs. Martin Luther King and other associates of her husband, won a pivotal strike of mostly black hospital workers whose impact was felt across the South.

A bank of elevators stood to the left. I hesitated for a moment, tempted to look at the paintings, but a glance at my watch told me it was already time to go up and see Moe Foner, executive secretary of the union.

I had met him a year before and I had discovered that he had two characteristics that are typical of many good union officials. First, tremendous energy and the ability to work under pressure, and second, the assumption that everybody else can do the same. In the course of three-fourths of an hour of talking with him, I found myself promising to make some phone calls on one matter and later ended up looking over the schematic diagram of the PA system to find out why the speakers in the meeting hall were buzzing, all because of a chance remark I made about having repaired radios several years before. It was a refreshing attitude, "There's work to be done, and as long as you're here you can help out." Foner and the other leaders of 1199 clearly believe that unions are still a social movement, not a business.

This passed through my mind as I rode up the elevator and the door opened. I got off and passed through a broad waiting room, and went into Foner's office.

I immediately had the feeling that he had not got up since I'd left him the year before. The phone was ringing and he had two projects underway. After a while, he stopped, sat back in his chair, spread his arms and said, "OK, what do you want to know?"

At one point, I asked him about the problem of corruption. Since I knew him personally, I was hoping for something a bit more substantial than the usual answers one gets when talking to union people about the subject—an answer equally composed of "Oh, there isn't much," and "Bankers do it too."

Foner agreed that the public image is far worse than the reality, but he continued beyond the generalizations and made one particularly fascinating point. He said: "A key problem, and one which is relatively modern, is the pension fund. Even a small union now has millions of dollars that it has to manage and invest. For a big union, it can run into the billions. On the one hand, big money and little supervision obviously invite misuse, but also there is a more subtle kind of corruption that is not even corruption in the legal sense.

"A union official who came out of the ranks and worked as a steward, for example, is going to have a militant outlook and some feelings for the ideals of the labor movement. But suddenly he is faced with the tremendous responsibility of administering several million dollars, and doing it well. So he has to become essentially an investment analyst. He starts spending his time with bankers and businessmen and moving around in that milieu. It's inevitable that his way of thinking undergoes a change. He loses contact with the things that motivated him before, and he starts to lose the sense of the union as a social movement.

"This kind of 'corruption' is far more common and really has a much greater effect on unions today, than the occasional guy who embezzles funds or builds himself a house with the union's money."

V

The answer which defenders of the unions give to the challenge of corruption is often the statistically proved fact that "More bankers are arrested for embezzlement than union officials." They might add, with equal accuracy, that corporate income tax evasion constitutes a theft of far greater magnitude than any financial chicanery by unions.

But such comparisons of blue-collar union crime with middle-class "crime in the suites," does not deal with the real issue. The existence of corruption and undemocratic practices has led many people to conclude that unions cannot be a force for change. One liberal political campaign manager I know said, "How can an institution with so much corruption and so little democracy in its internal life play a positive role in American politics?" *

* There is a real difficulty in dealing objectively with this problem. Many people get a negative image of all unions because, while the press presents excellent and necessary exposés of the worst offenders, descriptions of an uninspired but honest and reasonably open union local are not "news." Thus, many middle-class liberals are left with nothing but vivid descriptions of monstrous injustices, as in the United Mine Workers (before the victory in 1972 of an insurgent rank-and-file slate) where the pension funds were misused, demands for safety ignored, democracy completely stifled, and violence used against dissidents that culminated in the brutal shot-gun slaying of insurgent leader Jock Yablonski and his family. In fact, the press should have given even more attention than it did to exposing that ugly crowd, but it is wrong to imagine that the old UMW is in any sense "typical."

Industrial unions, in general, seem to be less corrupt than other unions, a result in part of their structure. The local industrial union does not control its members' jobs, which eliminates a crucial source of power, and the greater centralization of administration in industrial unions means there is less money floating around to provide temptation (pension funds, for example, invite the most abuse, and in large industrial unions they are nationally, rather than locally, administered).

An interesting illustration of this is that in the thirties, when meat products were handled by two unions, the skilled AFL butchers' union and the CIO packinghouse workers, which was organized along industrial lines, the butchers were generally recognized to be infiltrated by organized crime, while the Packinghouse Workers' Union, a truck ride away, was generally free of their influence. The militancy and dedication of the CIO organizers played a real part, but underlying it was the structural difference in the two kinds of organizations.[20] Exposés of corruption in recent years have, in fact, been mostly focused on nonindustrial unions.[21]

In any large union, however, there are some corrupt locals or officials. As one local UAW leader put it: "The UAW has a high reputation for honesty and it's deserved, but if you look you can find examples of bad locals. But, Christ, you're talking about an organization that has over a million members. The only place you'll find a million men and no crooks is in a graveyard." [22]

The 1950s offered some examples of the forms corruption can take. The leadership of the United Textile Workers in 1952 appealed to the AFL for an unusual amount of financial aid in an organizing effort. On investigation it was found that union funds were being used to purchase two houses and other personal possessions for the leaders. The Distillery Workers' Union in 1959 was charged by the McClellan Committee on

Union Corruption with "nepotism, careless bookkeeping and munificent salaries and expenses for union officers." [23]

The skilled trades, and construction in particular, has a far worse reputation. But in this area, it is vital to make a distinction between the most repulsive and inexcusable "corruption," which involves dirty deals between unions and management to exploit the workers (examples of which we shall see in a moment) and illegal activities that do not directly harm the interests of the membership.

Bribery runs through the whole construction industry. The contractor pays off the building inspector, the policeman gets a "piece of the action," city officials, state officials, and even the federal government is involved in a tangle of payoffs that have become an accepted system. [24]

Some union officials also get involved, forcing contractors to buy materials from their son-in-law's company, or otherwise using the threat of "labor trouble" to get benefits. But often such deals have little or no relation to the conditions of the workers themselves. Since the salaries of construction union local leaders are generally much higher than those of industrial union leaders, there is more opportunity for private investment deals, some of which may be shady (e.g., a contractor tips off a union official to the location of a new highway and the official buys land).

But at times such deals do harm the workers. Nonunion contractors have paid off union officials in return for tacit permission to use nonunion labor, while other contractors who refuse to pay are harassed. [25] Contractors may also pay off officials for the right to violate the safety provisions in the contract, manpower standards, and so on.

In fact, the entire system encourages corruption. As Frank Schoenfield, an official in the painters' union notes, "If the business agent doesn't play ball with the employers, then the employer won't hire his workers. It's a corrupt setup that rewards corruption. A corrupt business agent will have all his guys working, although maybe they'll have to do things that aren't in the contract. The honest agent tries to enforce the contract and his men don't work." [26] These opportunities arise because in construction and other similar unions, the union controls the jobs. As Jack Barbash says:

> There is a predisposition to racketeering in business agent situations which derives from the necessarily great power which the business agent exercises in the allocation of jobs . . . The racketeering may take the form of kickbacks by union members to the business agent in return for . . . job assignments as happened in the much publicized case of the longshoremen on the East Coast. It may also take the form of collusion between the business agent and employers in allowing deviations in the contract's labor standards in return for a bribe.[27]

But it must be noted that while corruption exists in the skilled trades' unions, on the whole they have won decent wages for their members.

The truly intolerable corruption, which preys on workers and harms their interests, is found in several specific areas and unions. The most important is in the hard-to-organize low-wage, temporary or "secondary" labor market in big cities. As Michael Harrington notes:

> The fact that the economic underworld is so hard to organize makes it a perfect place for two types of racketeers to operate: labor racketeers and their constant companions, the management racketeers . . . [in restaurants] the deal is very simple. The dishonest union man would demand a payoff from the dishonest restaurateur. In return for this money the

"unionist" would allow management to pay well below the prevailing union wage . . . There are Puerto Ricans who are members of unions they never even heard of. Their rights in these labor organizations are confined to the payment of dues. The businessman, who is so essential to racketeering unionism, makes his payment to the union leader. In return he gets immunity from organization and the right to pay starvation wages." [28]

Many of these unions are "independent," outside the AFL CIO, and others were in and out during the fifties.* In one case the leaders of a 20,000-member union were found by a federal court to have "embezzled, conspired or aided and abetted" in spending large sums (reportedly more than $50,000) from the union's pension fund. Other cases involved misuse of funds from a union optical plan and "sweetheart" agreements which virtually agreed to a permanent ban on strikes, even after the existing contracts expired.[29]

Some unions such as The East Coast Longshore and Maritime unions, and the old leadership of the Mineworkers and the Teamsters, for example, have bad reputations in regard to curruption. But in general, as Bok and Dunlop note in their study of the unions, "Union members have doubtlessly suffered more from inefficient and unimaginative administration than they have ever lost through corruption." [30] While hardly the most complimentary way the point could have been made, it does put the issue into perspective.**

---

* There are also some excellent unions outside the AFL-CIO, by the way, some of which were victims of the McCarthy hysteria.

** A few words need to be said about the Teamsters. One local UAW official who knows them extremely well tried to define them this way: "The thing you have to understand is that it's hard to even talk about the 'Teamsters' as a unit. The locals are unusually autonomous, and some of the guys I worked with were some of the most militant guys you ever met, while others were just plain crooks. In many areas of the country Teamster locals have a deserved reputation for being tough bargainers and getting really good contracts for their members. But, in some places, they sign real 'sweetheart' agreements. You really have to look at each particular case." [31]

The question of union democracy and rank-and-file participation is a bit more complex. Statistics on membership turnout for meetings or unopposed elections tell one little since, in some cases, members are basically satisfied or see little difference on the issues between two possible leaders, while in others they know the cards are stacked against them and that they can get in trouble for making waves.

In general, unions are probably about as democratic as a big city municipal government, a standard which is not very high. Union incumbents have many advantages and can offer rewards and punishments like any big city political machine. They sometimes use the union press without giving the opposition a chance to reply. The ballot can be made purposely confusing and a union meeting can be manipulated by a skillful chairman.

At the worst elections can be rigged, voting rules made patently unfair, dissenters fired from their jobs or occasionally threatened or beaten.

Attention has been focused on some of the worst unions, where violence and intimidation, as well as more subtle methods are used. The National Maritime Union, the United Mineworkers (before the victory of the rank-and-file slate in 1972) along with several others have been cited many times for dictatorial rule and violence against dissenters.[32]

But outright dictatorial rule is not typical. More widespread is the use of such tactics as denying jobs (in hiring hall situations) to union dissidents or the abuse of clauses in union constitutions which allow workers to be drummed out of the union on a patently phony basis. The UAW is one of the few unions which genuinely accepts caucuses and will even stick up for a critic if, for example, he is fired by the company. But in most cases dissenters or caucuses must be careful to stay within certain bounds or face the danger of being expelled from the union or at least of finding a variety of obstacles in their path. Industrial unions again tend to be better than those in other areas, but it must be said that, next to racism, a lack of full and open democracy and an intolerance for dissent is a central weakness of American unions.

But in attempting to judge the effect of these shortcomings on the labor movement's future role, it is vital to recognize that rank-and-file participation in most unions compares favorably with other social institutions in America. In the business world there is no democracy whatsoever. One secretary at a large corporation told me that her "lack of proper attitude" caused her to be called into the personnel office and asked if she would not "be happier elsewhere" because of a chance remark to another secretary who then "informed" on her. In university life the tenure system has been used against dissident professors probably as often as any of the tricks unions have used against rank-and-file dissidents. Even in universities with reputations for liberalism like Harvard, the University of Wisconsin, and University of Chicago, tactics have been used against unacceptable academic dissidents in many ways that would be familiar to a corrupt union leader. And in one regard, unions are uniquely democratic. The most important single issue for members, the contract the union negotiates with management, is voted on by the rank and file, and the wave of contracts rejected by workers during the sixties shows how important this right is to workers. Unlike national politics, where one votes for the man who makes the best promises and hopes that he will keep them, contract ratification gives workers the ability to have a say in the most important issue of the union's behavior.

Thus, while the problems are real and serious, it requires a severe double standard to dismiss the progressive potential of unions as that political campaign manager did. In fact, when we turn to politics, it becomes clear that on the national scene, unions have played a basically progressive role and their potential is tremendous for further action in the future.

VI

When I walked into Solidarity House, the headquarters of the United Auto Workers, I knew very little about Irving Bluestone, one of five UAW vice-presidents and head of the union's General Motors Department, the man I had come to see. Solidarity Hall is a large unassuming building in a black neighborhood that is only a few minutes from the center of Detroit, and directly across the river from one of the largest auto plants in the world.

I had heard Bluestone's name again and again in conversations and everyone had said that he was a man I had to meet. My appointment was for 11:00, and promptly at that hour his secretary ushered me into his office.

Bluestone fits no cliché expectations as to a typical union leader. His clarity of expression and breadth of knowledge make the word "intellectual" come to mind, and if he had chosen a career in that area, he would be the kind of professor whose classes are always overcrowded and whose students think up excuses to go into his office in the hope of a conversation.

Listening to him talk, one hears him systematically cut away the frills from ideas and focus on their useful core. One sees a man of action, but one who also thinks, and thinks deeply. The thing that makes Bluestone unique and so impressive, however, is that he so clearly uses ideas as tools, and does not just play around with them.

At one point, he said: "The labor movement should represent itself as a kind of quasi-public agency. It has to stand above the crowd in ethics and morals. There has to be a certain purity to it which is not generally expected within our kind of society. It has to be a movement which devotes itself to social causes far and beyond the immediate nickel-in-the-pay approach. And the difference between the two types of approaches within the labor movement are based on that problem. There are many labor unions in this country which operate on the basis of business unionism— 'What can I get for my people, that's what counts.' But there are others who think of the union movement in terms of what will do the most good for the broadest number of citizens in the country, and even the people in the rest of the world. This difference within the labor movement is a sharp one, and I would hope that eventually the total labor movement will move in the direction of seeing itself as a cause, as a movement, though even now we call it the labor movement. This means taking a very broad view of the welfare of the total, which on occasion might be in contradiction with the good and welfare of the immediate few who are represented by the union. It's a very difficult thing for a union to handle. I like to think that we in the UAW have been that kind of a union and will continue to be that kind of a union. There are those who pooh-pooh it in the labor movement and say 'these are dreamers,' 'these are impractical people,' but I believe that they are the ones who are impractical and unrealistic. It is the people who will dream and look ahead down the road and fight to move the whole of society in that direction who are, in the final analysis, the practical and realistic people."

The real issue behind the phrase "business unionism" is the question of the union's role in society, as Bluestone explained it, the degree to which they are forward-looking and deal with the whole society or restrict themselves to a limited and essentially defensive role. The "loss of idealism" and the charge that unions are part of the corporate structure ultimately come down to this question.

The content of "business unionism" lies in the change that occurred in the industrial CIO (Congress of Industrial Organizations) unions in the period after the Second World War. (The AFL skilled trade unions were always "business unions," and proud of it, even in the midst of the depression. They had ties with the Republicans at that time and startlingly *opposed* unemployment insurance, even in the face of millions of unemployed).[33]

The change was essentially the acceptance of collective bargaining at regular intervals and the use of strikes only when the contract had been violated.

Basically, the shop steward system and immediate redress of grievances was weakened. The national union made the best deal it could at contract time, but anything not specifically covered by the contract became management's "prerogative." Local unions, in general, lost the right to strike over local issues like hiring policies, occupational health and safety, work rules, and so on. Shop stewards were converted into lawyers who interpreted the contract, and spontaneous militancy was either channeled into that framework or exploded in wildcat strikes (i.e., strikes not sanctioned by the international union). A series of moves by management also made the grievance procedure more bureaucratic and cumbersome than before.[34]

Union leaders were caught on the horns of a very real dilemma. They could get a better contract at negotiation time if they demonstrated control over the rank and file. Thus, local issues and spontaneous militancy became a problem rather than something to be applauded. Management would not make as good a deal if they felt the union would not "live up to" its part of the bargain by preventing unauthorized strikes. And then, dues checkoff, the subtraction of union dues from the paycheck, while it freed the union for more important things, added a final element of distance between the worker and his union.

The loss of idealism about which liberals complain was in fact a loss of power, the acceptance of a crippling series of limitations on the spontaneous and militant role they could play. Most workers still support their unions and recognize their value in the daily operation of the plant. But there has indeed been a certain attrition of the union's role in the daily life of the people it defends.

The reasons for this change are more complex than a simple sell-out by leaders in return for "Cadillacs" and "room service."

First there was the disastrous Henry Wallace campaign in 1948. The base of his support came from CIO unions and when Truman preempted 90 percent of his rhetoric and a healthy part of his support, the CIO was isolated politically at a very difficult moment and Truman made completely free of debt to it.

Soon after came the Taft-Hartley Act which seriously restricted the prerogatives unions had before. And the expulsion of many left-wing union leaders and entire unions from the AFL and CIO also occurred at about this time, signaling the beginning of the McCarthy period. Finally, the widespread belief that the end of wartime production would lead to another depression led many unions to try to consolidate some gains in preparation for the crisis they anticipated. Most students do not remember that before the union contract, wages used to go down as well as up. The promise of guaranteed wage scales and certain other secure arrangements may sound petty today, but in 1948 they did not.

Understanding the reasons for this change, however, is not the same as justifying its consequences. "Business unionism," while its economic benefits are very real, is an insufficient philosophy in the best of times. In a period of rapid technological change like the fifties and sixties, however, it can be disastrous.

The unions did not respond with a realistic program to the challenge of technological advance. Instead each union has been forced to fend for itself, so to speak, with piecemeal programs aimed at lessening the impact of automation rather than integrating it into a new concept of work and workers in American society.

But again the central question is whether these changes have converted the labor movement into a conservative force in American society.

The answer must be no. The facts clearly indicate a decline of militancy and a partial triumph of "bread-and-butter" unionism over a broader social view. But a retrogression is not the same as a decisive change in social role. Many CIO unions were more militant and socially conscious in the thirties, but even today they are not "reactionary" in terms of the political spectrum or their role in helping American workers.

One "forgotten man" of the union movement, an old black organizer, a man who has fought in one of the least recognized struggles of the fifties and sixties, the attempt to "organize Dixie," made the following point:

You know, unions basically aren't radical institutions. Their job is to stick up for their members. Back in the thirties we were militant, all right, but the situation demanded militance. You had the whole damn country suffering like you young people wouldn't believe. My uncle used to eat garbage, literally. He'd go behind the restaurant and check out the garbage pails.

Now when things are like that, you're going to see some action. I'm a born troublemaker myself, I guess, and I couldn't deal with the pork chop stuff that goes on in an established union, but I recognize that once you win your union battle and your members start getting ahead in life you can't keep up the spirit like before.

But I'm a union man and will be until I die. Maybe you young folks are right, and we need a revolution. But I don't like it when I hear you people saying the unions aren't worth a damn. You ask some of the people we organized this year and they'll tell you straight out what a union does for a man. Don't get me wrong, there's too many Goddamn Cadillacs in this movement and a lot of crooks too. But I just went back to a meat-packing plant I organized in 1965 and, hell, you wouldn't recognize the place. You young people don't remember things like that, but I do.[35]

It is points like that which make one pause before dismissing the unions because they have fallen short of the progressive ideal.

VII

I was sitting in the tiny beaverboard cubicle that serves as the "office" of a congressional aide. I knew the man across from me from two years before when we worked on the congressman's first unsuccessful campaign.

"I've been thinking about what you said," the aide began, referring to a conversation we had had months before on the role of the unions. "And I really have come to see your point. I grew up in a little southern town where the one big union was corrupt and everyone knew it.

"But just sitting in the committees and watching the labor people in action, it's obvious that they're the only people who really put the pressure on for decent domestic legislation.

"On international affairs they drive me crazy,

"But you have to say that on domestic issues not only are they good, but they're the only ones with the muscle and balls to really get things done. Without them this country would move to the right so fast it would make your head spin."

More than any other area, the role the unions and the AFL-CIO in particular have played in American politics exposes the shallowness of the charge that they have somehow allied with reaction against progress. The factor which made such an interpretation possible was the foreign policy of the AFL-CIO and in particular the support that was given to the war in Vietnam. George Meany and the executive council of the AFL-CIO generally supported the war, while most progressives opposed it. In this area, there is a clear and basic disagreement.

But support for the war was by no means unanimous. The UAW was deeply disturbed by the stance of the Federation, and foreign policy was an important factor in their departure from the AFL-CIO. Other unions as well were displeased, and a meeting of trade unionists against the war in 1967, the "labor leadership assembly for peace," included 523 labor officials, including high-ranking officials from the UAW, the Amalgamated Clothing Workers, the Amalgamated Meatcutters and Butcher Workmen and the Woodworkers' International, along with many representatives of smaller unions and large ones whose official opinion was in favor of the war.[36]

By 1972, a second gathering of labor for peace supporters drew more than a thousand delegates, including the leadership of the American Federation of State, County and Municipal Workers and three vice-presidents of the Teamsters, along with other new additions to the unions who had come out in 1967.[37] But even granting labor's generally prowar bent in the mid-sixties, their record on domestic affairs is clearly progressive.

On the issue of black people, the 1963 and '64 civil rights bills not only received the support of the AFL-CIO, but this support was vital in ensuring their passage. In fact, labor itself insisted on the passage of fair employment provisions that would apply to unions as well as management (the reason for this seemingly contradictory position on union discrimination is that the leadership wanted to pass the "hot potato" to government and be able to cite national law as forcing them to make the needed changes). In addition, the unions have supported black candidates again and again and opposed the nomination of racial conservatives for the Supreme Court or other official posts. On virtually every social and economic program to aid not only union members but all underprivileged Americans their record of support has been constant and forceful. From funds for higher education to money for welfare, and rat control, they have been a positive force. On full employment their record is unmatched.

In addition, across a range of consumer and other "populist" issues, their role has been unparalleled. On tax reform, consumer protection, and election reform they have championed liberal and progressive causes.

Let us take, for example, the 92nd Congress. The following is a list of bills the AFL-CIO supported:

Jobs and the economy
(1) Equitable wage-price controls.
(2) Tax reform in favor of wage earners rather than corporations.
(3) Job creation and full employment measures including both public service and public works legislation to give jobs to the unemployed.

(4) Opposed revenue sharing as endangering social programs for the poor.

Housing and Mass Transit

(1) Lobbied for more low-income housing and a better rapid transit system to allow the poor access to jobs.

Pollution

(1) Supported laws protecting workers from "environmental blackmail" (the threat of unemployment if pollution standards were enforced). Labor also supported a bill for $24 billion in antipollution facilities and increased criminal penalties for pollution. In addition, labor supported pesticide, toxic chemical, and noise control legislation (they also supported Alaskan natives in their claim to 40 million acres of land promised by the government a hundred years before).

Health, Education and Welfare

The AFL-CIO supported

(1) National Health Insurance.

(2) Health personnel training.

(3) Increased aid to education.

(4) Busing and opposed all forms of segregation in the schools.

(5) Increased spending for free school lunch programs for the poor.

(6) Increased funds for the Office of Economic Opportunity, legal services, and comprehensive child development programs (day care was part of this).

(7) Increases in welfare benefits (including improvements in a number of areas).

Consumer Protection

(1) Supported creation of an independent consumer agency and measures to extend its powers.

(2) Supported product safety laws including criminal penalties for violation.

(3) Supported legislation for more meaningful product warranties.

(4) Supported no-fault insurance.

(5) Supported auto safety legislation improving auto collision standards.

(6) Supported better meat and fish inspection laws.

Civil Rights, Civil Liberties

(1) Supported stronger enforcement powers and coverage for fair employment laws.

(2) Opposed nomination of William Rehnquist for the Supreme Court as "antilibertarian" and racially conservative.

(3) Supported repeal of "Emergency Detention Act" (recommended for use against black rioters).

Election and Congressional Reform

(1) Favored campaign practices reform.

(2) Supported income tax deduction for political contributions by working people.

(3) Supported direct, popular election of the President.

(4) Supported home rule for the District of Columbia.

(5) Supported other reforms to make Congress more responsive.[38]

The list is long but it is important to see the number and scope of liberal measures the unions have supported.

And, in addition, as that congressional aide noted, labor's support for many bills is active and vital for achieving their passage. Between labor's lobbying activities under their Department of Legislation and the Committee on Political Education's (COPE) support for liberal candidates (many of whom they disagreed with on the war), labor is the central progressive force in Washington. Johnson and Kotz quote one AFL-CIO staffer as follows, "We are . . . the kingpin of any possible presidential election for a Democrat and very likely the only cohesive force that can assure relatively progressive majorities on the House and Senate."[39]

And they themselves note:

Beyond question, labor lobbying helped win crucially needed moderate and conservative votes for major social legislation, including a multitude of laws in the mid 1960s. "When you have a tough fight on any issue like day care or legal services," says Senator Walter Mondale (D-Minn.)," it's nice to say your bill has the support of the AFL-CIO. That support wraps the bill in a warm blanket of respectability." [40]

There is simply no avoiding the conclusion that, considering its power as well as its views, labor has been the chief force for progressive domestic legislation in America. Without them, there would be no Voting Rights Act, and therefore no black caucus. In Congress without a doubt many of the most valuable social programs would have been defeated and the very composition of Congress would have been far more conservative, without many of the key Senate doves who received labor support despite the AFL-CIO's support for the war. George McGovern, in fact, even as he was attacked by the AFL-CIO during the 1972 campaign, had a rating of 88 percent on the union's political scoreboard. This is not surprising since the AFL-CIO's Committee on Political Education ratings are generally identical to liberal evaluations except when the issue involves foreign policy or the loss of American jobs. In the first session of the 92nd Congress, for example, the positions taken by COPE were identical with the ADA except on Lockheed and the SST, two job-related questions. At the same time, labor and the right-wing Americans for Conservative Actions (ACA) disagreed on every single issue. [41]

Also the political viewpoint workers receive from their unions is solidly liberal and at times far more "radical" than that of the liberal critics who dismiss the labor movement as a force for change.

Here are some of the things workers read in their union press. On welfare, from the *AFL-CIO News*:

Lack of decent job opportunities, not unwillingness to work, locks millions of mothers in single parent families into the welfare system . . . 99 percent of the people in the Aid to Families with Dependent Children program are mothers and children in very deep poverty. . . .

Forcing welfare mothers into jobs . . . even if jobs existed, would leave preschool children without proper care and school-age children without the kind of supervision they need during afterschool hours and summer months. In most cases, "there is no alternative but for the mother to care for those children—and that's what's best for them."

On Martin Luther King, from a Steelworkers' union brochure:

As one of the great leaders of our nation, Martin Luther King, Jr., dedicated his life to the pursuit of non-violent resistance to racial injustice. He patterned his method after Gandhi, using non-violent means to fight social injustice . . . his speech, "I Have a Dream," moved the soul of a nation. In 1964, King was awarded the Nobel Peace Prize. He won worldwide acclaim, and became an international spokesman against war and poverty.

On military spending, again from the Steelworkers:

But the unhappy, bitter, ironic part of the Administration's misdirected budget cutting and impounding is the fact that it wants more money for the military. The Defense budget will be increased, despite an apparent end to our involvement in Vietnam. Such upside-down priorities do not make sense.

On gun control, from the Communications Workers' paper:

Not until we have the guts to get tough on eliminating unlicensed handguns will we stop the inhuman, senseless shooting and killing that is taking place in the United States.

On labor itself, from the *Machinist:*

> Someone once said that the story of mankind can be written in terms of the eternal struggle between those who "have" and those who "have not." It is hard to realize that only 40 years ago the vast majority of the working people of the United States and Canada were counted among the "have nots." Their wages were low. Their hours were long. Their claim to their jobs, or to fair treatment on the job, were non-existent.
>
> We have, by no means, corrected all the inequities of the work place. In fact, the power of concentrated corporate wealth is rising rapidly in both the United States and Canada. The "trickle down" theories of the 19th century are once more in fashion."

And, finally, a statement on George McGovern by the president of the Communications workers:

> His enemies have called him a radical. They say he favors unpopular causes (in much the same way Franklin Roosevelt favored the then unpopular Social Security Act).
>
> Well, every labor leader worth his salt was called a "radical" and has favored unpopular causes. Progress is not made by hiding in the musty attic of the old. Progress is made by venturing out into new wildernesses and conquering those wildernesses.[42]

Granted, these quotes were selected from pages and pages of more prosaic articles, and the conservative building trades, whose magazines have almost no political commentary are not included. But neither is the UAW, AFSCME, or any of the unions referred to as the "progressive exceptions" to the rule of union conservatism.

And one point must be recognized. Unlike the liberal magazines which do not reach workers and have circulations, at best in the thousands or tens of thousands, the union press reaches millions of workers and provides a solidly liberal counterpoint to the conservative views of *Reader's Digest* or other such magazines. And space does not permit giving even a tiny fraction of the articles on economic and working-class issues, where the viewpoint is uniformly progressive. There is simply no way to avoid the conclusion that unions, while they will not satisfy the "revolutionary," play an essentially progressive role and not a conservative or reactionary one in American politics, and in American society itself.

CHAPTER SIX

The Current Scene

ALL THROUGH THE FIFTIES and early sixties liberals saw labor as a "sleeping giant" who, they hoped, would soon awake. But in 1968, the Wallace campaign captured the nation's attention and suddenly it seemed to many liberals that the long-awaited "awakening" of labor signaled a threat to progress rather than the addition of a vital new ally. The 1970 attack on peace marchers and the misunderstood events of the 1972 elections seemed to cement this image in many people's minds and some liberals have now concluded that the best thing that could happen is for labor once again to go back to sleep.

But working-class America is not going to "go back to sleep" nor should liberals and progressives hope that it will. Wallace, "hard hats," and the blue-collar defection to Nixon in 1972 constitute only one aspect of the "awakening" of labor. And it was in fact time that blue-collar discontent was expressed. For it reflected two basic changes that occurred in the labor force during the sixties—the tremendous influx of blacks and the appearance of a new generation in the shops and factories of industrial America.

II

Ever since the strike of young auto workers in Lordstown, Ohio, in the winter of 1971, young workers have received a great deal of attention from the press. Reporters from *Life*, *Playboy*, *Newsweek*, and *Harper's* all flocked to that single plant and talked with the young employees, bringing back the news that they were a "new kind" of worker.[1]

But the change is not confined to Lordstown or auto workers alone. Many observers agree that all across America there is a kind of "youth rebellion" among the new generation of workers.

When I asked one local union leader about them, he replied, "They're different, all right, no damn question about it. They're better educated, make more demands and generally raise hell when something is wrong." Irving Bluestone brought up the subject himself when I spoke with him. "The generation gap exists in the plant as it does in the community at large. The younger worker coming in, whether black or white, is better educated than he was a generation ago. Studies indicate the worker currently entering the work force in industry has about twelve years of education on the average, as contrasted with eight years a generation ago, and with more education comes greater hope for what the future can hold. Aspirations are higher and part of our present scene is the individual 'doing his own thing' which I find to be extremely healthy, a damn good sign."

The rebelliousness of these younger workers has been expressed not only in greater demands, a lower tolerance for the abuses of working-class life, and simply wearing long hair, but also in some new and startling ways.

The most common has been absenteeism. At General Motors and Ford, absenteeism has doubled in the last ten years, and on Mondays and Fridays up to 15 percent of the workers in some plants fail to show up. Frequently they do not even bother to give an explanation or a forged doctor's note which is easy to obtain. In many auto plants, there is no longer any serious attempt to enforce the rules on absenteeism.

There is also a tremendous rate of turnover. Some workers simply work until they have enough to get by on for a while. A few just get fed up and walk off in the middle of a shift, leaving their post without a word.

Another manifestation of the discontent is shoddy workmanship which often extends to petty sabotage. It ranges from tools welded into fenders, scratches in the paint, and torn upholstery to deliberate acts of destruction such as a case in a pharmaceutical plant where several pints of cheap wine were poured into the small vat of mouth wash, or another where green dye was mixed with dog food.[2]

A sudden up-surge in the use of drugs is also part of the young workers' new style. Precisely because of the dull and frustrating nature of the work, marijuana, amphetamines, and even heroin have become more and more prevalent. Amphetamines in particular have become more and more popular as an aid to working long hours or on speeded-up lines. Heroin addicts in some factories have passed out right in the plant. During the break on the late shift where young workers are concentrated, it is not unheard of for a joint to be passed quite openly from hand to hand.[3]

Finally, increasing numbers of young workers are questioning and even refusing to accept both archaic regulations and the authority of the foreman. Their new assertiveness, unhampered by memories of the great depression, has been expressed in record numbers of grievances filed against employers and numerous charges of unfair labor practices as well as petitions and direct refusals to obey the rules. In one steel plant, disciplinary actions against workers for breaking the rules climbed from a few hundred in 1965 to 3,400 in 1970. While in the past, the worker would be fired after three disciplinary actions, some now have up to eight and are still working.[4]

However, while the signs of a new kind of spirit of dissatisfaction have appeared all over America, the place which has come to symbolize the insurgency of young workers was the protest and strike in the winter of 1971 in a single GM plant in Lordstown, Ohio. What made the struggle significant was not the specific issues nor the particularly heavy-handed approach of GM's management. Rather it was the unique spirit and aggressiveness of the young workers, a spirit that seemed to suggest the possibility of widespread pressure for reform developing in the coming years.

The roots of the Lordstown struggle go back to the fall of 1971 when several hundred men were dismissed and many of their tasks divided among remaining workers.

What the speedup generated was an uncoordinated but devastating retaliation. Many workers allowed cars to pass by on the assembly line without performing the required operations and occasionally engaging in deliberate acts of sabotage. When the question of a strike prompted a union meeting, an extraordinary 85 percent of the men attended and cast a virtually unanimous vote in favor of stopping work.

During the strike itself, workers refused to let nonstriking office employees enter the plant, and they coined the phrase "white shirts" to highlight the differences between them. The spirit of the strikers was captured in a few sentences by Gary Bryner, then the twenty-nine-year-old president of the local. "These guys have become tigers. They've really got guts. You used to not see them in a union meeting. Now we've got them in the cafeteria singing Solidarity." [5]

Although the strike was settled in three weeks and the

concessions limited to specific issues, the Lordstown strike had a profound impact on GM and the entire business community. While it was by no means the first time workers had ever struck over factory issues such as speedup, the spontaneous militancy of the workers was startling. Russell Gibbons, the longtime labor leader, called the strike, "The most dramatic instance of worker resistance since the 1937 Flint sit-down." [6]

But though the strike was dramatic, it was not unique. Union officials note that a far longer strike by older workers over similar issues was also taking place in Norwood, Ohio, and serious discontent not of strike proportions was apparent at other GM plants where pressure had increased.

But there is something very new in the attitude and life-style and behavior of young workers. The quiescence of labor in the fifties, although it has been exaggerated by writers who had no firsthand experience with the factories of those days, was to a certain extent very real. It was based on two factors and a part of the explanation for the current surfacing of discontent is that neither applies to the new generation.

The first reason for quiescence was the lingering memory of the depression. For the men who lived through those years the discontents of their work were always secondary to the simple economic fact that they were employed. While the workers of that generation were never in any meaningful sense satisfied with their jobs, they tolerated them because of the experience of the thirties.

The generation that has followed them, however, has begun to look at the factory not in comparison with the breadline, but in comparison with the jobs held by the middle class. Such a comparison not surprisingly favors the middle class and leaves workers with a deep sense of frustration and justified discontent, untempered by the gratitude their parents felt for finding work of any kind.

The second factor that held discontent in check in previous years was the myth of the American dream. While the middle class took the affluent society as fact, the working class took it as a promise, the promise that they were the last generation of factory workers, whose children would almost surely advance into the ranks of the affluent. It was, as we have seen, a comforting myth, but in retrospect a cruel one. In 1970 only 30 percent of all young people eighteen to twenty-four were in universities or even technical schools. Of the majority who were in the labor force, more than two-thirds were in working-class jobs.[7] The new generation of workers is entering the factories where their fathers worked before them. But unlike their elders they are entering without fear or illusions.

In addition to these underlying factors, the young workers now entering the factories are in a real sense part of their generation. In their lives they have seen protest and insurgency win victories for other groups. The unquestioning faith in the "system" often ascribed to "middle America" has been substantially eroded for young workers, not by the words of Herbert Marcuse and Charles Reich, but by the view from helicopters hovering over Da Nang and the Me Kong Delta. Although it is not codified in any clear alternative vision of what America should be, and attitudes vary widely, there is a profound cynicism which cuts across the whole spectrum, a feeling that something is basically wrong.

What this cynicism has generated, especially among single workers, is a new kind of working-class counterculture—a forceful rejection of the life-style of the older blue-collar generation. It is above all a rejection of security and possessions as the only goal to which present happiness must be sacrificed. While they drive the flashy "muscle cars" and do not engage in the college crowd's easy dismissal of material goods, young workers are just as able as other youth to sense a shallowness and lack of fulfillment in American society. Although they would express it in different words, the idea that one's life should have meaning and be lived is not lost on them. Many are deeply influenced by those elements of the counterculture which are not linked with the elitism and intellectual pretension of the student milieu.

One point about young workers that has not received much attention is their political attitudes. On the surface the situation is contradictory. On the one hand, young workers provided many of the blue-collar votes for Wallace, and when racial brawls do take place, they are often between the young.

In fact, although neither unions nor management like to talk about the problem of violence, it is very real. In Detroit, for example, B. J. Widick, one of the most informed labor reporters, and *Newsweek* magazine both note that many workers and even local union leaders carry guns with them for self-protection.[8] One incident, in which a black auto worker shot and killed two foremen and a worker, received national attention, primarily because he was found legally insane after the jury visited the plant and saw the conditions under which he worked. While such incidents are rare, there are other examples of similar shootings in other areas of the country.[9]

Less dramatic but more widespread are fights or simply tension in industrial plants or shops. Foremen, especially, have been assaulted, not only by blacks but by white workers as well. Widick's somber conclusion that "At best black and white workers tolerate each other in the plant" does describe the situation in many places.[10]

But at the same time, many young workers seem far more influenced by the progressive ideas of their student counterparts and often they are more open-minded than their elders. In the UAW, for example, it is often younger white workers who will cross over to vote for a black.

The common problems also tend to put them on the same side of the fence. A young black worker in a steel mill told one reporter, "Some of these white boys are all right. Not all of them, but a lot of them are getting hip. We had made a petition to get a new union man [steward] for the shop, and none of those lily asses upstairs [the older workers] would sign it. But those young dudes did." [11]

In the absence of any careful studies, it is hard to make solid generalizations, but one large and careful study of young workers' job attitudes did ask a few questions about politics. They found that more young workers called themselves "liberals" than older workers (by 43 percent to 30 percent), and they were far more concerned about the Vietnam War and pollution than were their elders.

Lastly, although far more likely to vote for George Wallace than older workers, most young workers also said that "blacks want to get ahead in the same way other Americans have," and only a minority felt that the company or union was doing too much for minorities. A vote for Wallace was clearly not identical with vicious racism. [12]

Turning to the opinions of people who had contact with them, one union official of the Steelworkers put it this way: "I don't think they are as hung up on race as the older workers. I don't know whether they learned that in school or training at home."

Irving Bluestone also hazards the opinion that "There is more antiwar feeling I would say, although this is too much of a generality. If you're thinking in terms of percentages and proportions, yes, a higher proportion. With regard to the racial prejudices, so much relates to experiences in the home and the community, totally unrelated to what happens in the plant, that it is extremely difficult to estimate. I think generally there is a much greater acceptance among young people of the facts of life regarding equal opportunity, civil rights, and the equality of people regardless of color than there was many years ago. But even then, if you go back to 1944 when a race riot occurred in the city of Detroit, there was only one oasis in the entire city where people worked together without violence, and that was in the UAW shops."

Mayor Richard Hatcher of Gary, when I asked him for his opinion of young workers, leaned forward and said with real feeling:

"They are my real hope for bridging the gap. Older workers tend to be critical no matter what I do. But I've found that the young workers are much more open and appreciate some of the things we are trying to do.

"I personally try to be understanding and relate to the young workers. I'm sure I'm the first mayor in the city's history ever to attend a music festival where the blue-collar kids were all walking around with hair down to their shoulders.

"In fact, many of the same politicians who had opposed me during my election began a campaign against permitting the rock festival.

"The blue-collar kids who were organizing the concert were acting very responsibly, but the politicians were really whipping up an hysteria and calling on all the 'red-blooded Americans' to stop those 'hippies' from running over them.

"The young workers finally called me and said, 'Mayor, we don't want to create a problem in this community, so maybe it's in the best interest of the community if we call off the concert.'

"But I told them I would support them if they wanted to go

ahead and they decided that instead of an outdoor concert they would have an indoor one which would eliminate the threat of any clashes. They also invited me to speak to them at the concert, which I did, and it came off beautifully.

"As a result of that episode, the young workers have found that they can relate to the city and hopefully we will build upon that. In general, though, I think that it is there that we may be able to break the cycle of racism, the way it is handed down from generation to generation. I think young workers are really the brightest spot on the horizon."

III

Along with the emergence of young workers as a new part of working-class America during the sixties, blacks also became a significant and sometimes pivotal new force, especially in certain industries and certain areas of the country.

In some cases, the increase is startling. In 1954 there were some 300,000 black craftsmen, foremen, and kindred workers. In 1969, there were about 750,000. Operatives jumped from 1.3 million to 2.1.[13] Add to this the increase in laborers and service workers, and the impact is clearly profound.

It can be seen in the growing black presence in the unions. There are today about 3,000,000 black trade unionists, which makes unions the largest organizations of blacks in the country with the exception of the church. In several important unions, blacks are now close to 20 percent of the membership, among them the UAW and Steelworkers. In the half-million American Federation of State, County and Municipal Workers, it is more than 20 percent, as in the Amalgamated Meat Cutters and Butcher Workmen, the Letter Carriers, Postal Clerks, and American Federation of Teachers. In unions like the Longshoremen the percentage rises to almost half.

Blacks control many locals in these unions. In auto and steel alone, more than forty key locals are largely or completely run by blacks.[14]

The labor movement has, in fact, become the most substantial power base black people have in America. Even with the significant black gains in national politics of recent years, a conservative estimate would be that their power and influence in the union movement is five to ten times as large.

This increased numerical strength has resulted in the development of black caucuses in unions like the United Automobile Workers, the Teachers' union, and the Steelworkers. In some locals of the first two, these caucuses have become an accepted part of the political life of local unions, and in others they are recognized, although grudgingly, as a real force. Often led by veteran black unionists, these black caucuses have focused on internal union issues like adequate representation for blacks and demanded greater trade union concern with the crisis in Black America. In steel, for example, they have raised the demand in the national conventions for a black member to sit on the five-man executive board, since blacks now constitute about 20 percent of the membership. This struggle is still going on.

Finally, the sixties saw the rapid growth of unions in two key areas: public employees and the South. The unionization of public employees is of great significance. It is bringing in hundreds of thousands of unskilled or semiskilled service workers like garbage collectors, postal workers, hospital workers, street cleaners, and prison guards into organized labor. These workers are universally underpaid in relation to the private sector, and are frequently black. As we shall see, they are often as militant as the most dedicated sit-down strikers of the '30s. They are injecting a fresh current of militancy into the trade unions.

The growth of public service unions has been astronomical. In 1957 the American Federation of State, County, and Municipal Workers had 155,000 members—today 600,000. The American Federation of Government Employees jumped from 64,000 in 1957 to 300,000 in 1970. The teachers (AFT) went from 50,000 to 213,000 in those years.[15]

The South also has seen a huge increase in unionization. Between 1960 and 1968 one million new union members were organized in the twelve southern states. In 1970 there were 2.7 million union members. By 1980 there will be perhaps four million or more. In addition to their impact on the unions, these new members will also have a positive impact on the politics of the southern Democratic Party.

Summing up these changes, Patricia and Brendan Sexton conclude:

". . . Unions in the seventies will more nearly resemble the Congress of Industrial Organizations of the thirties than the AFL of the sixties. Changing membership and leadership as well as a thrust into new unorganized areas will give the unions a strong new momentum. Many will have a membership which will be much blacker, younger, better educated and probably more militant. And these members will bring in new leaders who will more nearly resemble them."[16]

All these developments seem to indicate positive change in contrast to the common wisdom that saw labor in the sixties as simply becoming more and more reactionary and stultified.

As before, the common wisdom was indeed common but not very wise. A careful look at what was going on in labor in the sixties and early seventies shows that intellectual dogma and working-class reality were once again deeply at odds.

IV

The generally accepted interpretation of labor's behavior in recent years was well expressed by Richard Scammon and Ben Wattenberg in *The Real Majority*.

They saw the 1968 election as proof that the political awakening of labor, which seemed to have exploded almost overnight in the Wallace phenomenon, was something completely different from the labor militancy of previous years. This time it was the "social issue," a mixture of drugs, crime, pornography, and patriotism, that was generating blue-collar anger. The traditional "bread-and-butter" issues, in their view, clearly were taking a back seat and a new conservatism had taken over.

But the reality is far more complex. Working-class discontent did not suddenly appear out of nowhere in the spring of 1968 when Wallace began to show strength in northern working-class precincts. All through the sixties there was an increasing rank-and-file dissatisfaction over the "old-fashioned" economic issues, expressed in rejected contracts, wildcat strikes, and the replacement of old union officials with new, more militant ones.

The first and most obvious indication is strikes. In 1970 more than three million workers walked off the job despite the high level of unemployment. That is the largest number of workers involved in work stoppages since the Korean War and not since 1946 had so many different workers gone on strike for so long.[17]

Another indication of the growing discontent is the rising number of settlements rejected by the rank and file. Bok and Dunlop note that "Statistics compiled by the Federal Mediation and Conciliation Service reveal that membership rejections (in cases involving the active participation of Federal mediators) rose from 8.7 percent in 1964 to 14.2 percent in 1967. . . . There is no doubt the rejection rate has risen and that the ratification process must be taken seriously as an expression of rank and file discontent." [18]

Wildcat strikes unauthorized by national unions also flourished, sometimes lasting months. The UAW, which allows strikes over local issues, would sometimes have a majority of its locals on strike (in the late fifties and sixties) even after the nationwide bargaining had ended. In other unions, even under threats from the leadership, locals refused to go back to work after the contract was signed.

But the most interesting development in the sixties was the impressive series of challenges to incumbent union leaders and the very new kind of militancy that developed in those years.

These challenges occurred in a number of major unions. The United Steelworkers, for example, after the death of Phillip Murray, the well-respected and militant leader of the thirties, had been ruled by David McDonald, who was widely criticized for his "do-nothing, Cadillac" unionism. By 1965 discontent had grown and I. W. Abel replaced him in a tightly-fought election, mainly because of militant pressure from the rank and file.

In the electrical workers' union (IUE) James Carey was replaced by Paul Jennings in 1964, again in a hard-fought election in which the Department of Labor had to intervene to prevent ballot switching. The change resulted in greater militancy and better contracts. It was under Jennings' leadership that the unprecedented strikes against GE were undertaken.

Other unions also felt the force of rank-and-file pressure long before George Wallace appeared on the scene. The Oil, Chemical, and Atomic Workers in 1964, and the United Rubber Workers in 1966, saw new leaders elected because of widespread dissatisfaction with inadequate militancy of the old.

A last example of change was the election of Jerry Wurf to the presidency of the American Federation of State, County, and Municipal Employees in 1964. One of the youngest leaders of a major union, Wurf's victory signaled the change of AFSCME into one of the most militant and progressive unions in the AFL-CIO.

In general, as one author has noted, "By the autumn of 1966 it was possible to observe that, with the exception of the United Packing House Workers (UPW), all the major unions that contributed to the creation of the CIO in the 1930s had experienced a major revolt. Conditions in the coal, auto, rubber, steel, electric, and maritime industries in the sixties are now renovating the unions whose formation they stimulated in the thirties." [19] *Life* magazine, he notes, in 1966 referred to the "new union militancy" and *Fortune* also noted the trend. All this, it must be noted, was before the Wallace campaign occurred, and while students and liberal intellectuals were in the thrall of Herbert Marcuse's ruminations about the total integration of labor into the "system."

The final aspect of the "blue-collar awakening" that is often ignored is the growth of a genuine militancy in the rank and file, a militancy that was expressed in an increasing willingness to "take on" the company, that grew during the sixties. A few of the more well-known examples will suffice.

In 1964, the International Longshoremen's Union (east and west coasts) for the first time in history experienced an all-union wildcat strike that shut down all the ports in spite of the leadership. The issue was the loss of jobs agreed to in the contract that had been negotiated.

In 1966 the Airline Mechanics (affiliated with the International Association of Machinists) went on strike, stopping 60 percent of the nation's air traffic. They rejected the first contract worked out by their leaders. President Johnson intervened in the second round, trying to hold the settlement to the 3.7 percent wage guideline of that period. This also was rejected and, irritated by government interference, the four largest locals called for a formation of a third labor party to "serve the best interest of labor." The final settlement indeed broke the 3.7 percent guideline.

In 1966, and again in 1970, strikes against General Electric indicated the growing discontent. In 1966 the International Union of Electrical Workers created an unprecedented united front of eleven unions in a strike that broke the Johnson guidelines and the paternalistic approach of GE's management, who made only one offer and used public relations techniques to "sell" it to the membership. Even with this victory, thousands of workers stayed out over in-plant issues of working conditions and the grievance procedure.

In 1970 another GE strike lasted over three months and the unions again finally won what they were asking for. But *Time* magazine pointed out that the real significance of the strike was that the strikers were as "united in bitterness toward their employers as any band of workers who fought the industrial class wars of the thirties."

In 1970, the Postal Workers shook America with a wildcat strike, opposed by the unions, and in defiance of federal law. It signaled a new kind of militancy among the underpaid public service workers, hamstrung by antistrike legislation.

In June, 1971, the New York District Council of the American Federation of State, County, and Municipal Workers, along with some other unions, literally paralyzed New York City, closing the bridges, ignoring garbage destined for the incinerator, closing the sewage plants and letting the raw sewage pour into the rivers, along with a variety of other actions. The issue for the low-paid workers ($7,500 a year on the average) was a pension plan. But it also showed, like the postal workers' strike, a willingness to fight in the most militant way and no longer "play ball" with the rules, when they were blatantly unfair to workers.[20]

These facts expose how shallow the "social issue" is as a description of what was going on in working-class America. Far from having taken a "back seat" as the popular notion would have it, in national terms, it was the economic issue, not the social issue, that moved millions of workers in active protest.

In fact, where common interests united black and white workers, the struggle for economic goals actually overcame racial polarization at times. In the North, it emerged in the ethnic or neighborhood community groups, which put aside racism to deal with the real social and economic problems. For example:

Chicago, 1972, 1,600 black and white representatives of community groups from working-class ethnic neighborhoods all over America met in a national housing conference. The subject was "block-busting" and the enemy was defined not as blacks or whites but as the FHA and the network of financial institutions that exploit racial fear. The conference was extraordinary, not only as the most representative gathering of white working-class community leaders ever held, but also for the sophistication with which the common interests of black and white workers were mapped out and racism rejected by the delegates.

Hammond, Indiana, 1970, the Calumet Community Congress was established in a meeting of one thousand people, representing 143 organizations from the Gary, Hammond, and East Chicago area. It focused on community problems like pollution, corruption in government and tax reform, especially in regard to U.S. Steel. Local union leaders, housewives, professionals, and steelworkers along with blacks and Spanish Americans, were all represented. The Congress very strongly rejected any racial splits, which gained it the ire of the local KKK and Birchers along with the reactionary elements of the Democratic Party.

Detroit, a "Polish Conference on Greater Detroit" was formed several years ago by Polish clergy and black Congressman John Conyers focused on joint action by blacks and Poles in the areas of mutual need. The organization has gained support from community figures and has provided an ongoing progressive counterforce to polarization.[21]

But far more significant were the events in the South, where the struggle of low-paid workers to organize often created moving examples of racial cooperation.

In Mississippi, critically poor white woodcutters and haulers, some of them former members of the Ku Klux Klan, joined with blacks in strike action. They received help from Charles Evers, black candidate for governor, and the NAACP. Many of the whites later voted for Evers in the election.

In South Carolina, white steelworkers turned to the Southern Christian Leadership Conference for help in a strike. Support came from both the black and white community and the final victory was achieved only through that alliance, which kept the company from splitting the strikers along racial lines.

In Birmingham, Alabama, a struggle for union recognition among municipal workers began with blacks, but spread to whites as well as union organizers entered the picture. Again, in the face of attempts to split the movement along racial lines, the alliance persevered. Similar events have occurred in cities like Atlanta, Pensacola, Port St. Joe and many others.[22]

When reporters went to cover these stories, they found

white workers saying things like "Changing, hell yeah, things are changing. I guess with me and my boys and the other cutters, manning the picket lines with black fellows and my wife and daughter going down to Canton to buy supplies with them black ladies, has brought us a lot together." A black man in South Carolina said, "I never thought I would see black and white people working together like this in the South." Another white, this time from Mississippi, told a writer: "White against black is just not as strong in the state as it used to be. Before black and white couldn't get together and a nigger was a low-rated person. But I told my friend here (gesturing to a black officer in his local) I might not know what it is to be black, but I sure know what it is to be treated like a nigger by management. And blacks can see that whites are getting the same old shaft blacks get. We fought each other for a long time with the company egging us on, but now we are—some of us—fighting together." [23]

It is easy to dismiss such events in the South as "exceptions," but they have a special significance. Unlike the relationships in the North where there are, in certain areas, short-range economic conflicts of interests (between skilled craftsmen, for example, and unemployed blacks), the struggle for unionization in the South indicates the victories that can be achieved, despite racism, when the struggle is based on genuine common interest.

Putting all these events together, it becomes clear that, throughout the sixties, there were a rising discontent and militancy centered on the conditions of work and life in blue-collar America. It was an awakening that moved millions of workers to vote down old leaders, strike for longer periods, reject settlements, and in some cases raise new demands about job safety or the authoritarianism of factory life. George Wallace and busing protests were not the only signs of discontent. In fact, they were, in a way, tangential to this more basic thrust of complaints of black and white labor.

Yet, in the political arena, a drift to the right was apparent. Throughout the sixties, it was George Wallace and other conservatives who benefited from blue-collar discontent, rather than the liberal democrats.

As we have seen, the answer does not lie in working-class affluence, authoritarianism, or "innate" conservatism, since all of these are, in large measure, myths, rather than facts. Instead, to find out why workers have acted "conservatively" in politics, one must look not so much at workers, but at what was going on in the political system itself.

V

Although the blue-collar vote for George Wallace came as a shock to many people, all through the sixties conditions had been ripening for his appearance.

For one thing, the black population in the North had been rapidly increasing and had basically altered the composition of many northern cities. Since elementary democratic rights such as service at a lunch counter already existed, the demands northern blacks raised in the sixties immediately focused on the most sensitive issues of jobs and housing. The first major struggles that occurred, in fact, were directly aimed at union exclusionism and de facto segregation in housing. The conflict of interests between black and white workers was therefore far deeper and more directly threatening to white workers than the issues existing in the South.

Then the pent-up frustration which exploded in the ghetto riots dramatically intensified the fear and hostility of white workers. More important than the affront they constituted to workers' "law-abiding" ethos was simple fear. While the riots turned out to be strikingly free from violence toward people, to urban workers, who often lived so close to the ghetto that they could see the flames and sometimes hear the shouts, their impact was terrifying. One Chicago worker I know sat up with a shotgun all night, peering through his window and listening to the sounds of breaking glass a few blocks away. Considering the strong currents of racism that were already present in working-class America, the riots were certain to tip the balance and elevate working-class fear and hostility toward blacks into a central political issue. Combined with the growing polarization over the war in Vietnam, even the most astute and sophisticated strategy on the part of liberals could not have prevented a certain growth of conservatism.

But far from recognizing the growing discontent and danger of reaction in blue-collar America, most liberals in the sixties still considered workers to be affluent and smug. The myth that class no longer existed was in full flower, and liberals looked to blacks as a kind of "last frontier" of domestic social injustice. The AFL-CIO support for the war in Vietnam formalized for many the view of workers as no longer a sleeping giant soon to join the ranks of progress, but a permanently somnolent and conservative bulwark of the complacent white majority.

Thus, none of the social programs of the great society period were aimed at championing the new and growing social and economic grievances of all working people. Instead they were focused entirely on blacks or the very poor. The innovative social programs that had once made the Democrats the "party of the people" now appeared to workers as entirely for others while ignoring their needs. Just as a new level of discontent over legitimate issues began to surface, liberals turned away from workers. Workers' racism and militarism were often decried in the mid-sixties, but rarely were their real and unmet needs recognized.

The result was predictable. In 1968 Hubert Humphrey received only 43 percent of the vote and barely half the ballots of blue-collar workers. The remainder were split between Wallace and Nixon.[24]

Yet, in the midst of the chaos of 1968, blue-collar workers sent one "message" that was never understood. In the primaries, Robert Kennedy won in working-class precinct after precinct that had previously been ceded to Wallace.

Short of workers putting signs on their lawns which said, "I am discontented but not inevitably reactionary," there was no clearer way that workers could have indicated that such was the case.

This should have led to a serious reevaluation of liberal tactics and strategy, aimed at countering the disaffection of blue-collar workers with programs which would demonstrate that progressives were still the only force genuinely willing to champion workers' legitimate social and economic grievances and to show a real concern for their needs.

But instead, all the myths of authoritarianism and relative well-being were simply updated to include an explanation of why "backlash" or "conservatism" were now inevitable. Instead of taking the blue-collar worker vote for Nixon and Wallace as a call to fight for workers, many liberals interpreted it as proof that the situation was beyond hope.

As a result, a worker who voted for George Wallace in 1968 was given no reason to change his mind. Instead of seeing the liberal progressive forces reject the condescending myths and return to their traditional role as his advocates, he saw program after program that literally assaulted his real interests. In programs and in expression, what came through was condescension and indifference to the legitimate aspects of his discontent.

Thus, liberal strategy itself was a key factor in the "drift to the right." Though liberals did not consciously set out to drive workers into the arms of Wallace and Nixon, the appalling fact is that, objectively, that is precisely what they did.

Consider some of the key issues of the last few years.

On race, the myth that class no longer existed led liberals to lump workers with the middle class and fall into one of the oldest traps in the arsenal of reaction, playing white workers against blacks, rather than seeking the issues and programs to unite them.

The busing program was typical. It ignored the deeper problems of class injustice in education and the failure of the schools for both black and white workers. But more importantly, it was not fairly and evenly applied. People with the money to move to the distant suburbs, or to send their children to private schools could avoid the problems, while white workers, who could afford neither had no such pleasant alternative. To workers it appeared that liberals were willing to endanger the quality of blue-collar children's education for the sake of blacks, but not that of their own. Far from seeking the method of aiding blacks that would be the least provocative to workers, the busing program allowed the affluent to escape any sacrifice while concentrating the burden on the less well-to-do.

Black quotas followed the pattern. Until 1972 (when they were instituted in the universities), they were only applied to working-class jobs such as the construction trades, once again exempting the middle class from any sacrifice. The potentially unifying program of full employment was substantially ignored as a serious alternative. This tragic liberal myopia was skillfully exploited by Richard Nixon. As the *New Republic* noted:

> Unwittingly or not, the Administration could not have worked a better game plan to play off white against black labor for its own ends. Just as a nasty recession hit the unions in 1969, it began to talk about quotas for blacks, calling for preferential treatment for minorities in construction trades. (One of the Justice Department lawyers defending the Philadelphia Minority Hiring program was William Rehnquist.) Having split the AFL-CIO over the issue, the Administration never then delivered the jobs to blacks. And having whipped up blue-collar white resentment over "quotas," it used the resentment to club McGovern all through the campaign.[25]

The impact of public housing also fell heavily on workers. A map published in one large city's newspaper showed the location of the projects that had been built in white areas, and the neighborhoods of the men who had planned them. Every one of the projects outside the ghetto was in the southern working-class areas, while every one of the white planners lived in the middle-class northside areas of the city.[26] Once again, the affluent got off scot-free.

And, unlike the simple democratic issue of letting a black man live wherever he chooses, socioeconomic integration, putting the desperately poor side by side with those who have escaped from poverty, involves genuine social and economic issues. Public housing projects are often of higher density and less well constructed than the surrounding homes. Any real-estate agent will admit that such buildings do affect a neighborhood's value, even if the occupants are white. Working-class communities have often fought to keep out poor whites, or more recently, trailer parks for lower-paid white workers, for economic and social, not racial reasons. (In fact, stable black communities have also opposed public housing in their neighborhoods, when it was for lower-class blacks.) Again, liberal efforts to aid blacks pitted their needs directly against those of white workers.

And it was over these three programs, where class bias was most evident, that workers exhibited the worst racism. Although workers are overwhelmingly hostile to welfare and often deeply fearful of black candidates winning election to public office, neither of these areas produced violent clashes or widespread active protest. To be sure, there is substantial racism of the most overt and mindless type. But clearly, the hostility to busing, quotas, and public housing was made far worse, and many additional workers were alienated because, instead of seeking to meet black needs as part of a general assault on the social and economic problems of all workers, these programs put black improvement directly in conflict with the objective interest of white workers.

Nor is the list exhausted. If liberal programs with regard to race unnecessarily alienated workers, liberal actions in regard to peace and ecology were equally flawed.

On ecology: Not only did protestors ignore the problem of pollution inside the factories, but the often-expressed attitude was "shut down any plant that pollutes now and, in the next session of Congress, introduce something to help the workers."

The vote on the SST is a good example of how things worked out in practice. The environmental arguments against the SST were clearly sound. But at the same time, the AFL-CIO estimated that it would eventually generate

200,000 jobs. The AFL-CIO supported the SST because, for a change, it offered a peacetime alternative to building more bombers or jets.

The ecology forces succeeded in voting down the SST but where are the rapid transit systems they spoke of as more useful substitute projects? Where are the 200,000 new jobs in health, transportation, and pollution control that were going to employ those people?

Defense spending is a parallel case. By the mid-sixties, it was clear that a tremendous number of workers were dependent on military spending for their jobs. Unions like the UAW developed very sophisticated plans even before 1968 to ensure an orderly conversion to peacetime production which would not throw blue-collar workers out of work while the shift was made.

But in 1972, when George McGovern spoke at the convention of the International Association of Machinists, he had no clear and precise plan for protecting jobs during conversion. At that time, thousands of former aerospace workers were already driving cabs or doing jobs far below their skill level. The year 1972 was too late to defend those workers. Had a clear and consistent drive to defend workers been a key part of the liberal agenda, that issue could have been settled in 1968.

Even on a "bread-and-butter" issue like the wage-price freeze, workers did not see their erstwhile allies leaping to their aid. For anyone who had understood labor's demands for equitable controls in the late sixties, it should have taken about fifteen minutes to discover that Nixon's program was a probusiness caricature of a just program. Anyone seeking to champion American workers should have been crying "unfair" the minute he had finished reading. But when George

Meany did precisely this, many liberals joined with conservatives in denouncing his criticisms as the "selfish" demands of a special-interest group. It was a unique opportunity for liberals to show real understanding of blue-collar workers' economic discontent, and yet weeks passed before Democrats began to echo the charge. The mixture of silence and cries of "Greed!" during those weeks were hardly calculated to convince workers that Democrats were their defenders and friends.*

There are other issues as well where opportunities were missed, or destructive actions were taken, but the point is clear. The worker who had voted for George Wallace in 1968 had seen nothing since then to make him change his mind. Wallace's potent slogan, "Send them a message!" was precisely geared to the rising anger of blue-collar workers. One does not need elegant sociopolitical theories or the incomprehensible musings about "consciousness" of a Marcuse or Reich to understand the "drift to the right," or the "emerging Republican majority." The only way progressives have ever won a majority of the American people is by offering genuine programs that meet the needs of ordinary people. There is nothing strange in the fact that workers began deserting liberalism once liberalism so decisively deserted them.

Some, however, may object that McGovern, after Miami Beach, did pose such an alternative and yet he was decisively beaten. In the aftermath of his election, it was widely proclaimed that Nixon's victory "proved" the impossibility of progressives regaining the support of labor.

But while there has been a recognition that serious mistakes were made in the campaign, and McGovern was victimized by an unparalleled program of sabotage and subversion, it is worth

* Condescending liberals should remember Meany's action when they announce that Meany and other labor leaders are "out of touch" with their members. At the key moment, his was the only voice on the national scene demanding justice for American workers.

examining with some care what happened with the blue-collar vote, since the results hold clear implications for the future.*

VI

The McGovern campaign in many ways epitomized the worst mistakes and errors liberals have made in dealing with labor. Those who saw it firsthand know there was a pattern of arrogance and elitism toward workers and unions among many McGovern supporters that was simply unbelievable.

But McGovern was no lone sinner among saints. The lack of understanding and failure to champion the needs of working people in recent years has not been confined to McGovern or the "new politics" wing of the Democratic Party. George McGovern was still George "Who," when most of the programs described above were undermining the blue-collar support for the Democratic Party.

But to understand Nixon's landslide, and especially his labor vote, there is one key fact about George McGovern. In a very real and practical sense, he was never a serious candidate for president. This is not an insult but a simple statement of fact.

McGovern, from the time he decided to run two years before the election, to the middle of the primaries, was running what is usually called an "educational" or "issue" campaign, an attempt to use the exposure and attention of an election to present a point of view, rather than win the maximum number of votes.

Obviously, the politician whose main ambition is winning,

---

* The disclosures about Watergate, and, in particular, the still undisclosed role of the Nixon campaign in the sabotage of Muskie's and then McGovern's candidacy creates real difficulties in judging what was genuine error and what were "dirty tricks." However, while such activities may have significantly affected his vote, most of what will be said deals with McGovern's own positions and role, which, unless there was high-level infiltration, were not so readily affected.

carefully moderates his stances on the issues, cultivates the men and organizations he will need, and avoids taking positions on wildly unpopular issues, especially if they are of secondary importance.

However, press stories in the early part of the campaign noted that McGovern's real aim was in fact to consolidate his position as the major peace advocate liberal in the convention. This is a perfectly honorable role, and there would be little to criticize except that McGovern actually became the Democratic Party's nominee, and had the responsibility of beating Richard Nixon.

In a narrow sense, McGovern's nomination rested on his use of the reforms in the delegate selection process. By careful organization, pro-McGovern delegates were victorious all across the country, although they were often not genuinely representative of their community.

But the deeper and more important reason for McGovern's nomination was that the Democratic Party was split into two hostile camps, with labor on one side and a coalition of youths, blacks, and middle-class liberals on the other.

It is easy to make one-dimensional villains of labor or liberals. But this evades the point. George Meany has supported men like senators Gore, Hart, Kennedy, Metzenbaum, and other liberal "doves," although their Republican opponents were much closer to him on foreign policy. Equally, many of the most politically important liberals who were supporting McGovern during the convention had begun as Muskie supporters.

The fact is that McGovern, despite his disproportionate share of the delegates, would not have been nominated if the Democrats had had someone with a consistent progressive program that could appeal to blue-collar workers and liberals as well. Edward Kennedy was the only figure who was even on speaking terms with both sides, and with his refusal to run, there was literally no one who could bridge the gap, even in terms of style.

The problem in 1972 was in a basic sense the mirror image of 1968. Humphrey received 43 percent of the vote in that year, with Nixon and Wallace sharing the rest because he also could not forge an alliance.

As the campaign developed, McGovern did show strength in some industrial districts, especially after he suddenly "discovered" blue-collar workers in a Massachusetts shoe factory, and to some it seemed that he might actually succeed in winning large numbers of blue-collar votes in the election.

But unfortunately what McGovern said to Wisconsin workers during the primary was not what he had been saying on college campuses several months before. He had "discovered" blue-collar workers too late to develop a consistent approach and was saddled with all the positions he took to "consolidate the left." Along with the clearly unpopular issues like gay lib, amnesty, etc., were the more serious defects in this economic program. Even in style, with its scholarly jargon of demigrants and abstract notions of redistribution, it was inappropriate for appealing to blue-collar workers, and in fact it threatened them in two very real ways:

First, since it dealt with income redistribution separately from jobs, instead of suggesting full employment at decent wages, it is quite understandable that it appeared to workers as though it would make the working man support the guy who just laid around. Also the $12,000 cutoff point above which taxes began was about the worst choice that could have been made. It appeared to all workers, especially the young, to be a threat to bottle them up at their present level. Every assembler who hoped one day to become a tool and die maker, had to feel that the plan would keep him from any significant economic advance. Of course, when the mathematics failed to jell and McGovern had to reject it entirely, it was already too late to appear credible in many workers' eyes.

The other profoundly important defect of McGovern's campaign was the attitude he took in relation to the unions. Despite massive doses of self-righteousness on both sides, the real issue was not McGovern's allegedly antilabor record in the Senate or even his opinion on the war. It was something that was obvious when one watched the state delegate selections. McGovern and the unions were simply on opposite sides. There was no compromising, no attempt at amiability. In many states, McGovern's forces fought the AFL-CIO slates and often outmaneuvered them. Up until the final weeks of the campaign, George Meany was saying he would "support any Democrat except Wallace," because he felt sure the AFL-CIO would have a role in the convention through Humphrey and "Scoop" Jackson. His attitude changed when he suddenly discovered that McGovern had probably amassed a majority of the delegates and that labor had lost all its influence in the Democratic Party.

It is true that Meany and the labor leadership's intransigence about party reform and their dismissal of the "kids and kooks" did much to bring about their own isolation. They, too, had drawn the wrong lesson from 1968. The point was not that labor, by itself, had almost elected Hubert Humphrey, but that he only received 43 percent of the vote and barely half of the working-class total. It was, at best, short-sighted to think that some compromise did not have to be made.

But if Meany had the vain dream of a Democratic victory without middle-class liberals and students, McGovern went him one better in the weeks before the convention and announced that he didn't need the "labor bosses." They would have to tag along, the popular notion went, because they were "traditional Democrats" and had good reason to want Nixon out of office. The remarks about "labor bosses," the talk of winning with the "youth" vote or the "alienated" vote (thereby bypassing the unions), exposed the shallowness of McGovern's "populism" and ended any real hope that he could build an enduring majority. By pitting themselves against the unions in the primaries, the McGovern forces forfeited any moral claim to genuine leadership of the Democratic Party or social change in general. The challenge was to create a liberal-labor alliance, and in that central task McGovern failed.

It is not certain that a compromise could have been reached in the weeks before the convention, and the AFL-CIO Executive Council might still have refused to support Mc-Govern even if he had tried. But in failing to create a coalition of liberals and labor, he had already lost when he arrived in Miami.

All this was exposed in the convention itself. While McGovern tried to deny all the positions he had taken, he could not deny the social composition of his support. What was blindingly obvious on television was that McGovern's populism was rhetoric and not reality. A union steward who said, "The only workingmen I saw were wearing Wallace hats," put his finger directly on McGovern's central failure. What Americans saw was not a creation of a genuine liberal-labor alliance to defeat Richard Nixon, but a bitter factional struggle between the two groups with McGovern emerging the victor. Even though such extreme planks as legalization of marijuana and gay lib were voted down, they showed the concerns and issues that had won McGovern his early support. McGovern had discovered the working class too late to genuinely include it in his coalition. He left the convention with the nomination, but not the alliance that was needed to defeat Richard Nixon. No matter what they thought of his promises, workers could not feel that McGovern was truly "their" candidate for president. McGovern's student legions indeed defeated the unions in the 1972 convention but that was exactly what was not needed. With impressive organization and great political skill, they had split the only two forces that could guarantee progress in America, and McGovern, along with black people and blue-collar workers, were the real losers.

But despite all, one aspect of the subsequent campaign is of vital importance. While the AFL-CIO itself chose to remain neutral, the individual unions did not. McGovern received the endorsement of union after union until unions representing a majority of American workers came out in his favor. It was not only the traditionally liberal unions like the UAW or the American Federation of State, County, and Municipal Workers, but the Machinists, the Communication Workers and the Oil, Chemical and Atomic Workers along with many others.

For many of these unions, McGovern was not their real choice. They had hoped for someone whose style and positions would be easier to justify to their members. But not so much out of love of McGovern as a sense of responsibility for the future of the Democratic Party and the need for an anti-Nixon stance, they took a deep breath and went out on a limb as labor rarely has done, knowing McGovern was going to lose, but recognizing the need to support him.

And they worked for McGovern. In the face of titanic pressures and hostilities the industrial union leaders held their ground. Secret polls in certain unions indicated a frightening degree of support for George Wallace—in one it was 40 percent, in another smaller one close to a third. Yet many union papers splashed McGovern's picture across their covers and ran ads like one with a picture of a factory worker who was saying, "If you work for a living, how the hell can you vote for Richard Nixon?" [27] Some union leaders toured the plants, talked with workers, and although decent statistics are not available, those that exist suggest that northern union members such as in the UAW, were one of the few groups in America that gave McGovern a majority.

These facts are mentioned for one simple reason. In July of 1972, McGovern was criticizing "labor bosses," his campaign manager, Frank Mankewitz, was telling union officials that "The mood of America is against big labor and big business," and McGovern's student supporters were gloating over their "victory" against the labor movement. But in November, 1972, when America voted, labor in general and the industrial unions in particular "delivered," while their critics did not. Only one-third of the college-educated liberal elite voted for George McGovern, in comparison to close to half of American unionists. Were it not for those labor bosses so out of touch with their workers, George McGovern might very well have ended up running neck and neck with the vegetarian candidate. If all unions are now caricatured by liberals as the chief villains of the 1972 campaign, the reality is that many were in fact its unsung heroes.

It may seem that these events have been covered in excessive detail, but the conclusion that emerges is vitally important for the future.

The sources of the "drift to the right" among blue-collar workers are not some mysterious social-psychological processes that cannot be reversed. If workers were "traditionally Democratic" it was because liberal Democrats "traditionally" stuck up for them. The rising militancy and a growing dissatisfaction that arose among workers was in large part over legitimate grievances. Yet they found liberals and progressives were not even aware that they had any discontent at all. In fact, the steady erosion of Democratic margins among workers since the mid-sixties exactly parallels the indifference of middle-class liberals toward blue-collar workers in those years. Before George McGovern was even nominated the 1972 election had almost certainly been lost because the only viable progressive coalition, between liberals and labor, had not been established.

But the significance of the 1972 campaign goes deeper than political labels or offices alone. Nixon has demonstrated a competence verging on genius for harming the real interests of the black community and white workers at the same time. The desperate needs of both black and white workers have not been met nor will they be, so long as the coalition of interests Nixon represents holds power. The nature of that coalition requires that black be pitted against white, and little done for either.

Equally the only progressive majority that can defeat him or his successor is an alliance of liberals with black and white workers. The logic of their common interests is as powerful as the distrust and hostility that divides them.

CHAPTER SEVEN

The Future

THE PICTURE OF working-class America that has emerged in these chapters is very different from the popular clichés. Workers are neither affluent nor deeply conservative as many believe, and the so-called drift to the right had as much to do with errors made by liberal strategists as any inevitable growth of conservatism.

All this suggests that blue-collar workers can be a force for progress in America. There is clearly a wide range of issues where the real interests of workers, blacks, and liberals coincide and the basis for alliance exists.

But while very neat in the abstract, serious obstacles exist to making it a reality. Along with the real elements of racism and conservatism that do exist in working-class America, it will not be easy to overcome the legacy of distrust that has been created by the mistakes of recent years.

In addition, new issues and problems are arising. The kind of impact they will make is not yet clear but they may have a decisive influence not only on labor's coming political role and actions, but on the very future of blue-collar workers themselves. No productive considerations of working-class politics in future years can occur without recognizing both the threats and opportunities they impose.

II

The first and perhaps the most important issue is the threats which are developing to workers' jobs and job security. In a very real sense unemployment is still one of the most crucial issues facing not just blacks, but all American workers.*

At first glance, it seems hard to find evidence that this is true. A look at the changes in the unemployment rate in recent years shows that, while recessions still occur and send joblessness shooting up, unemployment in the sixties generally declined, at any rate until the Nixon recession of 1969–72. Even then the unemployment rate for blue-collar workers never suggested any return to the thirties, nor did it even equal the late fifties when 13 percent of operatives and 7–8 percent of skilled workers were without jobs. At its low point, in the mid-sixties, only 4–5 percent of operatives were seeking work and 2–3 percent of skilled workers.[1]

* Although the energy crisis is the most publicized aspect of the problem, its long-term impact is as yet impossible to gauge with any certainty. To the extent that layoffs were caused by the Arab oil boycott, the problem seems short-term, reversible and conceivably engineered as much by the oil companies as the Arabs. (The worst layoffs, in auto, in fact, could have been largely avoided, despite the boycott, had Detroit been willing to emphasize small-car production sooner.)

But on the other hand, petroleum prices are part of a broader, long-range trend. Prices for a whole range of raw materials and commodities, from foodstuffs to copper, bauxite and rare metals, have risen precipitously in recent years under the impact of the simultaneous 1972–73 world boom in the industrialized countries. This change, which could signify the end of the postwar era of cheap raw materials, does have the potential for a long-run threat to American jobs.

But any truly wrenching change would be felt far more in the virtually resourceless countries like Japan, rather than the United States, which remains one of the most self-sufficient countries in terms of resources. In fact, America's competitive position in relation to Europe and Japan could actually improve, though we too would be paying higher raw material prices.

But, even aside from the way the unemployment rate, as we have seen, understates the reality, this optimistic analysis really misses the point. Aggregate unemployment statistics like these seem to suggest that automation, for example, has not had any shattering impact on American workers. Nor, it seems, has the trend of industry to move to the South or the suburbs or more recently to other countries.

But all these trends have taken their toll on American workers, both black and white. They have not created mass unemployment like that of the thirties but instead generated a series of crises and victims all across America. Only by looking at what happened to specific individuals can the full impact be seen of a northern factory that is automated or shut down and relocated in the South.

One forty-year-old employee, for example, finds a similar job but loses his pension and eventually becomes part of the statistics of old age poverty. Another thirty-five-year-old man can only get work as a gas station attendant at half his previous salary. Automation and the movement of industry in postwar America have, in fact, had consequences like these for literally millions of workers, none of which show up clearly in the national statistics of blue-collar employment.

Automation, for example, is often ignored because it did not fulfill the predictions that it would literally end manual labor within a decade or so. The most comprehensive study, by the University of Michigan Survey Research Center, concluded that less than 1 percent of the labor force was directly laid off because of the introduction of automatic machinery between 1963 and 1967. It also noted that only 2–3 percent of the labor force per year encountered any change at all in their jobs because of new machinery.[2]

The labor force the study refers to includes professionals, businessmen, and everyone else along with factory production workers. But even if one assumes the effect to be five times as great for blue-collar workers as for others, the crisis still does not seem genuine.

But as the authors note, "Workers who might have been hired in the absence of technological change are not needed. The last to be hired have to wait longer for a job." This hidden effect of automation is supported by the fact that many unions negotiated attrition clauses in their contracts stipulating that only as workers retired or quit could automatic equipment be introduced.[3] It was the unemployed or young workers just entering the labor market who felt the impact most.

Also, in the areas where automation was rapidly introduced, it hit with disproportionate impact. In New York City, for example, automatic elevators eliminated 40,000 jobs in the space of a few years.[4] Another dramatic example of automation's impact can be seen in what happened in the late fifties when the Armour Company closed a number of midwestern plants. Almost half the workers laid off were still unemployed a year later in two of the cities where the change occurred. Three years after the shutdown, 30 percent of the East St. Louis Armour workers were still without jobs. This shutdown occurred during a recession, and not all plant closings have such disastrous effects, but as one commentator noted: "The burden of the change was simply dumped in the laps of the employees and the social service agencies. Some [employees] later received training from The Armour Automation Fund . . . but by November 1963, only 220 of some 2,500 eligible workers had been retrained and in virtually every case the new skills were at a lower rated job and less pay."[5]

One major group that is feeling the threat of automation today is the steelworkers. Completely automated mills are already in operation in other countries and each new facility which is built in the U.S. is more automated than the one before. More advanced technology in other countries has helped to give foreign steel a competitive edge and cheaper imports, as well as automation, have steadily reduced the number of steelworkers. To them automation is a very real threat.

Lastly, the massive unemployment and poverty in Appalachia and the migration of thousands of "hillbillies" to the cities of the North came about because of the mechanization of mining. Some of these men now live in cities and communities like Warren, Michigan, and work in Detroit auto factories. But there is a ten-year history of deprivation between their last day in the mines and their first in the plant. Only when one looks merely at figures about aggregate unemployment can that history be overlooked and the impact of automation seem negligible.

The figures also conceal the effects of industrial relocation. The trend of industries to move to the suburbs is a key factor in the crisis of black and poor white central city dwellers. Paul Zimmerer, a Chicago official, in testimony before a Congressional committee on industrial location policy said that "In Chicago's inner city alone, between 1955 and 1963 there was a net loss of some 400 manufacturing companies and some 700,000 manufacturing jobs. . . . Because of discriminatory housing practices, suburban zoning regulations, inadequate mass transit systems . . . most inner city workers could not continue to work at relocated manufacturing facilities in the suburbs." [6]

In New York, the *Times* notes that "manufacturing employment dropped from 54 percent to 51 percent from 1959 to 1965 and is expected to fall to 42 percent in 15 years." The head of the city's economic development agency estimates a loss of 200,000 manufacturing jobs over a twenty-year period.[7] In city after city, the pattern is repeated. Factories move to suburban industrial parks which can only be reached by car, automatically excluding poor blacks and eroding the tax base of the central city they leave behind.

There are a variety of reasons for this migration. Many factories function most efficiently spread horizontally for large distances, and land is cheaper in the suburbs. Construction costs are also lower and the congestion of central cities creates real problems in transporting raw materials and finished goods.

But, in addition, there are some less savory factors involved. As Kenneth Patton, the head of the New York Economic Development Administration notes, "The decision to locate a facility, especially in an industrial area, often has at its center, a question of evasion." [8] Suburban pollution regulations are often lax and taxes lower. Local communities often provide other inducements or services, competing with one another for the tax revenue the plant will supply. From a business standpoint, the move to the suburbs is an entirely logical development, but its inevitable by-product has been to make many northern central cities into a kind of urban Appalachia, burned-out pockets of permanent unemployment. Even for those who can make the adjustments, it has meant either long hours of commuting or going deeply into debt for a nearby home.

But industrial migration has not been limited to suburbia. The relocation of industry from North to South has also been accelerating. Between 1947 and 1965 employment in the Southeast and West grew by 57.4 percent, while in the Middle Atlantic and northeastern regions it grew by only 20.5 percent. In addition to textiles, the chemical and wood products industries have become major employers and the percentage of the southern population engaged in manufacturing is now close to that of the North. [9]

Low wages and the absence of unions are the magnet that attracts plant after plant to the South, along with important tax breaks and lax pollution standards that communities offer as lures to industry. An article in one corporate journal quite frankly summed up the advantages of locating in a depressed area. Along with the absence of unions, they note that in Appalachia the competition for jobs is so severe that workers will drive fifty and eighty miles one way to work for such "high wages" as three dollars and up an hour. One manufacturer they describe accepts a constant turnover of skilled and semiskilled workers with all the resultant loss of time and efficiency, because by keeping wages at about $2.25 an hour he comes out ahead.[10]

Many towns in New England became officially depressed areas with chronic high unemployment when the mills and factories left them for the greener southern pastures. In fact, as the authors of the study note, "For a number of New England communities, the wheel has come full circle. To towns like Fall River, Massachusetts, that saw its mills go south thirty and forty years ago, industry is returning, in many cases attracted ironically enough by the low level to which industry's defection ultimately depressed wages."

While black workers in many cases suffered the brunt of these changes, white coal miners, textile and paper workers were also affected.

To these, however, electronic, apparel, and auto workers must also be added because of the latest trend in industrial migration, the growing "export" of American jobs to other countries.

In recent months, this issue in particular has seized the headlines mainly because of labor's change from adherence to free trade to support for the very tough Burke-Hartke bill, a protectionist measure which would, among other things, seriously reduce the amount of goods that could be imported to America in order to protect American jobs.

No one denies that a real problem has developed. Whereas, in the early sixties, America exported much more than it imported and with the exception of textiles, the "made in Japan" label was a kind of shorthand for transistor radios, plastic toys, and other cheap marginal products, in recent years imports have grown in key areas such as auto, steel, and quality electronic equipment like stereos and color TVs. The balance of trade has, in recent years, shifted and in 1972, before the devaluation, the U.S. imported more goods than it exported. When the United Steelworkers began to feel the pinch, especially after the 1971 strike, the AFL-CIO shifted its pro-protectionist campaign into high gear.

Many American jobs have been lost. In March, 1973 *Fortune* magazine put the number at 87,000 in TV, radio, and electronic components since 1966. Paul Jennings, president of the International Union of Electrical Workers, said 121,000 jobs in electronics have been lost, affecting 50,000 members of his union. The United Shoe Workers, also hit by foreign imports, has lost 16,500 jobs over a ten-year period. The International Ladies Garment Workers Union lost 25,186 jobs in two years (1969–1971). Other more speculative estimates of foreign competition's impact on U.S. jobs are about 100,000 for steel and an equal number for auto.[11]

The *Fortune* article aptly dramatized the human cost with photographs of six older workers in their forties who were affected by foreign competition. Two are now unemployed, three found new work at lower salaries, and only one improved his economic situation as a result of the shutdown of his plant. Lost pensions, lower salaries, unemployment, and shattered lives have all been part of the effect this one change has had on American workers.

But questions of international trade are highly complex and several unions, as well as business, fear that import quotas may cause the loss of other jobs and actually make the situation worse.

Labor's previous support for free trade policies was based in large part on the disastrous experience of the thirties, when trade barrier generated trade barrier, a development which, if it was not the root cause of the worldwide depression of the thirties, certainly was no help in solving it. Even in 1971, before the issue had become a front-page topic, the Canadian affiliates of American unions were screaming bloody murder about the possible impact on their jobs of the Burke-Hartke bill, a reaction which forced the bill to exempt Canada from its provisions. European unions and the common market nations have also been increasingly concerned about the threat of protectionism and the newly formed European Trade Union Confederation has already suggested the real possibility of retaliation for any stringent limitation on imported goods.[12]

But labor is not unaware of these dangers. The most ferociously protectionist of the Burke-Hartke bill provisions are considered by many to be bargaining points, deliberately extreme, to force attention on the issues and achieve a workable compromise. The issue many unions hope to highlight is not foreign competition in general but the specific role of the American multinational corporations in the world's economy. The thing which makes "foreign" competition and the loss of blue-collar jobs today so different from previous years is that the cars and electronic components that come into America are often produced by American firms which have set up factories overseas. To the unions this is nothing but another variant of the "runaway shop" resembling the move many industries made to the South in previous years.

The free trade argument, as it is presented in economic textbooks, most often uses the example of a country like Equador which has the climate, soil, labor force, and so on to produce bananas cheaply. The U.S., on the other hand, has skilled engineers and sophisticated technology to make tractors at a low price. It is therefore in the interest of both, the textbooks suggest, to specialize so that the world may have the optimum number of bananas and tractors, rather than for the two to compete inefficiently in the production of both.

But this appealing argument (called "comparative advantage") hardly fits the modern reality. For many companies it is not soil, climate, raw materials, or other natural factors that make Mexico or Taiwan more attractive than Watts or Newark. Instead, it is a combination of low wages and weak or nonexistent unions, along with highly artificial inducements such as low taxes.

The foreign wages are indeed stunning. In Mexico they range from $2.80–$4.32 *a day* for factory employees. In Taiwan some assemblers get less than ⅛th of their American counterparts.[13] One apparel executive, who had just returned from a trip to Mexico where he was looking for a site for a new plant, candidly remarked that "A plant down there is going to be nothing but headaches for management. But how can you argue when they take for a full day's work what amounts to one hour's wages here in America?"

The absence of unions is also a key. Herbert Maier, representative of the International Confederation of Free Trade Unions, testified before Congress that multinational corporations "encourage favoring of antitrade union measures, permitting or even assisting companies to refuse to recognize trade unions and to enter into collective bargaining."

One union magazine, *The Machinist,* noted that "In Korea a special law takes away the right to strike and introduces compulsory arbitration for workers employed by multinational corporations . . . the Malaysian government offers any new industry moving into Malaysia a three-year period in which no trade union can operate." [14]

A special focus of the unions' criticism, however, is the tax advantages that artificially make foreign production more appealing than domestic. Because foreign taxes can be applied as credits to U.S. taxes the AFL-CIO *American Federationist* magazine notes that "American law rewards the corporation that does its work in Japan rather than in Pennsylvania. On one million dollars (in taxable income) the corporation that locates in Japan picks up 63 thousand dollars or 6.3 percent which is no mean tax break. . . . Actually the overseas producer can escape paying any tax on the profits he realizes abroad by the simple act of not returning the profits to the U.S." [15]

One major company, the article notes, closed down plants in Indiana and opened in Hong Kong. It paid no U.S. taxes at all, simply by investing the profits in Bermudan and Puerto Rican bonds.

Tariff advantages also promote job export. Parts and materials shipped abroad unassembled are only charged for the value added when they return as finished goods, instead of the way other imports are taxed. The result has been that hundreds of plants, including one which makes the Ford Pinto engine, are now located just across the Mexican border employing 40,000 Mexicans in place of U.S. workers. [16]

Finally, standards in other areas of corporate responsibility like pollution limits are generally lower or nonexistent in foreign countries.

It is unfortunately impossible to estimate exactly the

number of American jobs that have been lost because of the multinationals. The total loss of jobs due to imports has been variously fixed at anywhere from 500,000 to 1,000,000. Although a U.S. Commerce Department study suggested that only 14 percent of imported goods came from U.S.-based multinationals, this figure clearly underestimates the reality since it does not include joint ventures (the imports from foreign companies with significant though minority U.S. interests—GM for example has significant investments in Esusu Motors of Japan and Chrysler owns 15 percent of Mitsubishi Motor Company.)[17] A conservative estimate would be that several hundred thousand jobs have been lost and perhaps much more.*

* This topic does bring up one issue that has been ignored up to now in this section and in fact in the entire book, namely that the problems of American workers have been treated in isolation from the general world context. It might seem that this concern with American jobs ignores the far more pressing needs which the people of the third world have for industry and economic development. The fact that the U.S. uses one third the world's raw materials and American workers are "well off" in comparison with the poor of underdeveloped countries tends to reinforce this view.

But the nature of these investments, as well as the way in which they are granted, is not really in the interest of the developing countries themselves. As Leonard Woodcock, president of the UAW, notes, "Uninhibited by national loyalties the international corporations (with exceptions of course) advance their corporate interests by playing in the international arena the same "investment climate" game they use at home in dealing with large state legislatures competing for their favors. The 'climate' is deemed best in states where the business taxes are lightest (and public services consequently most substandard); where labor laws are least restrictive, unions weakest, and wages lowest; where toleration of environmental pollution is greatest; and in general where legislatures are most easily intimidated to do the bidding of the corporation.

"On the international scene similarly 'investment climate' backed up by threats to withhold or relocate investments is used to blackmail nations into mutually damaging competition, allowing the international corporation to extort concessions, subsidies, and special privileges that largely nullify whatever public benefits might otherwise flow from their investments. A kind of Gresham's Law operates under which bad social standards drive out good standards." [18]

Also as an article on the "global unemployment crisis" in *Foreign Affairs* notes, U.S. investments tend to be capital intensive (i.e., use a good deal of technology and few workers) when what underdeveloped countries need is labor intensive production which employs more people and whose products aid the economy of the whole country.[19] What a poor country needs for example is not an automobile engine plant that employs only a few workers and exports its product to the U.S. but something like a low-technology bicycle factory that employs more people and whose products help the development of the country. In many

Under the best of conditions, the loss of thousands of jobs like this would have caused serious problems for many workers. But although government "adjustment assistance" to aid workers with job training and financial help was demanded and won by the unions in 1962, it has been largely a dead letter. It placed an almost impossible burden of proof on the workers to show that imports and specific tariff concessions were a major cause of their unemployment. Five cases covering several thousand workers were filed in 1963, none were granted, and in fact only in 1969 did any workers receive aid. Even today only some 20,000 workers have received even modest assistance and less than 10 percent of the small group of eligibles have been trained for new jobs. Irwin Ross, author of the *Fortune* article noted above, called the program "totally ineffective" during the sixties and simply a "joke." [21]

What comes across very clearly in all of this is that the issue of job export and multinational corporations is not separate from the other aspects of unemployment and job security. Automation and the relocation of industries in suburbs and the South and other countries are all part of one complex reality. In all of these cases, the problem has been the closing of plants and the loss of income and security for thousands and thousands of workers, while readjustment programs for automation and job export have been, in general, dismal failures. There is no way to estimate the total number of workers who have been affected by one or another of these changes but they probably number in the millions.

More than anything else, however, the history of poverty and joblessness in black America puts the issue in focus. For

underdeveloped countries, foreign investment has tended to create a distorted economic structure called an "export enclave," a circular economic flow that only encompasses a tiny fraction of the population and has little value to the majority of the population that is locked outside.[20]

them automation and relocation have made the last forty years a grotesque kind of economic danse macabre, beginning with the mechanization of agriculture that displaced them from the land. Brought to northern cities by the promises of jobs and decent wages held out by Ford and GM labor recruiters, they quickly found that industry and jobs were passing them in the other direction, heading for the suburbs or down to the South from which they had so recently come. And now those plants are beginning to leave the South for Mexico and Taiwan, very possibly to begin the process of relocation all over again. (Now Japanese electronic plants are beginning to leave Japan for Korea, Malaysia, and Singapore because Japanese wages are higher than wage rates elsewhere.) [22]

It is now clear why, despite the statistics on aggregate unemployment, the question of unemployment and job security is still a big issue and possibly the most important issue for the future. Automation and the movement of industry played a very important role in generating the greatest domestic crisis of the sixties, the issue of black poverty and unemployment, and if it continues adding more and more white workers to its list of victims, it could become the major social crisis of the seventies.

To some business and intellectual writers, however, these threats to blue-collar jobs are seen rather astonishingly as a positive development. They evaluate the long-range trend as toward a "service economy" or "postindustrial state." The decline of manufacturing jobs is identified with upward mobility for all into the middle class.

The coming "post-industrial society," one writer says, "is based on services . . . what counts is not raw muscle power or energy but information. The central person is the professional for he is equipped . . . to provide the kinds of skills increasingly in demand. The post-industrial society is defined

. . . by the services and amenities, health, education, recreation and the arts which are now deemed desirable and possible for everyone." [23]

Nat Goldfinger, chief economist for the AFL-CIO, however, points out the central flaw in these kinds of projections. As he said, "Service jobs, most of them, are low wage, menial jobs. It's not all surgeons and research chemists by any means." [24] The AFL-CIO in general has characterized the service economy as "a nation of hamburger stands and soda jerks," a description which, although clearly exaggerated, is closer to the real outcome than any image of workers finding jobs as "white-collar" professionals or managers. As we have seen, much of the white-collar growth has been in clerical and sales occupations which pay so little that only women secondary workers will fill them.

Even if a significant number of workers could find their way into the professional and managerial group, the elimination of factory work would cut away the middle level of American society and create a huge class division with millions of workers facing a profound drop in income, not to mention growing unemployment.

In fact, manufacturing is still the largest single sector of employment in America, and all factory jobs are not going to disappear in the near future. But the march of automation, plant closings, and job export are eliminating blue-collar jobs. These changes are already a key source of concern, and if the loss of jobs accelerates, they could become a major issue for American workers, shaping their political stance in the coming years.

III

Unlike the threat that exists to workers' jobs, new attention to the issue of "job enrichment" seeks to help blue-collar workers by diminishing the boredom and alienation caused by many industrial jobs.

Although the issue has only recently become popular, it is not really new. Even in the forties some industrial planners and consultants were suggesting different ways of organizing production, ways which would give more autonomy and satisfaction to the worker. In the auto workers' rank and file, where the problem is intense, even in the late fifties and early sixties the slogan "humanize working conditions" was popular.

But only when a new generation of workers began expressing discontent by absenteeism, sabotage, drug use, and so on in the late sixties and early seventies did the question begin to be seriously considered by American industry.[25] Since then the Lordstown strike, and then the January, 1972, HEW report on job dissatisfaction have produced sequential floods of articles in the popular press and job enrichment has taken its place alongside "the blue-collar blues" as a public issue.

But while job enrichment is often referred to as though it is a concrete alternative to the present system of production, the concept is about as clear and precise as words like "happiness" or "fulfillment." The phrase covers a wide range of practices, ranging from very significant changes in the structure of authority and the work itself to innovations that are laughably superficial.

A small Gaines Dog Food plant recently built in Topeka, Kansas, which employs 24 men per shift, was designed from the beginning as an experiment in "enrichment." The workers are divided into teams which decide among themselves the way in which the work will be done and who does which job on a particular day. There are no foremen, only "team leaders," and each man can do a variety of tasks. The worst jobs, like loading and unloading, are done by everyone at some point. Employees themselves also do the hiring and firing, set the hours, and help make decisions about the purchase of new equipment and other choices which were formerly management prerogatives. Both productivity and satisfaction are said to have risen dramatically.

A Procter & Gamble plant in Lima, Ohio, has introduced many of the same innovations. Each worker has several skills, and routine jobs are shared by all. The employees decide pay scales, hiring and firing, again without supervisors. The work force is in fact referred to as "the community." Although the plant itself only employs about forty people per shift, other new facilities have been built along the same lines.

Chrysler Corporation has introduced a range of more modest modifications in thirty-one of its plants. Foot switches have been added to assembly lines in a few cases so that a worker can stop the line if he wants to pause for a drink of water or to go to the bathroom (the daily quota, however, is no lower than before). Some responsibility has been passed down to the lower levels, although rarely below the foreman to the workers themselves. Meetings are also held on company time where changes are explained and discussed with the workers. As *The New York Times* noted, however, "Almost no major changes have been made in the way workers scrape, wipe, lift and assemble cars and none is expected in the near future."

In a number of electronic and other small-scale production shops job rotation has been attempted or workers have been given entire subassemblies to complete rather than only one or two very simple tasks. At one such plant, a small Motorola factory in Florida, more workers are required than would be needed on an assembly line, but improvements in quality and productivity are reported to offset the additional costs.

At the other end of the scale from major innovations such as at the Topeka factory some very trivial changes have also been put forward as "job enrichment," among them painting factory walls in psychedelic colors, offering free coffee and nickel drinks, or simply "praise and recognition" from foremen for good work, the latter under the impressive title of "positive reinforcement." [26]

Even eliminating the more frivolous examples, it is clear that the only common element in these various programs is a focus on the work itself as opposed to wages, benefits, and so on. The first two cases involved genuine changes in the structure of authority and decision-making, while the others are limited to technical adjustments in the work process. The more significant innovations tend to be limited to small, newly designed factories, and The New York Times estimates that, in the entire country, only 3,000 workers have seen real changes in their jobs as a result of "enrichment." [27]

Several negative aspects of job enrichment are, however, already apparent. For one thing, because of all the attention the issue has received, the range of discontents of industrial workers are frequently reduced to the single issue of boredom by commentators and the press, isolating it from all the other problems workers face on the job. A UAW official, Frank Wallick, who wrote a book on the problems of occupational health and safety, remarked rather ruefully, "Somehow you never can get a major magazine to do a cover story on the noise, dust, and carcinogens in the work place, even though they kill so many workers every year." The validity of doubts like these are underscored by the fact that in the major articles, at any rate, job boredom and job enrichment are almost never placed in a broader context but instead presented as an isolated problem whose solution is already clearly in focus.

Also, there is a very real undercurrent of antiunionism, and occasionally elitism in the writing on job enrichment. Thomas Brooks, a labor historian and writer on this topic notes that

". . . I detect an underlying contempt for working people and a scorn for their unions as well as the creation of a new myth and a new conventional wisdom." [28] He quotes the point of Fred K. False of the Harvard Business Administration School, that many of the companies instituting job enrichment plans are nonunion and see these techniques "as a way to stay unorganized."

It is necessary to underline these facts because job enrichment on the surface is very appealing to intellectuals. As presented in the press, it appears very "visionary" or "radical" and for some progressives seems to provide a quick and easy answer to the problems facing working-class America. In practical applications where it improves the on-the-job conditions of American workers, it is of course entirely valid. But as a political issue, it must be viewed with caution, at any rate, until it is formulated in a way that overcomes its present isolation from all the other aspects of working-class discontent, and until its antiunion aspects are purged.

One last point about job enrichment, however, is that even on a simple economic level, there is a major roadblock to any widespread application of the idea. In certain areas like electronics, assembly-line techniques can sometimes be eliminated with little loss in productivity. In many other areas, however, where the handling of materials is a problem, the opposite is true. The routine and the pressure of the assembly lines did not occur by accident. In many cases, even with "alienation" and "absenteeism" or occasional sabotage, the line still guarantees that more will be produced per hour than by any more "fulfilling" organization of the work.

In the case of the auto industry, this is very clear. It is not an accident that the Chevrolet Vega assembly plant in Lordstown produces 109 cars per hour while the national average is only 59. The Chevy Vega has to compete with foreign imports from countries like Japan, where wages are lower. What this means is that from a businessman's point of view, an American factory has to produce more cars in the same period of time if the prices and profits are to be the same. It is thus only partially due to coincidence that the Lordstown line moves almost precisely twice as fast as the average in order to compete with the Japanese plants where wages are almost precisely one-half of what they are in Ohio.

Thus job enrichment, outside of a few special cases, is going to bang its head on the ceiling of competition and productivity. In Europe, for example, Saab and Volvo have designed auto factories that use teams rather than assembly lines. But the cars produced by these methods are not even intended to compete with lower-priced imports, and although very new, apparently their productivity is indeed lower than it would be if an assembly line were used.[29]

Ironically enough, it may turn out that workers and their unions will have their hands full in the coming years just struggling against management demands for higher productivity that would eliminate jobs and increase the pressure workers already face, rather than being able to mount a serious offensive for more "enriching" work. The fact that the steelworkers' union has already joined with management in "joint productivity councils" and other workers have been convinced to forego wage increases for fear of losing their jobs indicates the problems job enrichment will confront in moving beyond the limited circle of companies and occupations where it has taken root.[30]

IV

The final issue which will have critical significance for the future is the "wage-price freeze" and its consequences for the American economy in general.

While the details of Phases One, Two, and Three have been discussed back and forth many times in the press and media, one of the most basic results has rarely been mentioned.

Simply, it is that the freeze made the central economic issues for working-class Americans, the relations of their wages to prices and profits, *political* issues.

In the past such topics were left to the impersonal forces of the "market." If a worker's wage gains were eaten up by inflation, the only solution was to wait until the next contract and demand more money. During the entire postwar period, labor has basically placed a "catch-up" game with inflation, and while wage increases were often won, price increases kept real income at a far lower level.

Unions, in particular, recognized the merry-go-round workers were on but could find no practical remedy except to press again and again for higher wages to offset living costs. What the freeze has done, however, as Michael Harrington noted in an article written at the very beginning of Phase Two, "is to politicize the economy . . . wages, prices, and even profits [Nixon] has admitted are a fit subject for government action." [31]

Suddenly even the battle over the size of wage increases had to be fought politically before the pay board in Washington rather than simply in negotiation with the company. The sharp contrast between Nixon's "trickle down" approach, which quite clearly favored business, and the union's stance in favor of increasing the purchasing power of workers and meeting social needs made the most basic aspects of the economy—wages, prices, and profits—issues of clear practical significance for every trade-union official in America. [32]

This change presented two radically different future courses of action to the unions. As Harrington noted, "One response to the new conditions would be to raise national questions of income distribution [i.e., oppose the pro-business bias in the new economic program]. Another would be to parochialize the trade union struggle . . . the strongest unions would be able to protect themselves . . . but they would be unconcerned if the burden were then shifted to the unorganized and those living in poverty." [33] The strong unions in this case would tend to be offered rewards and increasingly become part of the business structure along with industry and government in return for their support. Today there is evidence of both trends within labor, although, in general, the more progressive alternative has predominated.

At first, despite their criticisms of the program, labor did join the pay board and, as Leonard Woodcock admitted, the strong unions gained decisions "they could live with, while the unorganized or much smaller unions were rigidly 'frozen.' [34] Several important unions, the Teamsters, Maritime, and sections of the construction trades, were won over to Nixon's stabilization program, and his campaign, by a variety of concrete inducements. But on the other hand, the AFL-CIO union leaders (along with Leonard Woodcock of the UAW) did walk off the pay board, despite the short-range penalties this move imposed. Since then the AFL-CIO has maintained a consistent stance in favor of curbing excess profits, ending the tax advantage the program gave to business, and generally insisting that the only acceptable stabilization is one which is fairly applied.[35] It seems now that Nixon has given up on the attempt to seduce the union movement as a whole into supporting his policies. Instead, an attempt is being made to outflank and undercut Meany and the AFL-CIO by strengthening the Teamsters and the Building Trades, who supported both Nixon and the stabilization program. The appointment of Peter Brennan, the head of the New York Building Trades, as Secretary of Labor, rather than another overture to the labor movement in general, is a step in the strategy. As B. J. Widick, labor editor for the *Nation* magazine noted, "Brennan's selection side-stepped the national AFL-CIO headquarters . . . [Brennan] is not Meany's first choice. Brennan has an independent political base and it is not George Meany." Later he says, "Now there are three big labor leaders in Washington, Fitzsimmons, Brennan and Meany, and that gives Nixon the kind of elbow room for political maneuvering that he has employed in the past to contain the trade unions . . . neither the building trades nor the Teamsters expect to retreat in 1973. They consider themselves 'in.' It's the rest of the labor movement that expects to feel the direct blow of Nixon's triumph over George McGovern." [36] Any uncertainty about Brennan's relationship with the AFL-CIO's leadership was erased by the latter's furious reaction to his very first official testimony on legislation during which he supported the administration against the AFL-CIO on the issue of lower minimum wages for teen-agers. Meany immediately charged that he had, "completely abandoned the trade union principles he espoused all his life," and was presenting "the discredited line of the Chamber of Commerce." [37]

In any case, the basic economic issues have become politicized and, depending upon the state of the economy, new pressures might drive other unions to follow the example of the Teamsters and the Building Trades.

Such pressures will be especially strong if the unions can find no other political allies on the national scene. Even the unions with a deep and sincere commitment to social and economic justice for all, ultimately have to "deliver" to their membership. And the notion of "conservative unions" could easily become a self-fulfilling prophecy if the only alliance that will benefit their members is an alliance with Nixon against the poor and the unorganized.

The three issues covered above, the growing threats to workers' jobs from automation and job relocation, job enrichment and productivity, and the political developments brought about by the wage-price freeze and its aftermath all offer both dangers and opportunities for progress. The impact they will have depends on how they are handled and, in particular, whether an alliance of liberals, blacks, and labor develops which can offer positive solutions.

V

There is, of course, nothing new about the idea of a political alliance for progress between workers and liberals. It has always been the foundation of the hope of winning a majority of American people to the side of progress.

The central thesis of this book has been that, far from being a quixotic dream, an alliance of black and white blue-collar workers and liberals *is* possible, despite the enormous obstacles.

Blue-collar workers have not disappeared nor been absorbed into the ranks of the middle class. Class divisions are still very real. Most workers do not earn enough for a decent life, and only a handful of workers can seriously be called affluent. The list of genuine problems they face is huge, ranging from the most outrageously bad conditions on the job to pervasive social and economic injustice in the community, politics, and other aspects of American life.

Workers' political attitudes and actions have also been seriously distorted. As we saw, neither they nor their unions are "inevitably conservative" and in many crucial areas, they actually emerge as more progressive than their "betters" of the educated middle class. Along with all the undeniable examples of conservatism and racial prejudice given so much attention by the press, there were other trends, ranging from growing militancy over their own concrete problems to examples of progressive sentiment that were totally ignored.

Finally, even the "drift to the right," that the vote for Wallace and Nixon supposedly demonstrated, was in significant part the result of a basic error in liberal strategy. It was noted that again and again liberal forces ignored or even assaulted workers' interests. It is worth considering how different the situation would be today if, in place of that long list of Democrat-sponsored social programs of the sixties, all of which antagonized workers, there had been instead, several pages filled with case after case of liberal proposals which championed workers' real and unmet needs and indicated a genuine concern for their interests.

In short, the evidence just does not support the belief that the current impasse between liberals and labor is inevitable or cannot be reversed.

Common issues certainly do exist. It is almost too obvious to state that since most blacks are employed in the worst blue-collar jobs, virtually every grievance of blue-collar workers applies with special force to the majority of the black population. Such things as full employment, higher wages, stronger health and safety provisions, pension reform, job security, tax reform, and equitable government economic policies are only the first examples that come to mind. Even the areas that are now explosive sources of confrontation, like better schools and housing, and reducing crime are at base common problems for all blue-collar workers and, in fact, for all Americans.

But it is, unfortunately, a sterile exercise to simply make long and detailed lists of the areas of common problems and interests. Genuine coalitions do not spring up in response to a list of issues or ideas. Only where groups are already in separate motion and people already galvanized into activity can real unity be created.

Some examples of cooperation have already been discussed, like the unity of black and white workers in southern strikes, and, to a lesser degree, in northern community groups.

But, in addition, in recent months the liberal ecology forces and sectors of labor have joined forces on a variety of issues. Most dramatic was the support the Oil, Chemical and Atomic Workers received when they called a strike and boycott of Shell Oil in the spring of 1973.[38] Major environmental groups, including the Wilderness Society and the Friends of the Earth, among others, backed the boycott, which was aimed at winning better health and safety provisions for the workers. One group referred to the action as an "historic first time alliance between labor and environmental organizations." [39] The Friends of the Earth stated:

> We have come to realize that working people are among the hardest hit by the hazards of pollution in the workplace. Further, we feel that American workers have as much right to participate in the decisions affecting the quality of the environment as does any other American. Moreover, it is the right of the worker to demand the safest and healthiest on-the-job conditions.[40]

A Washington-based group, organized by Senator Philip Hart, the Urban Environmental Conference, has also brought some black and labor groups together with environmentalists over issues like occupational health and safety (ending the threat to close down plants and fire workers if stiff pollution controls are enforced), and the problem of lead poisoning of ghetto children in the inner city.[41]

Other small-scale efforts have also taken place. In Boston, an OEO project, the Urban Planning Aid Office, has brought young scientists and health specialists together with workers in developing health hazard information and training programs for unions and workers. A Nader spin-off, the Health Research Group is similarly involved.[42]

Finally, there have been isolated examples of cooperation between liberals and labor in strike and organizing situations. The most important are, of course, the grape and lettuce boycotts of the Farmworkers' Union, but there are other local examples as well. But in realistic perspective, while these events suggest the possibilities that exist in the long run, they are at this time too small and isolated to provide anything more than a vision of what might be possible in the future. In the next two or three years, there is only one major area where real efforts at coalition can occur, and that is ironically in the area where much of the current polarization was created, the realm of electoral politics. Whatever the hopes or potentials in the long run, only the campaigns for local office as well as Congress and the presidency, provide concrete opportunities for liberals and progressives seriously to attempt to bridge the gap that now separates liberals and labor.

Unlike a particular demonstration or even a major strike, tens of thousands of blacks, students, and unionists are actively involved in political campaigns. The 1972 elections, for example, generated the active participation of more students than the peace marches, more trade unionists than any major strike, and more blacks than in any mass action at any time in the civil rights movement. In addition, for blue-collar workers, for blacks, and now for students, politics brings forward the crucial issues. Congressional and presidential elections now determine not only how a range of social issues will be handled but the previously apolitical question of how large wages will be and how high prices will rise. Also unlike other areas of labor action such as strikes, where there is really not much need for outsiders, politics almost inevitably demands coalition. Except in the rare cases where a liberal candidate need only appeal to one group to win, political campaigns force disparate groups to work together.

However, this does not mean that coalition will be easy. On the national level, in particular, the politics of vengeance seem to be carrying the day inside the Democratic Party. Just as the youthful delegates of 1972 took an understandable glee in excluding Mayor Daley, so the disastrous showing of George McGovern has strengthened the resolve of the top AFL-CIO leaders to purge the McGovernites.

To a fairly large extent, the AFL-CIO is justified both in its anger and its desire to regain a central role in the party. Even someone largely sympathetic to the "gay liberation" movement, for example, must grant that the passage of a resolution by the Minnesota State Convention in favor of legalized homosexual marriages (before a statewide television audience) was not an impressive example of either popular sovereignty or political realism.[43] Not only political expediency, but the basic idea of fair representation does demand that labor have a central place in the Democratic Party.

But, in their rhetoric, at least, some AFL-CIO leaders have been in favor of literally kicking the groups they call the "new politics" people, or the "kooks" completely out of the party. One reporter described their attitude as "those who aren't happy in the mainstream of the party might as well cut out." And "the Left must go."[44]

This is, one can hope, a kind of verbal overkill, a supertough first offer as in a contract negotiation, aimed at guaranteeing a more modest objective. But if by "kooks" labor means the whole liberal-McGovern wing of the Democratic Party, and labor seriously wants to get rid of them, the attitude verges on the suicidal. Such a move would eliminate many of the most prolabor forces in the party and strengthen the southern bourbon wing. Granted, this would cut down on "elitism" but only at the cost of replacing it with simple old-fashioned union-busting. Whatever the sins of liberal Democrats, they are better than the conservatives in the Democratic Party.

Fortunately, the AFL-CIO has always been realistic on this score. As was noted, they supported many liberal "doves," including George McGovern, despite the union's support for the war, because he did vote with labor on key domestic issues. As 1976 approaches, labor's self-interest alone will dictate muting intraparty divisions to keep the Republican party from holding office for the rest of the decade.

But, no matter what the precise degree of change in this attitude, the coming political struggles will inevitably offer the best opportunity for liberal-labor cooperation since the merger of the AFL-CIO. The reason is that many of the most politically active unions, because they supported McGovern while the federation did not, withheld some half a million dollars in contributions to the AFL-CIO Committee on Political Education, the political arm of the AFL-CIO. Even months later, larger unions like the Communications Workers, the Machinists, the Meat Cutters, and the American Federation of State, County and Municipal Employees, along with smaller unions like the 100,000-member Oil, Chemical and Atomic Workers are continuing the trend toward maintaining an independent political operation, as opposed to leaving politics to the Federation.[45]

For example, in early 1973 the independent United Auto Workers joined with the massive International Association of Machinists in the formation of a joint legislative "people's conference" in Washington, representing between them some

2,500,000 American workers, an alliance that by itself almost rivals the building trades in size. Their Washington conference was addressed by Senators Edward Kennedy, Hubert Humphrey, and Walter Mondale and focused especially on the problems of the industrial worker.[46] Equally, the one-half million member American Federation of State, County and Municipal Employees, in concert with other public service unions like the National Education Association and the International Association of Fire-Fighters, formed in March, 1973, a "Coalition of American Public Employees," a separately funded legal and legislative arm, representing some three million public service workers.[47]

Finally, the "Coalition of Black Trade Unionists," an organization of blacks within the labor movement, which was formed during the 1972 campaign, also continues its independent operation months after the election. Its leaders include the top black trade unionists in the country.[48]

It is vital, however, that one easily created misconception be quickly put to rest. It is absolutely wrong to identify COPE, the AFL-CIO political arm, as representing the conservative wing of the trade-union movement. COPE has, in fact, been consistently progressive and representative of the liberal, not the conservative, wing of the AFL-CIO. The major civil rights bills of the sixties, along with most of the good social legislation, was endorsed and aided by COPE. And, as was said, they have exhibited far more willingness to support candidates to their left than liberals have for candidates closer to the center of the Democratic Party. The genuinely conservative, Republican, wing of the AFL-CIO never supported COPE and often contributed money to COPE-opposed candidates.[49]

The importance of these new labor political groups lies more in the area of organization than the political differences that exist. In order to be an effective force COPE has become very tightly organized and "professional." This has inevitably limited the role outsiders, or amateurs, can play. In general, it has not offered middle-class liberals with a serious interest in trade unions much opportunity for making a contribution (though, in fairness, this aspect has changed somewhat in recent years, through voter registration efforts that reached outside the factory gates).

The new groups, however, and the independent political activity of many unions, on the other hand, offer wide opportunity for practical contact and joint action. Operating with lower funds and less manpower they will be far more receptive to aid from outside sources and offer far more opportunity for progressives outside the labor movement to use what skills they have while their concern will actually be visible, not only to union officials but to workers themselves. The liberal unions, in particular, who worked with George McGovern, and who did not share the same kind of bitterness toward middle-class liberals, will probably not only accept but encourage assistance of this kind, especially if such liberals are willing to listen as well as to talk.

The effects of such cooperation could be indeed profound. Whatever else they may be, both unions and blue-collar workers are decidedly pragmatic, and judge actions rather than words. The sight of significant and genuine liberal-labor cooperation in political activity will do more to erase the legacy of distrust than any rhetorical expressions of support and concern. At a minimum it would give a decent candidate a reasonable chance to put together a majority in the 1976 elections.

Such a change will require liberals to alter their essentially "top down," social engineering approach of the sixties (the essence of "elitism") to a genuine respect for the intelligence and basic decency of the "common" people, black and white. One need not accept every outrageous prejudice of working people to get rid of the equally outrageous prejudices often held against them.

Franklin Wallick, editor of the United Auto Workers' *Washington Report* and author of an excellent book on the problems of health and safety for blue-collar workers, devotes a whole chapter to the question of how students can relate to unions and workers. His conclusions, however, really extend to all liberals and groups who are outside the labor movement. Speaking in particular of the possibilities for students to work with labor on occupational health and safety drives, he says: "Union leaders, even of the most progressive democratic unions, deeply resent young people who come to save them from their ignorance. Students, for their part, have a difficult time fathoming the union clubbishness which tends to be suspicious of outsiders who go 'slumming' around union halls. . . . Mere competence and willingness to be of service to unions [are] not enough. The thing which unions resent the most is 'elitism.' It is an attitude that 'here we are, the bright enlightened product of college, and how lucky you are that we are here to help you.' It will take the most careful diplomatic moves by students and unions to make an alliance work, but it can work. It will not be an alliance of multitudes with mass meetings and fiery resolutions, although that could come—but it will be rather the quiet plugging work of sincere young people who are willing to do the unspectacular and are willing to make good on what they promise. To turn that help away would be rank foolishness by any union." [50]

Thus, a liberal-labor alliance, on at least this modest level, is not a romantic dream, but a very practical possibility. Unlike the weird collage of disparate groups and issues McGovern tried to fashion into an electoral majority, workers, black and white, are already united by similar problems and need similar solutions. They are a majority of the American people. These facts alone make a liberal labor alliance the clearest hope for progress in the coming years.

VI

Beyond the immediate practical political possibilities, there are also long-range implications to the problems and discontents of blue-collar workers, implications that point to a more human and democratic future for America. It is evident that all the hopes progressives have for fundamental improvement must relate in one way or another to the majority of American citizens, the blue-collar workers.

But the pop "theories" of social change have up until now focused on just about everyone but the worker as a key factor in a progressive future. The protests and discontents of blacks, of students, of women, and even the hippies have all been seen as posing radical challenges to the injustices of the present. Often such groups are presented as almost Promethean heroes, whose struggle will transform the very nature of society. Such popular manifestos as Charles Reich's *The Greening of America* or François Revel's *Neither Marx nor Jesus*, or Roszak's *Where the Wasteland Ends* are three very dramatic examples of such a trend in relation to the student-hippie cultural revolution.

Workers, on the other hand, have found at best apologists rather than champions when it comes to their role in basic social change. Frequently, a discussion of their potential role in the future will end with a caution that liberals ought not to expect too much. Sometimes their potential as a gradualist force for reform is suggested, but always with an insistence that workers are not a "revolutionary" force and are definitely not ready to mount the barricades in a burst of proletarian zeal.

But if workers are not about to overthrow the government, neither is anyone else, for that matter. The current crop of students, for example, seems quite as silent as their predecessors of the fifties.

The dismissal of working-class grievances and discontents as somehow less thoughtful or profound than those of other groups, in fact, smacks of condescension. It carries a certain implication that workers are a bit dull, lacking the sensitivity to desire fundamental improvements and genuine changes in society, unlike students, blacks, hippies, or other groups.

But it is hard to argue that workers are so very different that they alone of all social groups are inevitably shortsighted about progressive change.

In fact, all such discussions overlook the reality that basic progressive change does not spring from the reading of obscure and abstract manifestos. Rather it comes from the real and immediate needs of ordinary people. A majority of the participants in the American Revolution never heard of John Locke. The mobs that stormed the Bastille in France in 1789 did not know that a writer named Voltaire even existed. What "common" people know are their problems and that palliatives won't solve them.

Seen in this light, the significance of blue-collar discontent takes on a very different character. If one looks at the real and immediate problems workers face, in many cases the solutions are inevitably "radical," not in the sense of abstract theory, but of concrete reality.

One of the most immediate issues, but with profound implications, is simply the creation of genuine full employment. It is an immediate and practical issue for all workers, but it touches on basic questions of economic justice and social priorities. Full employment in combination with aid for those who cannot work would mean the virtual abolition of poverty in America.

The issue is, at present, locked in a maze of verbal and statistical contradictions that can only bring George Orwell's *1984* to one's mind. The "unemployment rate," as we saw, seriously distorts the real magnitude of the problem. In addition, however, from a business point of view, full employment does not even mean "full" employment. It means some compromise level of joblessness which ensures stability. Once this was judged to be 2.5 percent. Now the level is literally twice as high, and some economists argue that when 5 percent of the labor force is without jobs, that is the closest America can come to full employment.[51]

The labor movement, on the other hand, takes what is the only sensible view of the issue. As Nat Goldfinger, chief economist for the AFL-CIO says, "Full employment, as organized labor views it, means job opportunities at *decent wages* for all those who are able to work and seek employment."[52]

The most important part of that definition is the insistence on speaking of jobs and good wages together. It brings out the often forgotten central issue in the whole debate, that the point of jobs is to ensure a decent life. The fact is that anyone in America could be "employed" in a moment if he offered, for example, to wash cars for a nickel or work as a domestic servant for a dollar a day. The problem is not just simply jobs, but employment whose wages a worker can live on.

Black central city joblessness in particular brings this clearly into focus. In any major city, one can find pages of jobs like car wash attendants or dishwashers offered in the want ads and yet many unemployed people will not fill them. On this basis, much has been made about "cultural" factors and the "lack of the work ethic."

Yet only a few miles away, in the hiring office of a General Motors plant, for example, there are hundreds of blacks who have been up since 4:30 in the morning waiting their turn for an interview. Anytime a "high wage" plant opens up it is flooded with applicants, sometimes four and five times as many as there are openings. Some factories have bulging file cabinets filled with applications they will never return or consider, the oversupply of willing workers is so great.[53]

The point is obvious. A serious program for full employment cannot deal with national statistics that lump baby-sitters, newspaper boys, and hamburger stand waiters together with industrial or other kinds of stable jobs. The first group are genuine jobs only for special groups like teen-agers. Other employment such as the retail trades or laundry work can only be economically viable for single men or women. None of these jobs can support a family. A million jobs like these could open up in the black ghetto, but young blacks would still line up in the hiring offices of factories and other job sites, looking for jobs that pay better wages.

Seen in this light, the problem of the "unemployed" as defined by the census bureau becomes only the tip of the iceberg. Workers who can only find part-time jobs must be included along with workers now employed in low-wage industry who earn less than a poverty level income and cannot find a better job. As we noted, it is this group, not the unemployed, who constitute the majority of the black poor (and in fact the white poor as well).*

A variety of proposals exist, none of them complete in

---

* Liberal economists have referred to these other categories as the underemployed, and the sum of unemployment and underemployment as the total "subemployment." By this yardstick, one study found that in 1970 *31 percent* of central city dwellers, *black and white,* were subemployed in sixty urban areas.[54] The weakness of the concept, however, is that it rather artificially splits what is really a continuum and tends to conceal the common problems and interests of all workers.

themselves or exclusive of the others. Perhaps the most popular is creating jobs in the public sector. Jerry Wurf, head of the American Federation of State, County, and Municipal Workers, notes a study which "found some 4.3 million nonprofessional jobs in public and nonprofit agencies could be established to perform useful and needed services. These are not 'make work' slots," he added, "but real jobs that need doing." [55]

There have, in fact, been many legislative attempts to begin job creation, some directly related to welfare recipients, some for the unemployed in general, but the results have barely scratched the surface. The public employment program of 1971 created only 150,000 jobs, all of them temporary, and only one-third of them filled by the "hard-core" unemployed. The "workfare" provisions of the Welfare Reform Bill have to date created 6,900 jobs, about one factory's worth of employment. [56]

But a real potential quite obviously exists if serious attempts are made. Sweden, even though its unemployment problem is far smaller than America's, devotes three times as much money and reaches three times the number of unemployed. Their public works program includes "sheltered workshops," and government-supported factories, as well as public works programs. They have, in fact, virtually achieved full employment. [57] Even in the thirties, with a gross national product one-fifth of what it is today, the American government was able to put some four million Americans to work on federally subsidized public jobs, and it is hard to believe that an equally dedicated effort is not possible today.

But public service work alone cannot do the job. Unemployment and the welfare system as it exists today "acts to subsidize low-wage industry. A guaranteed public service employment program would push wages up and be very costly to industry, especially in the south." [58] Thus, needed changes in the private sector cannot be ignored.

One approach is tax incentives to business and government subsidies to low-income wage earners.[59]

However, the practical experience with the "let business do it" approach in the JOBS Program, a business-government cooperative effort, has not been impressive. A joint economic committee study of the four-year-old program found that "the program may have paid out subsidies to employers who would have hired unskilled laborers anyway, without government aid." And further it "has proven virtually useless in periods of high unemployment." [60] George Meany, in fact, accurately predicted that this would occur when he testified before Congress in 1968. As the AFL-CIO has noted, "it has simply proven wishful thinking to rely on tax incentives to business in this regard." [61]

The alternative is to recognize that the location of industries is as much a matter for public and government involvement as the garbage they spew out of their smokestacks. This issue is also basic to the discussions of job-export and consequent unemployment, but it must be extended to include all of the ways in which communities are devastated by the movement of jobs, and some regulation developed.

One possibility is legislation requiring that a certain proportion of new factories be located where unemployment is highest. Other more speculative possibilities include direct government subsidies supporting new industry, or the creation of cooperatives given solid government contracts to produce goods which America needs but which the market will not support. Especially if such industries are designed to be labor intensive, providing the maximum number of decent jobs, they could have a real impact.

But although the details of all these programs are highly complex and need to be worked out concretely with unions, management, and the unemployed themselves, the first step is the elementary one of establishing full employment, in the unions' entirely correct sense of the term, as a primary goal.

It is probably the only program that could seriously alter the polarization between black and white workers. At one stroke it would resolve the welfare issue by dramatically separating the question of jobs for able-bodied men from assistance for those who cannot work. It would put more money into the black community than any other government program, with obvious effects on housing, medical care, and so on. Finally it would have a profound impact on the explosive issue of crime that currently grips the big cities of America. Granted, the robbers and other criminals are a tiny fraction of the unemployed, and some would not be lured by the promise of a decent job, especially those who are making substantial money in the drug traffic. But full employment would dry up the massive well of recruits that joblessness and the loss of hope for a decent life creates.

The prospects for a serious struggle for full employment are actually promising despite the inevitable opposition from business. As Michael Harrington notes, "Organized labor would logically be the vanguard of any political movement for a guaranteed right to work. Unions fought for that very demand almost thirty years ago. And since then, they have battled for a whole range of manpower programs which would stimulate the economy, not by passing out windfalls to corporations, but by putting men and women to work, satisfying the urgent needs of society. Labor cannot, of course, prevail alone. But it has natural allies in the middle class. And the issue also is one on which the interests of both black and white workers must obviously converge. The formation of such a coalition around the demand for a guaranteed right to work would have ramifications for the entire society." [62]

If anything, this last assertion is an understatement of the facts. Full employment would make the greatest impact of any on the entire range of the social problems America faces.

But, although full employment is the most immediate and direct political goal that is possible, a number of other goals should also be mentioned. One progressive issue which workers care about is the quality of urban life. Workers' stake in the practical issues of reducing crime and pollution, and improving housing, medical care, and mass transit are obvious. But the deeper need to create "human communities" is not limited to middle-class intellectuals or the inhabitants of communes. Ethnic working-class neighborhoods are in fact often the most genuine communities in urban areas, and workers value that sense of community just as deeply as the most dedicated proponents of communes.

The issue is of real importance because many of the problems urban areas face can be traced to the way big cities systematically destroy organic communities. In contrast to the urban planner's ideal of an integrated community with employment, housing, and services all coordinated and planned, most urban areas are the chaotic product of special interests and a profit–loss mentality that inevitably subordinates human needs to economic imperatives. The same industrial logic of specialization and profitability that makes assembly-line jobs basically inhuman is what has made the cities equally so. Just as the logic of efficiency breaks down jobs into rote, repetitive tasks, preventing social interchange and satisfaction, the specialization of the cities into business districts, shopping centers, and drab residential tracts, instead of genuine integrated communities, leads to equally critical problems. Zoning laws and patterns of construction are based on the most overt class bias, almost guaranteeing that one's comfort, health, and even physical safety will be in direct proportion to one's income. The decaying central city, the trailer parks, and the walled fortresses of the affluent are all inevitable outgrowths of this fact.

The leap from the practical problems of full employment to solutions which would seriously deal with the restoration of community life is not as great as it might seem. The reality of community powerlessness in the face of special-interest groups is widely recognized by blue-collar workers. And some experiments with integrated "new cities" like Columbia, Maryland, have already occurred.[63] The race issue clearly looms large in this area and constitutes a serious roadblock, but the needs for decent working-class housing for black and white offers genuine opportunities for change. The overt desire for segregation will not suddenly disappear, but it is quite possible that it will be far less of a problem when new (or more likely redeveloped) racially integrated communities offer safe streets and better housing, along with improved transportation and social services, instead of the prospect today's cities offer to their residents.

Beyond these two issues are other even more speculative areas for the long-range future.

One is quite simply the abolition of completely rote and manual jobs. As was noted, some of the job enrichment programs give workers a wider role in the day-to-day operation of the plant. But beyond this lies the possibility of far broader involvement in the management of the enterprise as a whole. Scattered examples of workers' "self-management" already exist in western Europe and are, in theory, the norm in Yugoslavia.*

* The practical reality, as always, falls far short of the dream. Between the influence of the

Two basic ideas, however, are arresting. One is that the people who work in an enterprise and, by extension, the entire population ought to have a voice in what is produced, the kind and amount of new investments, and all the other aspects of the industry that are social issues, not technological or specialized ones.

The other is that no man should be "just" a worker, an hourly employee who does one simple task all his life. Upward mobility, as it exists today, is a limited escape for a few, from one static class to another. The long-range challenge is to break down the categories of manual and intellectual, of the man who only uses a hammer and the man who never uses one. And central to this is changing the structure of authority which concentrates all the power and decision-making in one group and leaves none for the other.

While for many years it has been popular to deny the very existence of class in America, class has remained a stubborn reality. As we have seen, not only in the factory, but in the community and the nation itself, blue-collar workers have always been second-class citizens in their own land. The *political* democracy that exists in America, the right to choose between opposing candidates, falls far short of the full meaning of the word democracy. The ultimate issue that has always been at the base of the progressive vision is genuine democracy, the rule of the people in all aspects of society, political, social, and economic. It is, in a way, the elimination of the job one does, or the income one receives, as a criterion of power or merit. It is the democratic vision in its fullest form.

To create such a democracy would be undeniably revolutionary in the precise meaning of that term. But it is a revolution that, while it has always existed as a vision, is so far

government and the managerial elite, the degree to which workers actually manage Yugoslav industries is open to serious question.[64]

from the reality of any existing country that it is a revolution without a name. The socialist revolutions of this century, although done in the name of working people, have (with the very exceptional cases of Czechoslovakia and East Germany) occurred in underdeveloped countries and socialism in practice has been a strategy of development, not of change, in the advanced industrial areas of the world. This paradox has often been at the base of the failure of students or intellectuals to deal with the real problems of working people as they exist today. The issues and policies that appeal to desperately poor, sometimes starving peasants, simply do not fit the needs of American workers. Whatever the merits or faults of any socialist country, they simply cannot be models for genuine progress in America.

Instead, it is precisely the extension of democracy to the central, social, and economic areas of American life, the creation of a society without injustice toward blue-collar workers that is the real issue. It is the fulfillment of the democratic ideal that goes all the way back to the French and American revolutions, the notions of equality and genuine popular rule that have lain dormant for all of our history.

All this, however, is in the future. To many, it may appear hopelessly romantic to discuss such issues, considering where we are today. But it is equally wrong to discount blue-collar workers as a genuine force for progress. The real needs of blue-collar workers can become the central engine of progress instead of a roadblock if all the myths and condescensions are put aside.

Shortly before his death, Martin Luther King said of the Negro revolt, "It has developed into more than a quest for simple equality. It is a challenge to a system that has created miracles of production, to create justice." [65]

He wrote those words in mid-1968, before the revolt of

white workers had even found its first confused political expression. But the years since then have shown in many ways that the same statement applies to all workers, black and white. In a real sense, the challenge to create more than miracles of production but also justice is the central challenge of every revolt and every progressive struggle of this century. It is also the central issue that underlies all the complex issues and events in the growing discontents of American workers. Thus, the confusion and disarray of recent years perhaps need not be the beginning of a "republican century," a permanent stalemate in the search for progress, but instead the beginning of a new stage in the ongoing struggle for a better world.

Notes and Sources

CHAPTER ONE

1. Campbell R. McConnell, *Economics*, McGraw-Hill Book Company, New York, 1966, p. 377.
2. John Kenneth Galbraith, *The New Industrial State*, The New American Library, Inc., New York, 1967, p. 276.
3. Herbert Marcuse, *One Dimensional Man*, Beacon Press, Boston, 1968, p. 27.
4. Alvin Toffler, *Future Shock*, Random House, New York, 1970, p. 16.
5. U.S. Department of Labor, *Dictionary of Occupational Titles*, 1965, Vol. 1 and supplement, 1966.
6. Calculated from Elizabeth Waldman and Anne M. Young, "Marital and Family Characteristics of Workers, March 1970," Table Q, p. A21 (Special Labor Force Report, 130, BLS, U.S. Department of Labor).
7. Calculated from *The Statistical Abstract of the U.S.*, 1972, Bureau of the Census, U.S. Department of Commerce, p. 222, Table #347.

There is one other question that could be raised about assuming the wives of workers to be "working-class."

Some sociologists have assumed that a working-class wife who spends her time in an office with middle-class people will pick up their values and carry them back to her working-class community and husband.

This is a realistic possibility and there are some weak indications that working-class women are more "with it" in terms of middle-class trends and styles.

But, first of all, the number of such women is small, since middle-class women tend to be hired for the jobs that put them in contact with the middle class—receptionists, for example, are usually selected for their ability in dealing with middle-class people, and few thirty-five-year-old welder's wives are hired in fancier business and financial establishments. Working-class women tend to work near their homes and in the working-class community. The general manager's secretary usually comes from a middle-class home, and telephone operators and cashiers are more often wives or daughters of the working class.

Richard Hamilton, in a study of clerical and sales attitudes shows that about 50 percent identify themselves with the working class.

Also, if we assume that contact with the middle class changes working-class wives so radically, then industrial psychologists, independent contractors, personnel managers, and any middle-class person who works with blue-collar workers could be assumed to carry working-class values into the middle class. Therefore, the use of male occupational figures is still the best rule of thumb guide to social class in America.

Also, in indicating women tend to follow their husbands' politics and life-style, the author is not implying approval, only an existing fact.

8. Calculated from *The Handbook of Labor Statistics*, 1970, Bureau of Labor Statistics, U.S. Department of Labor, p. 57, Table #19.

MAJOR OCCUPATION GROUPS FOR EMPLOYED WHITE MALES, 1969

Professional Technical	15.4%	31.0%	Middle Class
Managerial and Proprietor	15.6		
Clerks	7.4	13.6%	Lower Middle Class
Sales	6.2		
Craftsmen and Foremen	22.0		
Operatives	20.5	55.3%	Working Class
Service	6.3		
Laborers	6.5		

It may seem strange that black people should have so little influence on the totals. But black men in the male occupational structure constitute 10 percent, about 5 million of 50 million. And it is just in the nature of statistics that differences between black and white should have a small effect on overall figures. We will find this again and again. Things which are significant for the condition of blacks do not appear very large in statistics covering the whole country.

In general, when we compare working class to middle class, we will include black workers for the simple reason that, although they are invariably among the worst off, black workers are working-class and in the practical politics of the next decade, this is going to be a fact of key importance. Of course, in every case, we will also show what the situation is for white workers alone, so that black poverty, for example, does not hide the real situation of a typical "hard hat."

One other point also needs to be made. Foremen unfortunately had to be left in the category "working class," although, by our definition (and certainly in the minds of most workers) they are "straw bosses," lower-level managers and not workers. The reason is that virtually all statistics, of the Census Bureau as well as others, lump skilled workers and foremen together, and there is simply no way to weed the foremen out from the statistics on income and so on. However, since foremen are the highest-paid sector of the working class, and hence seem more "middle class," on most indicators, leaving them in the working class biases the statistics *against* the ideas being presented and certainly not in their favor. Thus, while less than precise, leaving foremen in the blue-collar category does not give any unfair advantage to the point of view being presented.

9. Seymour Wolfbein, *Work in American Society*, Scott, Foresman and Co., London, 1971, Chapter 1, and *op. cit.* Statistical Abstract.

10. Statistical Abstract, *op. cit.*

11. Calculated from "The U.S. Economy in 1980," BLS Bull. #1673, U.S. Department of Labor, p. 57, Table A-24.

12. Statistical Abstract, *op. cit.*

13. Herman P. Miller, "A Profile of the Blue Collar Worker—a View Through the Census Data," *Blue Collar Workers, a Symposium on Middle America*, Levitan, ed., McGraw-Hill Book Co., New York, 1971, p. 51.

14. "Guide to Living Costs, 1970," Special publication BLS, U.S. Department of Labor.

15. Calculated from Department of Commerce Current Population Reports, Consumer Income. Series P-60, #79.

16. "Wage Equity to Meet the Needs of G.M. Workers and Their Families," statement from UAW to General Motors Corporation, July, 1970, pp. 2–3.

17. Calculated from Current Population Reports, *op. cit.*

18. Department of Commerce, Current Population Reports, Consumer Income. Series P-60, #78, p. 6, Table 7.

19. U.S. Department of Labor, BLS, *Employment and Earnings*, Vol. 18, #1, July, 1971, p. 87, Table C-5.

20. Murray S. Weitzman, U.S. Department of Commerce, Bureau of the Census, Technical Paper 22, "Measures of Overlap of Income Distributions of White and Negro Families in the United States," p. 6, Table D.

21. The full distribution for white-collar family income is presented below.

WHITE COLLAR FAMILY INCOME 1970

Income	Total white collar		Clerical and sales		Professionals and managers	
	%	Cum %	%	Cum %	%	Cum %
0–7	17.7	17.7	26.1	261.	12.5	12.5
7–8	5.6	23.3	8.2	34.3	4.2	16.7
8–9	6.4	29.7	7.3	41.6	5.4	22.1
9–10	6.2	35.9	6.7	48.3	6.0	28.1
10–12	12.5	48.4	13.6	61.9	12.0	40.1
12–15	16.2	64.6	12.6	74.5	17.4	57.5
15 plus	37.2	100.0	30.1	100.0	42.2	100.0

This chart was calculated from Department of Commerce, Current Population Reports, Consumer Income. Series P-60, #79, p. 13, Table 3. Comprehensive data on all aspects of working-class and middle-class income can be found in CPR Series P-60, Nos. 70, 72, 73, 75, 78, 79, 80, 83, 84.

22. *The Statistical Abstract of the United States*, p. 128, Table #201.

23. *The Occupational Outlook Handbook*, U.S. Department of Labor, BLS, p. 376.

24. Richard F. Hamilton, *Class and Politics in the United States*, John Wiley and Sons, Inc., New York, 1972, p. 163.

25. *Ibid.*, p. 160.

26. *Ibid.*, p. 383.

27. *Ibid.*, p. 165.

28. Calculated from *Statistical Abstract*, pp. 856, 876.

29. Calculated from *Ibid.*, p. 210.

30. William Spring, B. Harrison, and T. Vietorisz, "Crisis of the Underemployed —in much of the inner city 60 percent don't earn enough for a decent standard of living," *The New York Times Magazine*, November 5, 1972, p. 44.

31. Calculated from *Handbook of Labor Statistics*, *op. cit.*, p. 57, Table 19, and Department of Commerce, Current Population Reports, Consumer Income. Series P-60, #80, p. 120, Table 56.

32. Calculated from *Statistical Abstract*, 1972, p. 222, Table 347 and Department of Commerce Current Population Reports, Consumer Income. Series P-60. #78, p. 6., Table 7, and #80, p. 110, Table 50.

33. Rex Hardesty, "The Changing American Workforce," *AFL–CIO American Federationist*, November, 1972, p. 16.

CHAPTER TWO

1. Although it is almost ten years old, Robert Blauner's *Alienation and Freedom in American Industry*, Chicago, University of Chicago Press, 1964, is still one of the best works systematically comparing the conditions of different kinds of working-class jobs. Its only limitation is the lack of any coverage of machine-operating kinds of jobs. His comparison is limited to printers, textile workers, auto, and chemical plant workers.

2. Peter Binzen, *Whitetown, U.S.A.*, Vintage, 1970, New York, p. 299.

3. John Haynes, "The New Worker," *New Generation*, Fall, 1970, p. 4.

4. Calculated from data in Reginald Carter "The Myth of Increasing Non-work Versus Work Activity," *Social Problems*, Summer, 1970, p. 60.

5. Calculated from U.S. Department of Labor, Bureau of Labor Statistics. *Area Wage Surveys*, Bull. 1660–91, p. 52, Table B-1.

6. Judson Gooding, "Blue Collar Blues on the Assembly Line," *Fortune*, July, 1970, p. 71.

7. Haynes, *op. cit.*, p. 6. It is worth noting that this article by a union community action director of IUE is even today the best short article on young workers. Even though it was written two years ago, it is one of the few pieces that is based on real firsthand interviews from several cities. See also John McGuckin's "Grist for the Arbitrators' Mill," *Labor Law Review*, October, 1971.

8. Both of these anecdotes are from William H. Leavy's "Arbitration and Insubordination of Union Stewards," *The Arbitration Journal*, pp. 22–23, March, 1972.

9. Barbara Garson, Luddites in Lordstown, *Harper's*, June, 1972, p. 68.

10. Haynes, *op. cit.*, pp. 4–5.

11. George Strauss, "The Shifting Balance of Power in the Plant," *Industrial Relations*, Vol. 1, No. 3, May, 1962, pp. 86–87.
12. The sources for these four incidents are respectively:
    Frank Wallick, *The American Worker: an Endangered Species*, Ballantine Books, New York, 1972, p. 157.
    Homer Bigart, "Lung Disease Problem Traced to Beryllium Refinery Plagues Hazelton, Pennsylvania," *The New York Times*, Sunday, October 29, 1972, p. 58.
    Robert Vare, "Asbestos Under Fire," *The New Republic*, July 8, 1972, pp. 13–14.
    Lawrence and Altman, "Doctors Find Many Work Related Diseases Difficult to Diagnose," *The New York Times*, March 20, 1972, p. 43.
13. Ralph Nader, "The Violence of Omission," *The Nation*, February 10, 1969, p. 44. Felix Belair, Jr., "U.S. Labor Agency Scored on Safety," *The New York Times*, April 16, 1972. Brendan and Patricia Sexton, *Blue Collars and Hard Hats*, New York, Random House, 1971, p. 103.
14. Frank Wallick, *op. cit.*, pp. 2, 4, 7, 42.
15. *Ibid.*, p. 53.
16. *Ibid.*
17. "Workmen's Compensation—Aiding the Injured," *The New Republic*, September 16, 1972, pp. 12–13.
18. See for example John Legget and Claudette Cervinka, "Labor Statistics Revisited," *Society*, November/December 1972, p. 99, and A. H. Raskin, "Unemployment—6% Is Only the Tip of the Iceberg," *The New York Times*, June 25, 1972, Section 4, p. 4. For the conservatives see James Daniel's "Five Million Jobless—How Much of a Crisis," *Reader's Digest*, June, 1972.
19. Ann M. Young and Kopp Michelotti, "Work Experience of the Population in 1970," *Monthly Labor Review*, December, 1971, p. 42.
20. *Ibid.*, Table 4, p. 42.
21. *Ibid.*
22. The income data is from the Department of Commerce Current Population Reports, Consumer Income. Series P-60, #80, p. 118, Table 55. The unemployment figures are from the Young and Michelotti article noted above.
23. Kenneth Lasson, *The Workers*, Grossman, New York, 1971, pp. 157 and 161.
24. Worth Bateman and Jodie Allen, "Income Maintenance, Who Gains and Who Pays," in Sar Levitan's *Blue Collar Workers*, McGraw-Hill Book Co., New York, 1971, pp. 307–14.
25. Quoted in "The World of the Blue Collar Worker," *Dissent*, Winter 1971, p. 29.
26. Quoted in Fred Harris, "Hot Under the Blue Collar," in Levitan, *op. cit.* p. 354.
27. Michael C. Jensen, "America's Pension System—A 135 Billion Dollar Question," *Saturday Review*, April 8, 1972, p. 42. The 50 percent figure is given in, for example, Robert D. Paul's "Pensions Are an Issue That Won't Retire," *The New York Times*, Section 3, p. 14, Sunday, October 22, 1972.
28. Peter Henle, "Recent Trends in Retirement Benefits Related to Earnings," *Monthly Labor Review*, June, 1972, p. 14.

29. "Private Pension System Termed Fraud by Nader," *The New York Times,* May 25, 1972, p. 65, and "The New Pressures to Safeguard Pensions," *U.S. News and World Report,* October 11, 1971, p. 40.
30. These anecdotes are found in:
   Jensen, *op. cit.,* pp. 43–45.
   Ralph Nader, "The Great Pension Fraud," *The Progressive,* October, 1971, pp. 18–19.
   "Private Pension Plans: Congress Considers Action," *Congressional Quarterly,* April 15, 1972, p. 848.
   "New Pressures to Safeguard Pensions," *U. S. News and World Report,* October 11, 1970, p. 41.
31. Henle, *op. cit.,* p. 17, Table 6.
32. Peter L. Peterman, "Fringe Benefits for Urban Workers," *Monthly Labor Review,* November, 1971, pp. 42–43.
33. *Ibid.*

CHAPTER THREE

1. Department of Commerce, Current Population Reports Consumer Income. Series P-60, #79, Table 3, p. 13.
2. Survey Research Center, ISR, *Survey of Consumer Finances,* University of Michigan Press, Ann Arbor, Michigan, 1970, liquid assets holding data p. 99, Table 6-2, vacations data p. 93, Table 5-18, installment debt data p. 23, Table 2-3.
3. *Ibid.*
4. Eli Ginsberg, "The Long View," in *Blue Collar Workers,* Sar Levitan, ed., McGraw-Hill Book Co., New York, 1971, p. 29.
5. Survey of Consumer Finances, *op. cit.,* Tables 2–3, p. 23.
6. *Business Week,* August 12, 1972, p. 85.
7. Brendan and Patricia Sexton, *Blue Collars and Hard Hats,* Random House, New York, 1971, p. 155.
8. Sources for these statistics are:
   Federal income tax data: Arnold Cantor, "The Slippery Road to Tax Justice," *The American Federationist,* April, 1973, p. 1.
   State and local data: Dick Netzer, "The Visible Tax System," *Blue Collar Workers, op. cit.,* p. 259.
   Social Security tax data: "Pension Benefits and Costs to Rise," *The New York Times,* December 24, 1972, p. 28, and Louis Hollander, "Reform in Social Security," *The New York Times,* January 3, 1973, p. 37, n.
   Property tax data: *Business Week,* "The Coming Change in the Property Tax," February 12, 1972, p. 50 and *loc. cit.,* Netzer.
9. Nat Goldfinger, "The Economic Squeeze on the Worker," *The American Federationist,* December, 1972, p. 7.
10. Edward Cowan, "Skeptics Find Economic Controls, After a Year, Had Worked Better Than Expected," *The New York Times,* August 11, 1972, p. 57.

11. Michael Harrington, "Labor's Radical Demands," *The New Leader*, February 22, 1971, p. 13.
12. Arthur B. Shostak, *Blue Collar Life*, Random House, New York, 1969, p. 113.
13. Peter Binzen, *Whitetown, U.S.A.*, Vintage Books, p. 81.
14. *Ibid.*, p. 228.
15. *Ibid.*
16. *Richard J. Krickus, "Organizing Neighborhoods: Gary and Newark," Dissent,* Winter, 1972, p. 108.
17. Binzen, *op. cit.*, p. 28.
18. William B. Furlong, "Profile of an Alienated Voter," *Saturday Review*, July 29, 1972, p. 49.
19. Barbara Brandt and Gordon Fellman, 'Working Class Protest Against an Urban Highway," *Environment and Behavior*, March, 1971, pp. 63–79.
20. Samuel Bowles, "Getting Nowhere: Programmed Class Stagnation," *Society*, June, 1972, p. 47, Table 2.
21. Binzen, *op. cit.*, pp. 56–57.
22. Evan Jenkins, "School Funding Viewed as Chaotic and Unjust," *The New York Times*, March 11, 1973, pp. 1, 52.
23. Bowles, *loc. cit.*
24. Robert Schrank and Susan Stein, "Yearning, Learning and Status," *Blue Collar Workers*, *op. cit.*, pp. 324–25.
25. U.S. Department of Labor Manpower Administration, *Career Thresholds*, Manpower Research Monograph No. 16, Vol. 1, p. 37.
26. Vera C. Perella, "Employment of Recent College Graduates," *Monthly Labor Review*, February, 1973.
27. Occupational Mobility Statistics calculated from Peter M. Blau and Otis D. Duncan, *American Occupational Structure*, John Wiley & Sons, Inc., New York, 1967, p. 496, Table J-2-1.
28. *Report of the National Advisory Commission on Civil Disorders*, Bantam, New York, 1968, p. 267.
29. Bill Kovach, "Study Finds Crime Rate Far Higher Than Reports," *The New York Times*, April 27, 1973, p. 1.
30. George Gallup, "Special Report on Crime in the U.S.," *The Gallup Opinion Index*, January, 1973, pp. 3–14.
31. "Crime Study Sees High Arrest Ratio," *The New York Times*, October 19, 1972, p. 12.
32. Donald Matthews, "The Social Class Background of U.S. Senators," *The Impact of Social Class*, Paul Blumberg, ed., Thomas Y. Crowell Company, Inc., New York, 1972, p. 314.
33. Haynes Johnson and Nick Kotz, *The Unions*, Pocket Books, New York, p. 92.
34. Irwin Ross, "Labor's Big Push for Protectionism," *Fortune*, March, 1973, p. 94.
35. *C.W.A. News*, November, 1972, pp. 6–7.
36. Data for this chronology come from:
Franklin Wallick, *The American Worker: an Endangered Species*, Ballantine Books, New York, 1972.
Felix Belair, "U.S. Labor Agency Scored on Safety," *The New York Times*, April 16, 1972, p. 44.

Felix Belair, "Labor Criticizes Work Safety Act," *The New York Times*, April 29, 1972, p. 63.

"Industrial Graveyard," *The New York Times* (editorial), September 30, 1972, p. 30.

Felix Belair, "Job Safety Suit Angers U.S. Aide" *The New York Times*, January 7, 1973, p. 48.

CHAPTER FOUR

1. Robert Coles, "Understanding White Racists," *New York Review of Books*, December 30, 1971, pp. 13–14.
2. Tom Kahn, review of Arnold Beichman's, "Nine Lies About America," *The American Federationist*, February, 1973, p. 23.
3. Seymour M. Lipset, "Working Class Authoritarianism," *The Impact of Social Class*, Paul Blumberg, ed., Thomas Y. Crowell, Inc., New York, 1972, p. 336.
4. Chandler Davidson, *Biracial Politics*, L.S.U. Press, Baton Rouge, 1972, p. 147. Davidson has a lengthy and excellent critique of Lipset; and Sidney M. Peck, "Ideology and Political Sociology: The Conservative Bias in Lipset's 'Political Man,' *The American Catholic Sociological Review*, Summer, 1962, makes the point about investigative bias. Richard Hamilton, *Class and Politics in the United States*, quoted earlier, also presents evidence against Lipset. Other sources include Louis Lipsitz, "Working Class Authoritarianism: A Reevaluation," *American Sociological Review*, February, 1965.
5. Richard Hamilton, *Class and Politics in the United States*, John Wiley & Sons, Inc., New York, 1972, pp. 456–57.
6. See tables for "Recommended allowances for sample errors of the difference" which are appended to the Monthly Gallup Opinion Indices.
7. Hamilton, "Liberal Intelligentsia and White Backlash," *Dissent*, Winter, 1972, and Hamilton, "Black Demands, White Reactions and Liberal Alarms," in Levitan's (ed.), *Blue Collar Workers*, McGraw-Hill, New York, 1971.
8. Hamilton, *Blue Collar Workers*, p. 135.
9. Derived from Hamilton, *Dissent, op. cit.*, pp. 225–27.
10. Hamilton, *Blue Collar Workers, op. cit.*, p. 141.
11. Angus Campbell, *White Attitudes Toward Black People*, Institute for Social Research, Ann Arbor, Michigan, 1971, p. 52.
12. Howard D. Hamilton, "Voting Behavior in Open Housing Referenda," *Social Science Quarterly*, December, 1970, p. 721.
13. *Ibid.*, p. 728.
14. James W. Vander Zanden, "Voting in Segregationist Referenda," *Public Opinion Quarterly* XXV (1961), p. 105.
15. Davidson, *op. cit.*, Chapter 7.
16. H. Edward Ransford, "Blue Collar Anger: Reactions to Student and Black Protest," *American Sociological Review*, June, 1972, p. 339.
17. Richard Hamilton, *Blue Collar Workers, op. cit.*, p. 149. And see also Andrew Greeley and Paul Heatsley, "Attitudes Toward Racial Integration," *Scientific American*, December, 1971.
18. Coles, *op. cit.*, p. 12.

19. Studs Terkel, "A Steelworker Speaks," *Dissent*, Winter, 1972, p. 12.
20. The unhappy advocate was Martin Patchen, "Social Class and Dimensions of Foreign Policy Attitudes," *Social Science Quarterly*, December, 1970. Additional support is given by James D. Wright in "Life, Time and the Fortunes of War," *Transaction*, January, 1972, and R. Hamilton, *Class and Politics in the United States*, p. 453 and Philip Converse and Howard Schuman, "Silent Majorities and the Vietnam War," *Scientific American*, June, 1970.
21. Calculated from Andrew Greeley, "Political Attitudes Among American White Ethnics," *Public Opinion Quarterly*, Summer, 1972, p. 215, Table L.
22. Robert P. Ableson and Philip Zimbardo, *Canvassing for Peace: A Manual for Volunteers*, Ann Arbor, Michigan, 1970, p. 29.
23. Harlan Hahn, "Correlates of Public Sentiments about War: Local Referenda on the Vietnam Issue," *The American Political Science Review*, Vol. 64, p. 1190.
24. Sources for this chart are, respectively, Ransford, *op. cit.*, p. 399 and Richard Lemon, *The Troubled American*, Simon & Schuster, New York, 1971, p. 163. The last three questions came from Blumenthal, Kahn, Andrews, and Head, *Justifying Violence—Attitudes of American Men*, Institute for Social Research, Ann Arbor, Michigan, 1972, p. 76.
25. Brendan and Patricia Sexton, *Blue Collars and Hard Hats*, Random House, New York, 1971, pp. 52–53.
26. *The New Republic*, November 18, 1972, p. 33.
27. Quoted in Richard M. Scammon and Ben J. Wattenberg's *The Real Majority*, Coward, McCann & Geoghegan, Inc., New York, 1970, p. 62. Thomas Pettigrew, Robert Riley and Reeve Vannerman also note the class nature of the Wallace vote in "George Wallace's Constituents," *Psychology Today*, February, 1972, p. 47.
28. R. Hamilton, *Blue Collar Workers, op. cit.*, p. 144.
29. *Op. cit.*, Scammon and Wattenberg, p. 191.
30. *Ibid.*, p. 192 and *Business Week*, "Candidate Wallace Talks Taxes and Jobs,' April 29, 1972, pp. 60–64.
31. *The New York Times* published three articles on Burton, the first on May 14, 1972, p. 58, the second on November 7, 1972, p. 23 and the third on November 8, 1972, p. 34. The selections quoted above are taken from all three articles.
32. *The Gallup Opinion Index*, November, 1972. If it seems I've gone against what was said earlier about these polls in using them at this point, the answer lies in two facts: first, only 13 percent of blacks voted for Nixon and, therefore, the Nixon totals are almost equivalent to a survey of whites only. Second, when one talks about national politics as opposed to attitudes, the subdivisions of men and women, North and South are not directly relevant.
33. *The Gallup Opinion Index*, October, 1972.
34. Louis Harris, "Poll Debunks Theory of Why Nixon Won," *The Atlanta Constitution*, December 14, 1972, p. 24-A.
35. Fred Harris, "Hot Under the Blue Collar," in *Blue Collar Workers, op. cit.*, p. 351.
36. Davidson, *op. cit.*, p. 219.

CHAPTER FIVE

1. Haynes Johnson and Nick Kotz, *The Unions*, Pocket Books, New York, 1972, p. 17.
2. Jack Newfield and Jeff Greenfield, *The Populist Manifesto*, Praeger, New York, p. 164.
3. *The Machinist*, "New Study Shows It Pays to Have a Union," December 7, 1972, p. 1.
4. Quoted in *AFL-CIO News*, March 31, 1973, p. 3.
5. Myra Wolfgang interviewed by B. Rosenberg and S. Wineman, "Young Women Who Work," *Dissent*, Winter, 1972, p. 30.
6. *Directory of National Unions and Employee Associations*, 1971, Bull. 1750, U.S. Department of Labor, Bureau of Labor Statistics, p. 74.
7. *Ibid.*, p. 75.
8. Ann M. Young and Kopp Michelotti, "Work Experience of the Population, 1970," *Monthly Labor Review*, December, 1971, p. 42.
9. See recent issues of *The Carpenter* and *IBEW Journal*.
10. "New Moves to Curb Violence in Building Industry," *U. S. News and World Report*, May 28, 1973, p. 101.
11. Johnson and Kotz, *op. cit.*, Chapter 8.
12. Personal interview.
13. Personal interview.
14. H. Hammerman, "Minorities in Construction Referral Unions," *Monthly Labor Review*, May, 1973, p. 44.
15. Johnson and Kotz, *op. cit.*, p. 187.
16. Hammerman, *op. cit.*, p. 44.
17. Brendan and Patricia Sexton, *Blue Collars and Hard Hats*, Random House, New York, 1971, p. 269.
18. *Business Week*, "The Fight Against Bias in Seniority," February 10, 1973, p. 56.
19. Sexton, *op. cit.*, p. 269.
20. Personal interview.
21. See for example Burton H. Hall, *Autocracy and Insurgency in Organized Labor*, Transaction Books, New Brunswick, N.J., 1972.
22. Personal interview.
23. J. Hutchinson, "George Meany and the Wayward," *California Management Review*, Winter, 1971, pp. 56–57.
24. David Shipler, "Study Finds $25 Million Yearly in Bribes Is Paid by City's Construction Industry," *The New York Times*, June 26, 1972, p. 26.
25. Charles Stevenson, "The Tyranny of Terrorism in the Building Trades," *Reader's Digest*, June, 1973, p. 89.
26. Quoted in Johnson and Kotz, *op. cit.*, p. 171.
27. Jack Barbash, *American Unions*, Random House, New York, 1967, p. 40.
28. Michael Harrington, *The Other America*, Penguin, New York, 1964, p. 28.
29. See B. Hall, "Restaurant Workers: Thumb in Labor's Soup," *The Nation*, January 22, 1968, and M. Kaplan, "Union Fraud Laid to Retired Judge," *The New York Times*, February 16, 1973, p. 26.

30. Derek Bok and John Dunlop, *Labor and the American Community*, Simon & Schuster, New York, 1970, p. 90.
31. Personal interview.
32. Hall, *op. cit.*
33. H. W. Benson, "Apathy and Other Axioms: Expelling the Union Dissenter from History," *Dissent*, Winter, 1972, p. 220. See also B. J. Widick, *Detroit: City of Race and Class Violence*, Quadrangle Books, Chicago, 1972, p. 43.
34. G. Strauss, "The Shifting Balance of Power in the Plant," *Industrial Relations*, Vol. I, No. 3, May, 1962, pp. 86–87.
35. Personal interview.
36. *Labor Voice for Peace*, January, 1968, p. 3.
37. *Business Week*, "Labor's New Left Launches an Attack," July 1, 1972, p. 15.
38. *Labor Looks at the 92nd Congress*, an AFL-CIO Legislative Report, December, 1972.
39. Johnson and Kotz, *op. cit.*, p. 77.
40. *Ibid.*, p. 96.
41. *Congressional Quarterly Weekly Report*, "Pressure Group Ratings of All Members of Congress," April 29, 1972, pp. 934–41.
42. These quotes are taken from the following sources:
    (1) *AFL-CIO News*, January 20, 1973, pp. 4–5.
    (2) *Steel Labor*, "These Are Our Roots," December, 1972, p. 10.
    (3) *Ibid.*, March, 1973, p. 16.
    (4) *The CWA News*, May, 1972, p. 3.
    (5) *The Machinist*, September 14, 1972, p. 8.
    (6) *The CWA News*, September, 1972, p. 3.

CHAPTER SIX

1. (a) "Boredom Spells Trouble on the Assembly Line," *Life*, August, 1972.
   (b) Barbara Garson, "Luddites in Lordstown," *Harper's*, June, 1972.
   (c) *Newsweek*, "The Bullet Biters," February 7, 1972.
   (d) Geoffrey Norman, "Blue Collar Saboteurs," *Playboy*, August, 1972.
2. Judson Gooding, "Blue Collar Blues on the Assembly Line," *Fortune*, July, 1970, p. 71.
3. Bennett Kremens, "No Pride in This Dust," *Dissent*, Winter, 1972, p. 24.
4. *Ibid.*, p. 24.
5. Agis Salpukis, "Young Workers Disrupt Key G.M. Plant," *The New York Times*, January 23, 1972, p. 41.
6. Russell Gibbons, "Showdown at Lordstown," *Commonweal*, March 3, 1972, p. 523.
7. Calculated from 1972 Statistical Abstract, p. 105.
8. B. J. Widick, "Black City, Black Unions," *Dissent*, Winter, 1972 and *Newsweek*, "Violence in the Factory," June 29, 1970, p. 142.
9. Widick, *ibid.*, and *Newsweek*, *ibid.* See also *Time*, "Hell in the Factory," June 7, 1971, and *Atlanta Constitution*, "Worker Gets Fourteen Years in Shooting at Meade," December 18, 1971. And John H. McGucken, Jr., "Grist for the

Arbitrators' Mill: What G.M. and the U.A.W. Argue About," *Labor Law Journal,* October, 1971, p. 647.
10. Widick, *op. cit.,* p. 142.
11. Kremens, *op. cit.,* p. 25.
12. H. Sheppard and N. Herrick, *Where Have All the Robots Gone?* The Free Press, New York, 1972, pp. 134–44.
13. Thomas Brooks, "Black Upsurge in the Unions," *Dissent,* Summer, 1971, p. 125.
14. B. J. Widick, "Minority Power Through the Unions," *The Nation,* September 8, 1969; see also William B. Gould, "Black Workers in White Unions," *The Nation,* September 8, 1969, and Brendan and Patricia Sexton, "Labor's Decade—Maybe," *Dissent,* July, 1971.
15. William Abbott, "The Public Worker Transforms Labor," *The Nation,* May 24, 1971, and Sexton, *op. cit.,* p. 649.
16. Patricia and Brendan Sexton, "Labor's Decade—Maybe," *Dissent,* Summer, 1971, p. 365.
17. U.S. Department of Labor, *Handbook of Labor Statistics.* pp. 340–41, Table 153.
18. Derek Bok and John Dunlop, *Labor and the American Community,* Simon & Schuster, New York, 1970, p. 244.
19. The information from the preceding section is from Stanley Weir, "USA—The Labor Revolt," in *American Society Inc.* (Maurice Zeitlin, ed.), Markham Publishing Co., Chicago, 1971, p. 480.
20. The information for this section comes from Weir, *op. cit.* and *Newsweek,* "Up Drawbridges," June 24, 1971, and Burton Hall (ed.), *Autocracy and Insurgency in Organized Labor,* Transaction Books, New Brunswick, N.J., 1972.
21. This list comes from the following sources:
    (a) *Newsweek,* "Here Come the Ethnics," April 3, 1972, p. 86; Fred Barbash, "Coalition Against Blockbusting," *The Nation,* April 17, 1972, pp. 496–97; John Herbers, "1600 from Ethnic Groups Organize Protest Against Institutions They Say Are Destroying the Cities," *The New York Times,* March 20, 1972, p. 29-c.
    (b) Richard Krickus, "Organizing Neighborhoods: Gary and Newark," *Dissent,* Winter, 1972, p. 25. And Krickus, "The White Ethnics," *City,* May–June, 1971.
    (c) Frye Gaillard, "Poles in Detroit Ally with Blacks," *Race Relations Reporter,* n.d.
22. These facts come from:
    (a) Pat Watters, "Workers, White and Black in Mississippi," *Dissent,* Winter, 1972, p. 70; William T. Lundberg, "Black and White Woodsmen Form New Union in the South," *The New Leader,* March 6, 1972, pp. 10–12. Steve Martin, "Anger in the Southern Pines," brochure from the Gulf Coast Pulpwood Association, n.d.; *Newsweek,* "Mississippi: Strange Alliance," November 9, 1971; Bill Gray, "Woodcutter's Appeal," *The Great Speckled Bird,* February 21, 1972, p. 15; Kathy Kahn, "Pulpwood Strike: Black, White Join Forces in Mississippi," *South Today,*

n.d.; Peter Barnes, "Pulpwood Peonage," *The Nation,* March 18, 1972, p. 15.

(b) Carl E. Farris, "The Steelworkers Strike in South Carolina," *Freedomways,* second quarter, 1971, p. 178.

(c) Chandler Davidson, *Biracial Politics,* Louisiana State University Press, Baton Rouge, 1972; Gene Guerero, Jr., "Textile Walkout: Interracial Effort Typical of New Spirit Among Workers," *South Today,* n.d.; (Institute for Southern Studies) "Florida Agribusiness Fights Unions," *The Great Speckled Bird,* February 14, 1972, p. 14.

23. (a) Lundberg, *op. cit.,* p. 12.

(b) Farris, *op. cit.,* p. 187.

(c) Watters, *op. cit.,* p. 71.

24. *The Gallup Opinion Index,* November, 1972.

25. *The New Republic,* "Black Labor and White," January 27, 1973, p. 12.

26. Hugh Nations, "Most Public Housing in Small Area," *The Atlanta Constitution-Journal,* April 4, 1971, p. 11.

27. See, for example, *The Machinist,* August, 1972.

CHAPTER SEVEN

1. U.S. Department of Labor, Bureau of Labor Statistics, *Employment and Earnings,* Vol. 19, No. 9, March, 1973, Chart 7, p. 11.

2. Eva Mueller, *Technological Advance in an Expanding Economy,* Survey Research Center, Institute for Social Research, University of Michigan, Ann Arbor, Michigan, 1969, p. 10.

3. Some examples can be found in Section IV-B, "Approaches to Control of Technological Change," *Critical Issues in Labor* (Max Wortman, ed.), London, Collier-Macmillan, Limited, 1969, pp. 175–224.

4. Donald N. Michael, "Cybernation: The Silent Conquest," *The Corporation Takeover* (Andrew Hacker, ed.), Anchor Books, New York, 1964, p. 193.

5. Ben Seligman, "Automation and the Unions," *The Radical Papers* (Irving Howe, ed.), Anchor Books, New York, 1965, p. 223.

6. Paul N. Zimmerer, "Statement Before the House Ad Hoc Subcommittee on Banking and Currency Hearings," *Industrial Location Policy,* Washington, U.S. Government Printing Office, 1971, p. 316.

7. Statement by Kenneth Patton, in Zimmerer, *op. cit.,* and Linda Greenhouse, "Rise in Jobs Poses Problems in the Suburbs," *The New York Times,* August 18, 1971, p. 47, col. 1.

8. Patton, *ibid.*

9. Bill Collins, "South Factory Growth Exceeds That of Nation," *The Atlanta Journal,* August 21, 1972, pp. 10–11, and James L. Stern, "Unions and Automation," *The Progressive,* February, 1967, p. 25. See also "The Industrial Shift South That Never Stops" *Business Week,* July 19, 1973, pp. 62–64.

10. John Greene and Allan Gussack, "Labor: The Search for Insularity," *Corporate Financing,* March–April, 1971, p. 60.

11. *Forbes,* "Where Have All the Jobs Gone?" August 1, 1972, p. 17, and Leo

Fenster, "Detroit Goes Multinational," *The Nation,* March 12, 1973, p. 326, and Irwin Ross, "Labor's Big Push for Protectionism," *Fortune,* March, 1973, p. 95.

12. *Business Week,* "A Pact Against U.S. Protectionism," March 31, 1973, p. 78.
13. *Business Week,* "A Business Boomlet on Mexico's Border," January 22, 1972, pp. 36, 38, and Robert D. A. Shaw, "Foreign Investment and Global Labor," *Columbia Journal of World Business,* July–August, 1971, p. 329.
14. This quote from Herbert Maier's statement during *Hearing Before the Subcommittee on Foreign Economic Policy of the Joint Economic Committee, Congress of the United States, a Foreign Economic Policy,* U.S. Government Printing Office, Washington, D.C., 1970, p. 823. The data on Korea and Taiwan come from Ben Sharman, "Free Trade," *The Machinist,* May 24, 1973, p. 8.
15. Gus Tyler, "Multinationals: A Global Menace," *American Federationist,* July, 1972, p. 4.
16. *U.S. News and World Report,* March 27, 1972, pp. 57–59.
17. Tyler, *op. cit.,* and Fenster, *op. cit.* The main document in the continuing debate over the number of jobs exported is the *U.S. Department of Commerce* report on "The Multinational Corporation."
18. Leonard Woodcock, "Force Social Responsibility on International Companies," *The New York Times,* January 7, 1973, Section III, p. 34.
19. James P. Grant, "The Global Unemployment Crises," *Foreign Affairs,* October, 1971, p. 116.
20. See, for example, Ann Seidman, *An Economics Textbook for Africa,* London, Methuen & Co., 1969, Part IV, Foreign Trade.
21. Irwin Ross, *op. cit.,* and U.S. Department of State, *Issues,* publication #8546, Washington, D.C., U.S. Government Printing Office, 1971, p. 20.
22. *Business Week,* "Japan: A Stepped Up Search for Cheap Asian Labor," March 31, 1973, p. 40.
23. Daniel Bell, "Labor in the Post-Industrial Society," *Dissent,* Winter, 1972, p. 166.
24. Forbes, *op. cit.,* "Where Have All the Jobs Gone?" p. 17.
25. See, for example, Judson Gooding, "It Pays to Wake Up the Blue Collar Worker," *Fortune,* September, 1970, and "Blue Collar Blues on the Assembly Line," *Fortune,* July, 1970.
26. The data for this section are contained in the following articles (although there is some overlap, the listing roughly follows the order in which they were presented). David Jenkins, "Democracy in the Factory," *Atlantic,* April, 1973; *Newsweek,* "The Job Blahs: Who Wants to Work?" March 26, 1973; *U.S. News and World Report,* "Latest Moves to Fight Boredom on the Job," December 25, 1972; Agis Salpukis, "Auto Workers Given Assembly Line Voice," *The New York Times,* June 19, 1972, p. 1; *Business Week,* "Motorola Creates a More Demanding Job," September 4, 1971; *Newsweek,* "Factories: Art Against the Wall," August 2, 1971; Andrew H. Malcom, "More U.S. Companies Reducing Worker Boredom," *The New York Times,* May 15, 1972, p. 53; *Business Week,* "New Tool; Reinforcement for Good Work," December 18, 1971.

27. Phillip Shabecoff, "Redesign Dull Jobs: Leaders Wary," *The New York Times,* January 7, 1973, p. F-17.
28. Thomas R. Brooks, "Job Satisfaction: An Elusive Goal," *American Federationist,* October, 1972, p. 3. See also William Gomberg, "Job Satisfaction, Sorting Out the Nonsense," *The Federationist,* June 1973, pp. 14–19, and Levitan and Johnson "Job Redesign" *Monthly Labor Review,* July, 1973, pp. 35–41.
29. *Newsweek,* "Manufacturing: The Assembly Team," August 21, 1972, p. 69.
30. See, for example, U.S. Department of Labor, Bureau of Labor Statistics, *Improving Productivity: Labor and Management Approaches,* Bulletin 1715, September, 1971.
31. Michael Harrington, "Mr. Nixon's Reactionary Revolution," *Commonweal,* November 26, 1971, p. 200.
32. See, for example, AFL-CIO Legislative Report, *Labor Looks at the 92nd Congress,* December, 1972 and previous year.
33. Harrington, *op. cit.,* p. 200.
34. David Deitch, "Phase Two: Will It Work? For Whom?" *The Nation,* December 27, 1971, p. 680.
35. See, for example, *American Federationist,* "Labor Views the Economy, 1973," March, 1973, p. 10.
36. B. J. Widick, "Nixon's Hard-Hat Strategy," *The Nation,* December 18, 1972, p. 615.
37. George Meany, "Brennan's Retreat," *AFL-CIO News,* April 14, 1973, p. 4.
38. "New Allies Among Environmentalists," *Business Week,* February 2, 1973, p. 86.
39. *Ibid.*
40. *Business Week,* February 24, 1973, pp. 19–20.
41. Daniel Zwerdling, "Poverty and Pollution," *The Progressive,* January, 1973.
42. Personal interview with Frank Wallick, editor of the UAW *Washington Report.*
43. Paul Wieck, "Labor's Al Barkan," *The New Republic,* March 24, 1973, p. 15.
44. *Ibid.*
45. *Ibid.* See also "Labor and the Democrats," *The New Republic,* June 30, 1973, p. 10.
46. See *UAW Washington Report,* March 12, 1973, and *The Machinist,* March 15, 1973.
47. *The Public Employee,* Vol. 38, No. 3, March, 1973.
48. *The Public Employee,* "Coalition of Black Trade Unionists Schedules 2nd Annual Convention," Vol. 38, No. 4, April, 1973. See also "Black Trade Unionists Hold Initial Convention," *The Public Employee,* June, 1973, p. 7.
49. The New York Building Trades are one example.
50. Frank Wallick, *The American Worker: an Endangered Species,* Ballantine, New York, 1972, pp. 142–44.
51. See *U.S. News and World Report,* "Jobs for All: Any Time Soon?" August 2, 1971, and *Business Week,* "The Debate over Public Jobs for the Jobless," December 9, 1972.
52. Nat Goldfinger, "Full Employment: The Neglected Policy," *American Federationist,* November, 1972, p. 7.

53. Personal interview: A hiring manager for one of the big three auto companies made this statement.

54. *Business Week,* December 9, 1972, pp. 102–4.

55. Jerry Wurf, "Crisis in Jobs—Tapping the Public Service Potential," *American Federationist,* August, 1971, p. 24.

56. Paul Delaney, "82,075 Found Jobs Under Workfare," *The New York Times,* April 20, 1973, p. 34-C, and Michael Harrington, "Government Should Be the Employer of *First* Resort," *The New York Times Magazine,* March 26, 1972, p. 44.

57. Although there are many lessons that could be learned from the Swedish experience, there are also economic and technological differences that would require too much space to delineate here. The following articles give some indication of Swedish manpower policies: *Forbes,* "Trouble in Paradise," April 1, 1972; Charles D. Stewart, "Swedish Labor Market and Manpower Policy," *Growth and Change,* January, 1970; U.S. Department of Labor Manpower Administration, "Special Job Creation for the Hard to Employ in Western Europe," *Manpower Research Monograph No. 10,* 1970; Eli Ginsberg, "Sweden's Manpower Policies," *Manpower,* November, 1970.

58. Frank Reisman and Alan Gartner, "Employer of First Resort," *The Nation,* April 5, 1971, p. 434.

59. See, for example, Dean A. Worcester, *Beyond Welfare and Full Employment: the Economics of Optimal Employment Without Inflation,* Lexington, Mass., D. C. Heath and Co., 1972.

60. "The Debate over Public Jobs for the Jobless," *Business Week,* December 9, 1972, p. 106.

61. See George Meany's testimony before the *Joint Economic Committee—Congress of the United States,* on May 28–29 and June 4–6, 1968, Washington, D.C., U.S. Government Printing Office, 1968.

62. Harrington, *op. cit.,* p. 62.

63. See, for example, the testimony of Thomas C. Wolfe, Jr., before the *Ad Hoc Subcommittee of the Committee on Banking and Currency on Industrial Location Policy,* Part Three. Washington, D.C., U.S. Government Printing Office, 1970, p. 67.

64. Even more so than Sweden, Yugoslavia tends to be a Rorschach, in which anything can be seen. On workers' self-management, in general, see the following:
J. Obradovic, J. R. Fench, and W. L. Rogers, "Workers' Councils in Yugoslavia," *Human Relations,* Vol. 23, No. 5; W. F. Glueck and D. Kavran, "Worker Management in Yugoslavia," *Business Horizons,* February, 1972; John Case, "Visions of a New Social Order," *The Nation,* February 14, 1972.

65 Martin Luther King, "The Trumpet of Conscience," Lectures delivered over CBC Radio in Winter, 1967.

Index